SPIRIT WARRIOR III

Solace for the Heart in Difficult Times

B.T. SWAMI

HARI-NAMA PRESS

Copyright © 2000 by John E. Favors

All rights reserved. No part of this book may be reproduced, stored in a retrieval system, or transmitted in any form,by any means, including mechanical, electronic, photocopying, recording, or otherwise, without prior written consent of the publisher.

Hari-Nama Press gratefully acknowledges the BBT for its use of verses and purports from Srila Prabhupada's books. All such verses and purports are © Bhaktivedanta Book Trust International, Inc.

The publisher gratefully acknowledges the kind permission of Goloka Books in allowing us the use of their artwork for incorporation into our cover design.

First printing 2000
Second edition printing: Amazon KDP 2020

Cover design by Stewart Cannon / Ecstatic Creations
Cover artwork by Philip Malpass / Goloka Books

ISBN 9798639983047

SPIRITUAL WARRIOR III

Solace for the Heart in Difficult Times

I dedicate this book to all
spiritual warriors who have come to
re-spiritualize society.

Contents

Acknowledgments 1
Foreword 3
Editor's Preface 7
Introduction 9
Chapter 1: The Choice Before Humanity 15
   Humanity is at a Crossroads! • A World at War • The Nature of the Choice • A Forgotten Heritage • Distortions in the Materialistic World View • Lack of Community • A Distorted View of History • The Evolution of Modern Society • Deficiencies of Modern Society • The Renaissance: Boon or Bane? • The Reformation's Oversight • A Degradation of Consciousness • Emptiness of the "American Dream" • Denial of the Soul's Eternality • The Need for Simplicity • Need for Healing • A New Type of Human Being • A Call for Courage • Questions & Answers

Chapter 2: Predictions and Prophecies 35
   The Word Is Falling Apart • A False Sense of Security • Why Is This Happening? • A Major Transition Ahead • Need for Higher Consciousness • Warnings throughout History • Psychics View the Future • Astrologers Report from around the World • Predictions in Dreams • Insights from Hypnosis and Regression • Dr. Raymond Moody's Psycomantium • The Message of the Dinosaurs • The Evidence of the Pyramids • Native American Timelines

• Buddhism's Vision of the Future • Islam Predicts Civilization's Downfall • The Virgin Mary's Warnings • Other Warnings in the Judeo-Christian Tradition • Vedic Predictions • Comets • Extraterrestrial Contacts • Growing Public Interest in UFOs • Cloning • Increasing Turmoil • Disasters Expose Our True Motivations • Wide Availability of Higher Knowledge • A Wake-up Call • Questions & Answers

Chapter 3: The Condition of Society Today 61

Technology is Not Neutral • Superficiality of Knowledge • Poor Quality of Life • The Extent of Human Need • Misguided Worship • Improper Role Models • The Need for Real Leadership • Corruption Is Commonplace • Corrupt Police • Short-Term Self-Interest • Ecological Devastation • Economic Exploitation • A Debt-Driven Economy • Houses of Worship in Decline • No Sacred Havens • Hypocrisy of Religious Leaders • Atrocities in the Name of God • Subtle Corruption • Egocentricity in Excess • Lost Children and Youth • Skewed Values • The Problem of Pharmaceuticals • Dependency is Widespread • War and a Weapons Culture • Guns at Home and in Schools • Widespread Crime • Unrestrained Lust • Illicit Behavior is Self-Perpetuating • Distorted Sexuality • The Tragedy of AIDS • Pornography around the World • Rape and Violence • Increasing Incest • The Harm of Abortion • Denial Does Not Help • Questions & Answers

Chapter 4: What is Behind it All? 93

Negative Forces Throughout the World • What is Evil? • The Historical View • Conflict and Fragmentation • A Strategy of "Divide and Conquer" • Demigods and Demons • Who Are the Demons? • A Real-life Example • The Demonic Agenda • How it Works • Enslavement Already Exists • The Pace of Modern Life • Plans for Manipulation • Psychic Manipulation • Domination through Propaganda • Drug Addiction to Control Society • Deliberate Creation of Problems • Governments Have Betrayed Our Trust • Secret Societies • The "Invisible Government" • Some Important Questions • Relativity and Suppression of Higher Knowledge • Questions & Answers

Chapter 5: We are Easy Victims 127

Mind Control • Manipulative Techniques • Psychic Control • Manipulation by the Media • The Influence of Advertisements • Television's Power • Obsession with the Body • Glorification of Suicide • Collective Suicide • One-dimensional Thinking • The Failure of Our System • Poor Relationships • Obstacles to Loving Interactions • Decline of Families and Community • The Mental Health Crisis • A Challenge to Psychiatrists • Physician, Heal Thyself! • The Importance of Role Models • Truth Must Not Be Distorted • Need for Positive Examples • Our Link to Collective Consciousness • Misusing the Mind • Self-destructive Patterns • We Can Make a Difference • Questions & Answers

Chapter 6: A Spiritual Warrior's View of the World ... 157

We Are Not the Body • The Search for Ecstasy • True Liberation • The Deluding Qualities of Material Nature • Three Modes of Material Nature • Reincarnation: Fact or Fiction? • Our Karmic Patterns • Sense Control • The Kingdom of God • A Personal Approach • Questions & Answers

Chapter 7: 12 Qualities of A Spiritual Warrior 179

Spiritual Warriorship • Spiritual Warrior Checklist • Sense Control and Mastery of the Mind • Humility • Fearlessness • Truthfulness • Compassion and Pridelessness • Material Exhaustion and Disintrest in Material Rewards • No Idle Time • Patience and Selflessness • Firm Faith • Perseverance • Curiosity and Enthusiasm to Learn and Grow • Surrender to Divine Will • Questions & Answers

Chapter 8: How to Strengthen Ourselves 203

Spiritual Life is Challenging • Even Great Teachers Were Tested • Working on Our Own Consciousness • Weeding Out Saboteurs of Devotion • Self-Protection • The Value of Discernment • "Normal" is Not Natural • The Impact of Subtle Phenomena • Sound Vibration • Dark Night of the Soul • Choosing Our Path with Care • The Importance of Commitment • Purity is the Force • Calling on the Names of the Lord • Devotion • Health and Healing • Karma and Healing • Keep the Goal in Mind • Questions & Answers

Chapter 9: Guidelines for Responsible Action 229
> We Are Always Acting • Helping and Serving • The Humility of Service • Seeking Divine Empowerment • Understanding Power • Identifying Types of Power • Physical Power • Institutional Power • Emotional Power • Academic Power • Intuitive Power • Sacred Power • Divine Power • Keeping Spiritually Attuned • Being Responsible Leaders • Being Alert and Strategic • Acting as Revolutionaries • Being Revolutionary in Today's World • Standing Firm • Evaluating Our Actions • Questions & Answers

Chapter 10: Serving the World Community 255
> Creating a Viable Future • True Culture • A Spiritual Nucleus • Combining the Best from East and West • The Sacred Art of Dying • Reestablishing True Culture • Tolerance and Interfaith • Connection with Nature • Simplicity and Self-Sufficiency • Strength in Community • Creating Community • Four Principles of Community Building • Building Strong Families • Cooperation and Community • Addressing Conflicts in Community • Maintaining a Positive Community Environment • Make the Commitment • Questions & Answers

Index 287

About the Author 297

Acknowledgments

I would like to express my deep appreciation to all the people who dedicated time and effort to make this book possible. Greg Gurewitz reproduced countless tapes so that others might transcribe them. Lisa DeSoto, Christina af Wetterstedt, Laurice Stuart, Michelle Stanfill, Isis Bey, Lauren Kossis, James Parks, Marcus Laurence and Walter Howard carefully transcribed the tapes from which the text was taken. Frederick Waddell, John Papazagalou, Leigh Clements, Adam Kenney, Robin Cannon, Marylin Wood and Krista Oliver provided invaluable editing assistance. Stewart Cannon did the wonderful layout and cover design. I would also like to thank Phillip Malpass of Goloka Books for his generosity in again allowing us to use a drawing from the first volume of *Illustrated Bhagavatam Stories* as part of our cover design.

Through your perseverance in the development of this book, you have manifested the wonderful qualities of true spiritual warriors.

Foreword

In 1893, the World Parliament of Religions gave birth to an organized religious summit and marked the beginning of a dialogue between the religious traditions of the East and West. A century later, in 1993, the Parliament of World Religions was reborn in Chicago, and the dialogue intensified. Over eight thousand people from around the world came together to explore religious and spiritual responses to critical issues that confront the international community. This gathering powerfully celebrated the role of diversity in creating harmony among peoples.

In 1999, it was no coincidence that the Parliament of World Religions conference was held on the African continent in Capetown, South Africa. Many felt it was a testimony to emerging patterns of unity in the world. South Africa represents a microcosm of the rest of the world, and its history in the last decade of the twentieth century is a testimony to the capacity of people to work together to create new levels of material and spiritual liberation for society. As it pursues the thorny path of reconstructing its society in the next decades of the new century, South Africa is forging new ways for people to live and work together. This process embodies the spirit and purpose of the Parliament of World Religions, and South Africa proved a fitting matrix for the expression of our purpose as the new millennium dawned.

The 1999 Parliament of World Religions conference brought the religions of the world together at a most critical moment in human history. As the twentieth century ended, some of the greatest problems facing humanity were those of sectarianism, racism, tribalism, nationalism, gender conflicts and religious fanaticism. These problems are fragmenting the planet and decimating the foundations of human societies the world over.

How critically important, then, it was for religious people and institutions to come together to confront these planetary adversaries through the sharing of perspectives and spiritual solutions, and the initiating of practical initiatives for change. The wider circles of unity created at the Parliament are even now unleashing a collective will to combat the problems of the age and develop a world that preserves the honor and destiny of every soul.

A major goal of the 1999 Parliament was to inspire individuals, organizations, nations and religious communities to offer gifts of service designed to make long-term differences in the world. His Holiness Bhakti Tirtha Swami Krishnapada has designated this new book, *Spiritual Warrior III: Solace for the Heart in Difficult Times,* as such a gift of service to the global human community. This is but one more offering in his long record of service to the advancement of human consciousness and spirituality.

Spiritual Warrrior III and his previous book, *Leadership for an Age of Higher Consciousness,* both present ways of addressing material problems with spiritual solutions. Bhakti Tirtha Swami's outstanding international record in interfaith dialogue, international relations, conflict resolution, consultation with world leaders and development of self-sufficient communities is evidence of his commitment to creating a healthy, global mindshift.

As the world's only African-American Vaishnava Guru, a Princeton scholar and an African high chief, he brings together Eastern, Western and African world views in all of his books and in his daily life. He is a truly loving and tender soul, and his very life is his message. He exemplifies the power and peace that come from serving humanity and creating unity through diversity.

May all who read this precious gift of service be inspired to reflect upon what gifts we ourselves can offer to help usher into being new levels of human consciousness and unity.

    Dr. Amy Marks
    Co-Chair
    Parliament of World Religions
    South Africa, 1999

Editor's preface

Spiritual Warrior III: Solace for the Heart in Difficult Times consists of lectures given by His Holiness Bhakti Tirtha Swami (Swami Krishnapada) to a wide variety of live, radio and television audiences around the world, over a period of several years. Because the topics were originally presented in spoken form, the style is conversational and informal. In the editing process, we have modified the text to enhance readability, yet sought to preserve some of the verbal nuances that would maintain the mood of the original presentations. By so doing, we hope to create an atmosphere that literally makes you part of the audience, where you can experience the powerful presence of the speaker as he shares essential nourishment for the soul.

We would like to mention a few other stylistic considerations. In the course of his discussions, Bhakti Tirtha Swami includes perspectives from many different spiritual philosophies, however because his audiences are composed mainly of people in the Christian and Vedic traditions, he makes the most extensive references to these scriptures. At times he uses Sanskrit terminology from the Vedas, a vast body of ancient scriptures originating from the area of the world known today as India. We have translated and removed these terms wherever possible, but where the use of the terms seemed important to the point, we endeavored to explain them within the context of the discussion. Also, the end of each chapter includes a few of the many questions and answers exchanged during the original lectures. We hope that these will respond to some of the concerns that may arise in the course of your reading. These discussions between Bhakti Tirtha Swami and the audience may also give you different angles from which to view the topics presented.

This book is the third volume in our *Spiritual Warrior* series. The first two volumes, *Spiritual Warrior: Uncovering Spiritual Truths in Psychic Phenomena* and *Spiritual Warrior II: Transforming Lust into Love,* are already in print, and have been translated into several additional languages along with His Holiness' other works. The information presented within these pages is extremely rare, and we hope you will make the most of the knowledge they contain. If you take these teachings seriously, they can transform your life into a most sublime, loving adventure.

Introduction

Spiritual warriors are unconventional, to say the least. We do not fight with conventional weapons, we do not fight on conventional battlegrounds, and we do not fight for conventional objectives.

Many of the wars in human history have had some religious overtones, but a closer look generally reveals that the combatants are actually more interested in some political or territorial gains. In these cases, religious differences are simply held out as banners, like race, gender or class, to minimize the humanity of others and justify unjustifiable actions. Spiritual warriors have nothing to gain by such exploits—we see that the assets and power these groups fight so viciously for are transitory, and do not bring true happiness.

There is a difference between religion and spirituality. Religion can play an important role in our development of spiritual understanding, but it can also promote divisions and sectarianism. Whether we follow the Bible, the Torah, the Quar'an or the Vedas, we must recognize that true spiritual pursuits seek the common ground between all things and all beings, and this is developed by a careful study of all of the ancient wisdom we have available to us.

The true spiritual warrior strives to master the weapons of love, humility, compassion, faith and self-knowledge. Our battleground is the realm of human consciousness, where we wage war against the ignorance and lust that now pervade human society like an occupying army. Our objective is a civilization where people live in harmony with each other and with God, awakened and in tune with the effulgent spiritual environment that is available to us. Toward these ends, we endeavor to develop ourselves and share our understanding with the people we meet, giving them the tools they need to discover and experience the truth for themselves.

Spiritual Solutions to Material Problems

The problems we face today are so vast and so varied that even the most paranoid have difficulty knowing what to worry about on any given day. War, racism, crime, disease, natural disasters... The list goes on. Each of these issues is so overwhelming and complex that it seems any one of them could easily be the downfall of our existence.

Humankind has experienced periods of great calamity throughout history. Mysteriously yet without fail, every time these calamities have reached crisis levels a great guide or prophet has appeared with a powerful message. These revolutionary teachers have come in different races, they have appeared in different parts of the world and they have presented different religious systems, yet at the same time, each of their messages has embraced the same three basic tenets: Love the Lord with all of your heart, love your neighbors as yourself, and this world is not your true home.

We have all heard these sayings, in one form or another, so many times that they have become trivialized in most societies. Just think for a moment, though, about what kind of world we would live in if we all truly took these three basic principles to heart.

There are two ways to water a tree. You can go from leaf to leaf carrying a small drop to each, or you can simply pour the water on the roots. The latter requires far less effort, and actually does a better job of delivering the water to where it is needed. The complexities of the material world have far more "branches" and "leaves" than we can perceive, but according to our great teachers the roots of our problems lie in our relationships with God and with each other.

Spiritual warriors seek to heal and nourish these relationships first by learning to identify and honor the true self, then learning to recognize the God-essence in ourselves and everyone in our environment.

Divine and Demonic Consciousness

In much the same way as the light hurts our eyes when we first wake up in the morning, opening our eyes to the true nature of our existence can at first leave us wanting to roll over and pull the covers back over our heads. This is a natural reaction, and it is the duty of those who have already awakened to help others adjust to the light.

Unfortunately, not everyone is interested in sharing the truth. There are those who have awakened to some degree, but who actually prefer to keep others in darkness. By feeding their fears of the unknown, impious individuals endeavor to keep the masses of people confused, sedated and completely dependent on them for sustenance, simply to feed their own egotistical convictions that by manipulating people and resources they can make themselves powerful gods in their own domains.

Such people have existed since the beginning of civilization. They are referred to in the Vedas as *asuras,* or demons, because they work actively to usurp the Lord's power for themselves.

We must keep in mind, however, that even the distinctions between the devotional and the demonic is really a matter of consciousness. Nearly every great prophet has encountered resistance from powerfully demonic individuals, but overwhelmed them with such love and purity that even these wicked individuals were redeemed in the process. This is the true essence of spiritual warfare.

These are Difficult Times

The modern world is filled with contradictions between the environment we want to live in and the environment we actually create for ourselves. We all seem to want peace, yet there are numerous wars raging even as you read this. Nearly everyone is seeking deep love and companionship, yet even within relationships so many people are feeling a deep sense of loneliness. Workers want to feel valued and want a sense of job security, but the machines created by our own industry devalue many skilled workers. Students dedicate years studying at universities, only to find themselves inadequately prepared for the fast-paced business world in which their skills are already obsolete. Parents want their children to grow up healthy and happy, yet so many children end up depressed, angry and self-destructive.

We turn to our friends for comfort and understanding, but are often left feeling stranded because nobody has time for anybody anymore. We look to social and political leaders to improve the quality of our lives, only to be taken advantage of *en masse*. In many parts of the world, even the police exploit and abuse the people who approach them for protection. Even as people retreat from the modern paradigm and try to move into more natural settings, weather shifts and natural disasters devour their communities. Those who run for the shelter of drugs for some escape from the misery find themselves more miserable than ever.

Finally, in frustration, some people look to their religious leaders to bring some sense and direction into their lives, only to be disappointed by impotent spiritual leaders who are even more confused and sinful than those they are supposed to be guiding. These and other overwhelming disappointments have led to global increases in depression, mental illness, homicide and suicide.

It is the duty of the spiritual warrior to connect with divine power and develop the strength, compassion and selfless love that will guide and give solace to the hearts of those whom the Lord entrusts to our care. Beloveds, the time has come to re-spiritualize society, and great adventures await those who are willing and able to rise to the challenge of becoming true spiritual warriors.

14   Spiritual Warrior III

Chapter 1

The choice before humanity

Humanity is at a crossroads!

Humanity stands at the brink of a spiritual emergency—and of a profound spiritual awakening. The spiritual forces engulfing the planet are intensifying, causing those who are less grounded to become completely bewildered, while at the same time reinforcing the commitment of those who genuinely desire spiritual advancement.

A World at War

Today, it seems that everything that can go wrong is going wrong, and most people are feeling completely out of control. Right now, it actually appears as if the demonic forces are more successful than the spiritual ones. Every day, people are becoming less capable of regretting their sinfulness, because aberrant behavior has grown more and more to be the norm. Our history is filled with periods like this, where insanity reigns for some time, followed by a massive polarization and cleansing—similar to what is happening now.

Despite certain appearances to the contrary, we are a world at war. For example, we are at war in the political and social arenas, being bombarded with such scourges as tribalism, sexism, religious intolerance and racism. Meanwhile, we have become a morally depraved culture that indulges in child abuse, elder abuse, incest, pornography and of course, abuse of ourselves. All these behaviors are symptoms of the ongoing decline of human values.

Let us take a serious look at the material situation in the world today. It is always important to recognize the intensity of the problem at hand, so we will not make any miscalculations. If we underestimate the capacity of an enemy or an opponent, we may approach our defense in a dangerously superficial way. Such a miscalculation can guarantee failure. But when we appreciate the potential power of our opponents and know their track record, then we can better judge how to deal with them, how to pace ourselves and, ultimately, how to defeat them.

Only a few years ago, our world was basically a bipolar one, with demarcation and rivalry between two major world powers. We now find ourselves in a more multipolar world, in which almost every social and political coalition is completely unstable and transitory. The international balance of power is subjected to constant change, and this is extremely dangerous.

The Nature of the Choice

The true lines being drawn across the planet are not based upon nationality, complexion, language, creed, style or fashion. Instead, they are based upon degrees of piety and purity. Around the world, the polarization is increasing between those of us who are spiritual and devoted to higher consciousness and those of us who are materialistic, even demonic. The once broad middle ground is giving way. Those who migrate toward materialism and anesthetize themselves against their feelings of incompleteness, hoping to gain some measure of peace through artificial means, are becoming more and more degraded. On the other hand, those whose feelings of incompleteness drive them to pursue a deeper understanding of the human condition and their relationship to God are finding greater realization and empowerment.

The intense pressures people face daily are leaving many dumbfounded—sometimes even totally crazy and delusional. Others, who have had their fill of the madness, are striving for greater sanity and balance by returning to more holistic paths. Still others are seeking complete transcendence, attempting to move past the limitations of the material world and the mundane patterns of simply eating, sleeping, mating and defending.

By nature, human beings in the material world are neither totally good nor totally bad. Instead, we stand on the borderline, and can be swayed in either direction. Unfortunately, the more negative influences are temporarily dominant in the world today, as evidenced by many of the calamities we are facing—such as drug abuse, war, AIDS and natural disasters. Many consider these to be direct chastisements from God and His agents in response to the number of sinful acts being performed by the world's population. However, for those of us who view these calamities as incentives to rise to the occasion, these very problems present us with a great opportunity to make positive changes.

A Forgotten Heritage

Spiritual warriors face many challenges, especially in the Western world. The West no longer has a culture of reverence and order. Western society is losing its basic value system, and tends to pull people down spiritually rather than supporting their upward rise. For example, we no longer show respect to our parents and elders. We have lost much of our understanding about how to contact angels and other divine beings for guidance. Indeed, we have even lost our fear of and reverence for God. We are no longer willing to perform the austerities and make the sacrifices that could summon divine intervention.

In brief, we have all but forgotten that we are products of a tremendous heritage, and of profoundly powerful divine interventions that have taken place throughout our history. It is this very forgetfulness that is bringing this planet to its evolutionary crossroads. Without understanding our spiritual roots, we are increasingly relying upon unstable, illusory forms of fulfillment, such as money, prestige, distinction and adoration. We tend to substitute the transitory for the substantial, even though the purpose of real culture is to aid in the expression of our genuine individuality and creativity. True culture is highly spiritual and allows us to get in touch with our deepest essence.

Distortions in the Materialistic Worldview

As we enter the twenty-first century, the Western materialistic model of society has gained predominance around the globe. Unfortunately, because of the serious distortions inherent in the materialistic worldview, humanity may not have a viable future unless we change our outlook and our behavior.

When we consider other human beings, and this planet, simply as physical entities and objects to be manipulated for our own selfish ends, then we are not motivated to examine the ramifications and implications of what we do. We only think about what is economically feasible for the moment, or what will bring power and control now, without considering future consequences. Without factoring in both the physical and spiritual, there is a great potential for us to cause harm to others—and eventually to ourselves.

The Choice Before Humanity 19

A few years ago, I attended meetings with then-President Kaunda of Zambia. He wanted to have a banquet in our honor to show appreciation for our Institute's service in his country. Naturally, he invited the members of his Central Committee, most of whom were Marxist. This proved to be extremely interesting.

In our discussions, I tactfully challenged the members of his committee to take a serious look at their contradictory sense of identity: "You call yourselves Marxists," I said. "Yet, you are also Africans and spiritual people. You have grown up surrounded by ancient prophecies and ancient wisdom. Don't you see how incongruous Marxism is with your Afro-spiritual orientation? Marxism is a behaviorist perspective that presumes that a human being is merely a mechanical entity, not coordinated with the universe or with any higher scheme of existence. How can these two philosophies harmonize when they are naturally opposites?"

Once I had their attention, I acknowledged that Marxism has good intentions, because in essence it deals with being your brothers' and sisters' keeper. It also attacks class distinctions and racism. Despite its good intentions, though, it does not follow through on its own premises. How can you be your brothers' and sisters' keeper when you deny the existence of your divine Mother and Father? What makes you brothers and sisters unless you have common parents? Similarly, how can you be your brothers' and sisters' keeper when you rely solely on material commodities that are completely transitory and temporary?

We see now that, worldwide, the communist order has fallen apart. But, spiritually speaking, there is little or no difference between a so-called capitalist nation and a communist one, because neither truly encourages higher consciousness. Both of these political and economic systems share a similar materialistic view of reality. They also have a common core motivation: exploitation. What does it matter whether you are exploited by the communists or by the capitalists, by a monarchy or by an oligarchy? Exploitation is exploitation.

Lack of Community

Another issue causing difficulty is the fact that modern materialistic culture lacks a strong sense of community. Once, while visiting with Nigeria's president, General Olusegun Obasanjo, he cited an interesting example of the differences in the Western worldview from those of his own country. In his younger days, when he was studying in England, his next-door neighbor's husband passed away. What surprised him most about this event was that it took a month before he knew of it. Even though he lived right next door, he never had any conversations with his neighbors. Even when they came out to get their newspaper or their milk, they tried to avoid eye contact. This whole approach was quite foreign to him. He told me: "In my country, not only would we have been aware of the death in the family, but we would have been there, offering condolences and support, and we would have felt that our neighbor's loss was our loss."

In most ancient cultures, a natural communalism still exists—a natural sense of family and a natural appreciation of the responsibility of human beings to their brothers and sisters. Unfortunately, even many of these cultures are now becoming absorbed in the modern materialistic mindset, typified by the philosophy of Descartes: "I think, therefore I am." This is an extremely "I-" or "me-" centered outlook. In contrast, a healthier view is: "I feel, I relate, I serve, I associate, I experience, I care, I love—therefore I am." If we are not valuable to others, if we are only concerned with what value others can provide to us, then we are missing the point of human existence.

A Distorted View of History

Most of the world has been caught in a powerful, seductive, materialistic trance—in a dream that masquerades as reality. As we all know, no matter how real they appear, dreams always consist of illusory content. Illusion is in fact the nature of the dream state. We have nevertheless greatly indulged ourselves in both waking and sleeping dreams of hedonism. When a dream extends past the sleeping state into waking consciousness, it becomes a delusion. When many people share the delusion, it becomes part of a public mindset that can be extremely insidious and contagious.

Of the many collective dreams and delusions shared by Americans, a primary one is our perspective on history. If we consider the historic trends in this country and in most Western nations, we notice that we have gradually moved away from our original agricultural civilization into a much more production-oriented and consumer-based one. However, a society centered on agriculture is far more natural, and affords people more control over the variables in their lives. In such an environment, individuals can select the kinds of foods they want to grow, plant medicinal herbs, arrange for a fresh water supply and even make their own clothing. When people are self-sufficient in this manner, they acquire useful skills and feel a natural sense of purpose and accomplishment.

The Evolution of Modern Society

This way of life has been largely replaced by mass manufacturing—a change that has caused the displacement of many of those who once worked at home. As a result, a sizable proportion of the population has become dependent on uncaring employers. In this alienated state of existence, children—rather than being viewed as assets who share the workload or potential heirs to a trade—are instead seen as greater burdens, imposing the requirements of more mouths to feed and bodies to clothe. Further, urban environments have created intense stress, become breeding grounds for disease, and have produced high degrees of crime, congestion, and pollution.

In more recent years, we have moved from a society of mass production and consumer goods to an even more "advanced" technological and scientific model known as the "information age." This move has essentially redirected the focus of society from manufacturing to the more intangible areas of knowledge, data and communications. In such a society, information becomes a commodity unto itself, and data processing has emerged as a new survival skill.

The majority of jobs in the American workplace now deal with data collection, processing and communications. There is certainly no lack of data in our society. Thousands of scientific journals are published worldwide every day. Fueled by the spread of computers into every area of life and by the phenomenal growth of e-mail and the Internet, the explosion of information threatens to bombard each and every one of us to such an extent that we all suffer to some degree from information overload. Every few years, the amount of available raw information in the world literally doubles. In our educational institutions, the information we acquire is often rendered obsolete before we even graduate.

Deficiencies of Modern Society

Something is extremely wrong. While the facilities for communication are far greater than ever before—with our fax machines, computers, satellite dishes and other communication technology—our mutual intelligibility and ability to relate to one another are declining drastically. Modern humanity has traded wisdom for data and replaced serenity with insanity. Much of the increase in racism, gender problems, religious sectarianism, tribalism, and fanaticism around the world relates directly to our overemphasis on data processing and minimization of true knowledge and wisdom.

Although we are surrounded with constantly shifting information and changing codes of behavior, it is not true that everything is transitory and relative. Many values and needs are universally present in every human being. For example, whether we are male or female, American, African, Indian or European, we all experience the need to love and be loved, and the need to understand ourselves and our Creator. When human interactions are based on what we have in common, differences then serve only to enhance and deepen our relationships. Indeed, such diversity within a framework of unity actually helps to create a stronger, more balanced society. Unfortunately, today's world order ignores many of these universals and instead emphasizes differences, no matter how superficial, to the point of fragmentation.

The modern worldview encourages such fragmentation because its fundamental values include individualism, competition and self-gratification at the expense of the whole. Because members of modern society have selfish concerns in almost everything they do, they create a "gimme" atmosphere in which groups and individuals vie to get as much for themselves as they can, rarely concerning themselves with the hardships they may cause others.

The Renaissance: Boon or Bane?

Most of us in this culture have unthinkingly accepted the idea that Western civilization's historic changes have been signs of inexorable progress. In this view, each major change has replaced old, primitive ways of being with newer, superior methods. But is this really the case?

For example, many contemporary history courses teach that the Renaissance was a period of exquisite human development—an extremely progressive time in the evolution of Western society. During this era, people supposedly began to free themselves from older ways of thinking and allowed themselves much more creativity and expression, contributing to the general progress of human civilization. However, there is another view. Because this expression was largely unbridled, the Renaissance actually paved the way for a decline in human values. Like many of the other periods that have such an admirable reputation, the Renaissance should in some ways actually be considered as a leap backwards that has contributed to the degradation and mass chaos that much of the world is experiencing now.

Let us explore this a little further. A statement from the *Columbia University Encyclopedia* sheds light on the accomplishments of this period, saying: "The Renaissance tended to develop an emphasis on the individual; [it] brought new importance to individual expression, self-consciousness and worldly experience; culturally, it was a time of new currents and brilliant accomplishments in scholarship, in literature and in the arts… More generally, it was an era of emerging nation-states, of exploration and discoveries, of the beginning of the commercial revolution and of a revolution in science."

Probing beneath the enthusiasm and idealism of this statement, we could conclude that the Renaissance actually set the stage for increasing conflict between individuals and nations. For example, we can consider the phrase "emerging nation-states" to be a nice way of saying that new divisions arose between formerly unified entities. Meanwhile, if we look at the biographies of some of the renowned personalities of that time, we find that many of them were not just exploring new techniques in art and literature, but were also exploring new outlets for their carnality and greed.

The Reformation's Oversight

The Protestant Reformation was another distinct time in Western history that produced massive confusion in the minds of this planet's inhabitants. We do not mean to imply here that Lutherans, Presbyterians or Baptists are misguided because they emerged from the Protestant revolution. Rather, we wish to point out that during this period, much of the sacred autocracy of the formerly intact divine system was minimized and attacked, and this was a great loss.

There were, of course, legitimate reasons for this rejection of the teachings of the Church. Priests of the time were exploiting and cheating their parishioners, so naturally the people rebelled and tried to create a system that was less bureaucratic—one in which everyone had direct access to the prayers, scriptures and methods of worship. Although the intention behind this was good, the result was still imperfect and left many people adrift.

In fact, the material world is full of this kind of paradoxical duality. In order to correct an evil, we often destroy the positive aspects of a particular situation as well. It is as if we decided to blow up a dam in order to douse a raging fire in the valley. Although we may succeed in putting out the fire, we would also cause massive water damage to the village we are attempting to save. To some degree, Protestantism doused the fire of priestly exploitation and corruption, but it also created another problem in the process. It fostered the beginnings of religious anarchy and rejected many potent processes for spiritual deliverance that had been, and could continue to be, of great benefit to humanity.

A Degradation of Consciousness

Another major source of mass confusion on this planet came from the European emigration to the Americas. Before this influx of Europeans to America, approximately 80 million indigenous people lived on the continent. Yet, after a few years of European presence, only 10 million people survived. European behavior in the New World conformed to the collective consciousness of imperialism at that time, when one power after another traveled to foreign lands in order to acquire resources and commodities, sometimes by force, sometimes by barter and sometimes by trickery and deception.

Such an examination of social and political history can give us a clue as to the direction modern materialistic culture is taking. With this in mind, we may note that until the seventeenth century, almost all sociological, astronomical and scientific research was based on a theistic acceptance of the reality of the Supreme Being. From this point of view, the purpose of human life was to understand each person's position in relation to that Being within His cosmos, and to offer service to the Divine. Later, the Renaissance and other backward leaps encouraged people to throw away the notion of a Supreme Godhead altogether.

This trend away from God and toward a materialistic view of life increased greatly as we moved into the scientific revolution, the industrial revolution and the information revolution. Now, unfortunately, we can spend our lives sitting in one spot flipping television channels or browsing the Internet. As a result, the majority of people who once had a strong belief in God have now redirected their faith to new, lesser gods, including science, technology, television and computers. In the long run, these gods may not be as benevolent or reliable as we would like to believe.

Emptiness of the "American Dream"

As we look at our immediate situation here in America, we must begin to acknowledge the illusory nature of our so-called "American Dream" and the steep price we have paid for it. For example, in the last ten years, several million jobs have disappeared in the United States alone, largely because of modern automation that can replace tens, hundreds and even thousands of people at a time.

Another effect of our growing dependence on technology is that people are becoming increasingly impersonal. It is a phenomenal tragedy that people actually believe in the possibility of simulating an experience by watching it on a flat screen. As we watch romance and adventure on television or the silver screen, we begin to believe that we ourselves are involved in such experiences. By constantly relating to fantasies, virtual realities and images that we can control, that do not talk back and that we can dismiss at any time, we are losing our ability to relate to real, imperfect people in our everyday world.

Denial of the Soul's Eternality

The "American Dream" is gradually becoming a nightmare. Perhaps the most nightmarish component of this "American Dream" is all the suppression of information about reincarnation. Throughout the world, major religions and widely accepted bona fide philosophies have accepted the concept of reincarnation. Reincarnation is in fact an integral part of Native American philosophy, African philosophy, Hinduism, Buddhism, Taoism, ancient Greek philosophy, mystical Judaism, and mystical Islam. Scholars who study religious history can also confirm that reincarnation was an integral part of early mystical Christianity.

It was only in the sixth century, after the Emperor Justinian proclaimed that reincarnation was no longer acceptable and would be considered a heretic doctrine, that Christians began to denounce it. The writings of earlier Christians such as Saint Jerome in the fourth century explain that reincarnation was considered an esoteric doctrine that should be understood and defended by Christian philosophy. In the second century, Origen discussed themes of reincarnation in his book titled *On First Principles,* which is still available in the library today. As we research different scriptures, we can still find hints of reincarnation in all of them.

The truth is that ancient philosophers, modern mystic yogis and broadminded spiritualists have always recognized the eternality of the soul. Indeed, the concept is so widely accepted in many parts of the world that those who do not believe in reincarnation are the ones considered to be misguided. Here in the West, though, the repression and trivialization of this concept are so pervasive that even those who recognize the soul's eternal existence eventually are tempted to reject this depth of understanding.

This rejection is extremely denigrating to the soul and to all higher reasoning, because it convinces people that they must live only in the physical "here and now" and abandon everything of a higher, more subtle nature. Of course, maintaining such a dream requires that we sleepwalk, and everyone knows that sleepwalkers encounter a great danger of accidents, falls and injuries.

The Need for Simplicity

Families in agriculturally based societies used to master a trade or two—enough for one or two adults to feed an entire family, including the extended family, while at the same time imparting that trade to their children. Today, a whole staff or faculty is needed to teach vocational or professional skills. Yet, in many cases as the economy goes through unpredictable cycles, these skills can be insufficient to supply the necessities of life.

For example, as we enter the new millennium, there is no guarantee that those with college degrees will in fact be able to support themselves or a family. In fact, the likelihood that a college education will be useful gets slimmer with each year, as the increasing pace of technology makes last year's learning obsolete and replaces human beings with automation. As a culture, we have become increasingly vulnerable as we stray further and further from the basics of what people genuinely require for survival.

In simpler societies, trades were directly related to

fundamental, immediate needs. People grew their own food and made everyday items such as shoes, clothing, blankets, candles and soap. They learned essential skills, including carpentry, medical care and midwifery. With these relevant trades, community members could then barter to acquire the goods and services they needed from one another and all their necessities were provided.

In the information age, however, our commodities are so extraneous and intangible that the whole system becomes a bit absurd. Many of us get caught up in the extravaganza of consumerism and end up working, earning and spending an inordinate amount of money to accumulate a variety of possessions and experiences. Ironically, we often fail to meet our most basic human needs. We are often lonely and unfulfilled, unable to find meaning in our lives. Our quest for material gratification has obscured our deep, genuine longing for loving relationships and a sense of community. At an even more profound level, we have ignored the most fundamental human needs of all—to inquire into higher knowledge, to understand the purpose of human life, to develop an intimate relationship with God, and to offer ourselves in loving, devoted service.

Need for Healing

Indeed, the quality of human relationships is emphatically on the decline—and has been for a long time. Right now, some of the greatest threats to human progress, security and survival are toxic individuals, toxic physicians, toxic workers, toxic institutions and toxic communities, which are combining to produce a toxic society and a toxic planet. As a world, we need serious healing.

As for our future, the World Health Organization projects that over the next twenty years one of the greatest worldwide health problems will be mental illness. This is to be expected, as people experience increasing difficulty from trying to merely enjoy material pleasures without acknowledging that we are far more than just physical beings. Our increasing reliance on technology as a replacement for human relationships and community, combined with our competitive pursuit of material gain and power, can only deepen the loneliness and alienation so many of us experience.

The materialistic western view of the world attempts to break every subject down into component parts in order to understand and control its causes more effectively. However, this is not an invariably successful approach. Indeed, contemporary events are demonstrating its shortcomings. For example, if any lesson emerges from the spectacular failure of Western medicine to eradicate disease, it is that disease cannot be reduced to a single cause, nor can it be explained within prevailing linear, scientific parameters. In other words, complexity is the hallmark of disease.

Our reductionistic worldview needs to accept a holistic model and a way of living that is more spontaneous, pluralistic, joyful, integrative, constructive and life-sustaining. We need a cosmology that helps us view the big picture and be aware of the context of every problem. Our solutions must become holistic, transnational, transgenerational and hopefully transcendental in focus.

When we look at such proliferating worldwide problems as ecocide, matricide, genocide, homicide and suicide, we can see that these various symptoms of dysfunction are systemic and all-pervading. Very few people would question the need for serious healing on this planet. However, for such healing to occur, we must recognize and accept the necessity of a profound shift in our generally accepted paradigm. We must be willing to adopt a less materialistic view of what constitutes true happiness; we must acquire an understanding of the ultimate spiritual purpose of human life and of who we actually are as human beings.

A New Type of Human Being

As we meet the challenges that confront us and choose survival instead of destruction, a new type of human being is emerging who can express spiritual realities in the midst of the turmoil of daily life. At the same time, another kind of human being is on the decline. Individuals absorbed in selfishness, whose only thoughts are of the economics of sense gratification, are voluntarily moving down a path of self-destruction. They may be drug addicts or alcoholics whose lives are being shortened by their addictions. They may be politicians or business people whose stress-filled, egotistical lifestyles destroy their families and sap their health. Whatever path their focus on sense gratification takes, they are gradually distancing themselves from their own humanity, becoming increasingly enmeshed in materialistic concerns and attachments.

To emerge victorious from this struggle, and to choose the path of higher consciousness available to humanity, each of us must possess the characteristics of a powerful spiritual warrior. We must tune in to the spiritual and metaphysical realms in order to receive the support that is available there, and we will need courage and understanding to utilize the ammunition God has given us to help others.

A Call for Courage

Despite the gravity of the situation, we must not let our awareness of the degradation in today's world demoralize us or activate our fears. Rather, we should use this information as a catalyst to accelerate our pursuit of higher consciousness. If we simply "freak out" and run for cover, we will only make ourselves an easier target for these negative patterns. Instead, we must remain calm and centered, remembering that worry is a prayer for something we do not want. When we obsess and overreact to our fears, we are focusing on negativity.

Consequently, since energy follows thought, the concentration of our attention upon our fears tends to bring about the very conditions that we were trying to avoid.

Yes, it is true that we are at war—a spiritual war. Humanity stands at a critical crossroads. Forces are aligning themselves for a powerful struggle between the pious and the impious influences. The societies that dominate our world are not truly "cultures." They are devoid of God-consciousness, lack reverence and do not reflect a spiritual understanding of life. The great spiritual cultures of the past are no more, and the way of life that we see every day is morally depraved and toxic. To move beyond our degraded culture, we must first recognize it for what it is and understand the power it has over so many of us. Only then can we take wise and effective action as spiritual warriors.

Fear and love do not go together. Fear is constricting, self-centered and self-conscious, whereas love is expansive, selfless and directed toward service. To become effective spiritual warriors, we must learn to cultivate genuine love, courage, and compassion and come to depend on our inner faculties rather than externals. This allows us to understand our own true nature more deeply, and to behave more like the children and servants of God that we are. Then, firmly established in a higher state of consciousness, we can serve others—and the world—from the deepest, most aware and loving aspect of ourselves during these challenging times.

Questions & Answers

Question: I have read newspaper articles about some of your meetings with diplomats and presidents of various countries. I also know some professionals who took your leadership course at Montgomery College. Do you only deal with leaders and the "elite" class of society? Is your message only for them?

Answer: In warfare, one must use many different types of weapons and be able to reach all classes of people. History has shown that to effectively change consciousness, one must be able to influence the leadership as well as the average person. For example, early Christians were thrown into lions' dens, murdered and harassed in all sorts of ways. However, when Emperor Constantine was converted to Christianity, these same Christians suddenly had full support, and the morals and values of the culture were uplifted. Buddhism had so many difficulties, but when King Ashoka Maurya accepted it, it began to spread. When Srinivasa converted the king of Visnupur in West Bengal, the king made Vaisnavism a state religion. Narottama Das similarly converted the king of Manipur, who in turn made Manipur a Vaisnava state.

I am not moving about in the global community just to convert people, but as a warrior, I am definitely on a mission. My goal is to help people face and overcome their difficulties, with particular emphasis on spiritual solutions to material problems. However, crises in leadership are at the root of many of the world's current problems, and I therefore frequently target the leaders.

Question: You discuss the need for healing the planet, emphasizing that we not only have a toxic planet, but also toxic leadership, toxic institutions, toxic physicians and toxic individuals. In spiritual warriorship, which area is most affected by this toxicity?

Answer: Ultimately, everything comes down to a personal level. The family is a microcosm of the race, the tribe, the nation, even the planet. When our family units are healthy and spiritualized, this will affect every aspect of our existence. We must look closer at the family as we look at the individuals.

One of the themes we discuss at our medical conferences and leadership classes is the role that feeling loved and valued plays in health and productivity. From a medical point of view, people who feel alienated and not loved are four to five times more susceptible to disease and about five times more likely to meet premature death. When we feel unloved, our subconscious literally sends messages of self-destruction to various tissues of our body, and this plays a part in bringing on disease.

From a business point of view, as competition becomes more fierce, management must constantly struggle to produce their products faster, cheaper and with better quality than before. Many top business leaders have discovered that the key to success lies in the empowerment of one's staff. Successful management is actually only about 20% technique and 80% relationship. When employees are not feeling sufficiently valued and cared for, they will not produce sufficiently to keep-up or surpass the competition.

Jack Collins emphasizes this point in his book *When Your Customer Wins, You Can't Lose.* According to his research, only about 9% of customers will stop patronizing a business simply because the competition offers something better, and only about 14% will switch because of product dissatisfaction. On the other hand, about 75% of patrons leave when they perceive that they are not valued. All of this brings attention to the fact that giving proper care to the individual will naturally bring about healthier families, healthier institutions and a healthier planet.

Chapter 2

Predictions and prophecies

We have all heard predictions of calamities and global changes, especially as the new millennium dawned. Scholars from various religious traditions have pointed out that the current world order bears a frightening resemblance to the circumstances that their scriptures claim will precede devastation. Indeed, many people claim to have had mystical visions, and some have proven remarkably accurate. Other predictions have been propagated by fanatics and have proven to be remarkably destructive.

Although many of these predictions have not proven true, many claim that they still have some merit. We have all had a "bad feeling" that prevented us from walking down a particular alley or driving at a particular time. We may never know what dangers we were protected from in those instances—we may even feel a little embarrassed—but the fact remains that we were none the worse for following our instincts. Some believe that these predictions and prophecies serve a similar purpose in the world community: They serve as warnings that our present course of action is leading us down a dangerous path, and if we are attuned to the root message of these warnings and change our behavior in time, we can often avoid the catastrophes.

Let us spend some time examining a few of the most prevalent predictions for the coming years, how they have begun to manifest in our current reality, and what we as spiritual warriors can do to improve the global outlook.

The World Is Falling Apart

Many people today feel that the world is falling apart ecologically, geologically and economically. Pollution has become serious enough to affect the whole planet, not just one region, one country, or one continent. Almost every week there is a volcanic eruption, hurricane, flood or drought somewhere on the globe, causing great suffering to countless human beings and other forms of life.

We have due cause for concern. The Earth has become extremely sick. The normal remedy in the face of sickness or disease is to do some cleansing, and indeed, Mother Earth is trying to cleanse herself in order to reestablish balance. Many of the disasters predicted in various scriptures have begun to unfold as this cleansing process progresses.

In 1998 alone, 300 million people were displaced because of earthquakes, floods and tornadoes, and over 50,000 people lost their lives in these disasters worldwide. We should take heed of these omens instead of numbing ourselves with diversions.

A False Sense of Security

Some people are indeed watching these situations very closely, but others do not see the big picture yet because the events are happening in a fragmented way. Unfortunately, because news reports place so much emphasis on the news of the day, there is a tendency for us to overlook the general patterns. We tend to think these calamities only happen to the "other guy." We do not see the forest for the trees, and we do not acknowledge the fact that Mother Nature is claiming lives on this planet with increasing frequency.

Nature is not irregular and temperamental. She responds appropriately by reciprocating our actions towards her. Humanity has been and continues to be very abusive toward Mother Nature, and her natural first reaction is to withdraw her services and assistance. If the harmful behavior continues, she must ultimately rebel and defend herself. That is what is happening now.

Why Is This Happening?

Such turmoil and devastation may seem perplexing. If everything is well-ordered by cosmic arrangement, then why is there so much resource depletion, crime, racism, tribalism, greed, and aggression? Why do massive holocausts occur time after time, when a preordained cosmic order is supposed to exist?

As sentient beings, we are naturally inquisitive about enduring truths and important matters. When we look at all these questions, we must first employ a little detachment and realize that everything made of matter goes through transitions. All matter, whether animate or inanimate, experiences a cycle that we can loosely characterize as birth, maintenance and deterioration. Nothing made of matter escapes this process. From this perspective, there is nothing surprising about profound changes happening on the Earth.

A Major Transition Ahead

We are at a transition point in history. As one era fades away and another begins to unfold, the way people see themselves and their reality begins to shift. This is God's mercy, preparing us for the next chapters in what we call human history.

When divisive attitudes come to the fore, it is only a matter of time before God must adjust things so that His devotees do not suffer too severely and innocent people are not too badly misled. The Lord will arrange for tribulations in the lives of those who love Him, because by enduring difficulties, devoted individuals become stronger, more faithful and ultimately more glorious. These challenges show us that Mother-Father God is not indifferent or neglectful and has not forgotten us. This alone should give us hope.

The real reason for all this global suffering is that humanity is in the process of taking its final examinations. Everyone on the planet is undergoing important tests, the results of which will determine how well humanity will pull through the coming challenges—if we pull through them at all. The power to change is within us, but it is up to us to do what is necessary.

Unfortunately, many of us are indifferent or apathetic and unaware of the seriousness of the situation. Ultimately, our own lifestyles may prove more dangerous than the threat of public apathy. Societies that have not developed an appreciation for simple living, kindness to nature and self-sufficiency will take the hardest blows. People who have been overly spoiled and have developed huge appetites for luxury will be rudely awakened, and many will simply not have the emotional mettle to survive sudden hardships.

Need for Higher Consciousness

When discussing earth changes or impending calamities,

the first thing most people ask is "How can I save myself? Where is the safest place to find shelter? How much time do I have? How can I store food and water?" Most people of the present age are so entirely "me"-centered that they lack character, integrity and generosity. There is no thought or appreciation of sacrifice. It is rare for someone to ask, "What can I do to help my neighbor or that invalid who may not be able to flee from the fire or run for shelter?" Most people think solely about themselves.

Trying to correct a situation by means of the same consciousness that created it in the first place will never work. Unless we gradually elevate ourselves by exercising love in action, we will never experience our inherent divinity. Divine consciousness brings immense protection and fulfillment as well as other boons that defy description. But ultimately, human beings are only *potentially* divine. We must do our part.

None of this should surprise a spiritual warrior. A spiritual warrior is acquainted with the nature of the human mind and its tendency to rationalize. The conditioned mind is always inclined toward wishful thinking. The mind has the tendency to ignore and deny frightening and unpleasant truths no matter how obvious they are.

Warnings throughout History

Warnings about cataclysmic events have come from many directions all around us for centuries. Some of the world's most pious, ingenious and contemplative minds have endeavored to alert us to the dangers of technology and of tampering with nature.

Throughout history, science fiction writers, novelists and satirists have tried to awaken us to the ills of human pride and greed. Jonathan Swift, Lewis Carroll, Charles Dickens and Mark Twain gave poignant warnings of the harmful direction in which society was headed, as did Aldous Huxley, H.G.

Wells, George Bernard Shaw and Isaac Asimov. All of these great minds saw the signs of human demise. Many of them, such as Aldous Huxley in *Brave New World*, even turned to eastern mysticism and transcendentalism after modern materialism made them cynical.

Questions like these arise in the minds of intelligent persons. Although we should not overly obsess on potential crises, we also cannot be oblivious, especially in light of what so many ancient prophecies have foretold. Let us therefore look directly at some of these prophecies to deepen our awareness of what messages they hold for us.

Most of these predictions find their origins in various spiritual and metaphysical traditions. There are few disaster prophecies from atheists. Is this because spiritual people suffer from mass paranoia, or is it because such people are endowed with second sight and deeper vision? I leave that to you to answer for yourselves.

Psychics View the Future

Some people are born with psychic abilities. Perhaps some of these people were yogis in previous lives and came into this world with certain gifts of sight. Others may have come from other realms, where they possessed higher faculties. These gifts are rare, and when such gifted people come into this earthly realm, they stand out as extraordinary.

Some of the psychics now making predictions are in this category. They have unusual karma. There is something special about them, and they shine because of their positive karma and experiences from previous lives. Many of them possess or will soon possess higher faculties.

Over the last millennia, there have been several prophets whose predictions have proven astonishingly accurate. Well, hold onto your seats, because many of these same prophets have predicted some incredible changes on this planet in the near future. Some of them have even suggested that up to two-thirds of the people on this planet will die.

Throughout history there have been personalities like Edgar Cayce and Nostradamus, persons of extreme piety and purity who seem to be "carryovers" from another age. An extremely high percentage of Nostradamus' predictions have been correct.

Edgar Cayce displayed incredible powers of prediction. At his institute in Virginia Beach, VA, the Association for Research and Enlightenment (A.R.E.), countless records exist of predictions Cayce made while in trance. Almost all of these were accurate. Cayce predicts that Japan will sink into the Pacific Ocean and that earthquakes will destroy California around the turn of the century. He had much to say about how these events will increase over the next few years.

Astrologers Report from around the World

In Bangalore, India, a top astrologer by the name of B.V. Rama made a rather unique study. He contacted several of his colleagues—leading astrologers from around the world—and compiled a book of their predictions. Amazingly, all but one saw intense catastrophes and calamities occurring worldwide in the early years of the 21st century. Some of them attributed the devastation to wars, others to floods and earthquakes, and others to broad-scale earth changes, but nearly everyone's astrological analysis produced a vision of tremendous disasters plaguing the entire planet.

Predictions in Dreams

Dream investigations are another source of prophecy. Because I write and speak about psychic phenomena a great deal, I often get letters from people around the world with similar experiences. According to the reports I have received, numerous people are having dreams suggestive of massive future calamities. Interestingly enough, the dream content seems to be similar in all parts of the world, independent of language and culture. This tends to agree with Chet Snow's research on mass dreams, which indicates that these kinds of visions are occurring all over the world.

Insights from Hypnosis and Regression

As a student at Princeton University, I wrote an interdisciplinary dissertation on Eastern philosophy and Western psychology. As a result of my research into hypnotic regression for this thesis, I became convinced of the reality of life after death, and that subjects were able to view both their past and future lives during hypnosis.

People who are skeptical about reincarnation should consider the fact that many of reincarnation's strongest proponents were originally great skeptics themselves. Dr. Jess Stern and his hypnotherapy subject, novelist Janet Taylor Caldwell; the leading psychic Ruth Montgomery; and even Edgar Cayce were all skeptical of this reality until they were faced with overwhelming evidence.

There was another rather chilling element in our study. During moments of intense hypnotic progression, when subjects were taken into the future—say, the twenty-first and twenty-second centuries—the majority of people did not see themselves as existing in a future incarnation. In fact, almost none of the subjects studied saw themselves alive in the twenty-second century.

Some of the subjects who were fast-forwarded to the twenty-first century did see themselves existing, and gave incredibly similar accounts. Many saw nothing but tremendous calamities and immense changes in the world. While in the trance state, they perceived that most people did not survive the disasters, and that those who did survive were living very isolated lives in rural environments created outside the pitfalls of modern technology.

Dr. Raymond Moody's Psycomantium

There is another method of divination called a psycomantium—a darkened room in which people can see the future or communicate with departed loved ones by gazing into mirrors. Dr. Raymond Moody created a room in which people could do precisely this. His instrument proved to be so accurate that many articles were written about it. In many cases, people who used Dr. Moody's device experienced similar visions of the future. They saw great calamities in which millions of people suffered and died, followed by the emergence of a new civilization.

The Message of the Dinosaurs

There have been recent discoveries of the remains of dinosaurs frozen for millennia beneath ice and snow. Scientists have been able to look at the fossils and even at entire dinosaur carcasses to see them as they were in their original form. In certain cases, scientists have examined wooly mammoth stomachs and discovered undigested remnants of tropical plants.

At first, scientists were perplexed because the dinosaurs were found in arctic regions where such plants and foodstuffs did not exist. Eventually, the scientists were able to deduce from their studies just how severe the climatic changes in these areas had been. Apparently, within these dinosaurs' life spans, the earth's climate had severely changed from tropical to arctic.

The Evidence of the Pyramids

Turning to the wisdom of ancient Egypt, experts studying the Great Pyramid of Giza appear to have uncovered predictions that what we now consider world civilization will end by the year 2001.

Native American Timelines

Native Americans have a tradition of being attuned to nature and of interacting with their ancestors, as well as disembodied beings and extraterrestrials. The Mayan worldview predicts that technology will gradually turn on people and betray them. According to their calendar, by the year 2012 much of the technology that modern people depend on will produce a backlash that will literally destroy the world.

We might be wise to heed their warnings. For centuries, the Mayan calendars have accurately predicted the number of popes. The Mayan system predicts that one more pope will reign after the current one, and then no others. The reason given for this in their predictions is that civilization will basically be destroyed. The Mayan scriptures also say that a completely different scheme of life will have to exist in order for people to function. The Aztecs and the Hopi Indians have made similar predictions. Both of these oral traditions predict extreme calamities in the near future.

Buddhism's Vision of the Future

Many religious traditions are making predictions similar to those of individual psychics. For instance, Buddhism has long predicted that its lineage and tradition will last for 2,500 years, then change drastically or disappear altogether. By the end of 2000, Buddhism will have existed for 2,500 years.

Tibetan Buddhist theology predicts that after the fourteenth Dalai Lama, there will be no more heirs to the Dalai Lama's throne. The fourteenth Dalai Lama is enthroned right now.

Islam Predicts Civilization's Downfall

Islamic texts also claim that soon after man goes to the moon, world civilization as we know it will crumble. Many traditions have also predicted that the present era would be characterized by an increasing incidence of mind control. Esoteric Islamic texts, for instance, refer to a one-eyed monster that would control every household from within. Of course, this is the television set.

The Virgin Mary's Warnings

Recently there has been an increase in the frequency of the appearances of the Virgin Mary around the world. In the last several years, her appearance has been reported in many different places, such as Medjugorje, Bosnia. She has appeared to hundreds of thousands of people around the world. In almost all these appearances, the Virgin Mary has given a consistent, basic message that the world can be saved if—and only if—enough people change their lives, repent and turn to God. The second part of her message is that if people become increasingly sinful, we can expect incredible devastation.

Other Warnings in the Judeo-Christian Tradition

Similar information can be found in Judaism among the Kabbalists in their codes of the Zohar. The Zohar describes intense tribulations and global upheavals. Likewise, millions of Christians who have read the Bible's Book of Revelation are totally convinced that these are "the last days and times," and that there will be a serious devastation of our planet.

Religious movements such as Elizabeth Clare Prophet and the Ascended Masters have channeled revelations corroborating these ideas. Both these groups and the Mormons/Latter Day Saints have been making predictions and preparations for twenty-first-century disasters for years.

Vedic Predictions

According to the *Mahabharata,* whenever two eclipses take place in close succession, inauspicious events are bound to occur. Another inauspicious sign is the alignment of seven planets in one sign or house of the zodiac. Both of these events happened right before the terrible war described in the *Mahabharata.* Modern Astrological predictions indicate that two eclipses will take place in the year 2000, and that the same type of planetary alignment described in the *Mahabarata* and the *Bhavisya Purana* will happen again in May of 2000.

Another aspect of earth changes concerns the concept of *pralayas. Pralaya* is a Sanskrit term meaning a time of destruction or withdrawal, a cessation of manifestation. *Pralaya* is often defined as the state of latency or rest between two *manvantaras,* or great life cycles. These *pralayas* are generally preceded by periods of calamity or destruction. The Vedas give different types of situations that can bring down human civilization. In the contemporary world, there are a number of phenomena that could be indicators of an impending *pralaya.* It is of course difficult to know for certain, but any one of these circumstances by itself could extinguish the majority of the planet's inhabitants.

Greenhouse Effect. The first indicator of a possible *pralaya* is the greenhouse effect. Global warming is an increase in the Earth's temperature caused by too many greenhouse gases. Excess amounts of carbon dioxide, methane, and nitrous oxide trap too much infrared heat from the sun, causing an increase in the Earth's temperature. Over the past fifty to sixty years, scientists have noticed that the planet is getting hotter and hotter, as it tries to withstand ever greater levels of pollution. If this continues at the current rate, this could devastate humanity worldwide. This gradual global warming may also cause the polar icecaps to melt, causing devastating floods as water levels rise and possibly submerge entire countries.

Ozone Depletion. The second indicator is the phenomenon known as ozone depletion. Let us quote a few recent article headlines in the news. One of them simply says "The Ozone Vanishes, and Not Just over the South Pole." Another recent headline says, "Manmade Pollutants Are Producing Changes in the Earth's Climate that May Prove Catastrophic." Still another headline says: "Increasing Greenhouse Gases May be Worsening Arctic Ozone Depletion and May Delay Ozone Recovery."

The ozone layer is a covering that shields the whole planet. It is a part of a divine design that, among other things, protects us from being scorched to death by the sun's rays. Because of various unnatural pollutants and extreme emissions from human-made products, the ozone layer is now thinning, and ultraviolet rays are penetrating the upper atmosphere.

There are now large holes in the ozone layer located in the Antarctic and elsewhere. Scientists at first ignored the problem, hoping it would go away, but instead it has gotten worse. The holes are expanding and allowing harmful radiation to enter. The danger is that this radiation can harm millions of people and other forms of life. Already, there is an indication that this factor is increasing the skin cancer rate in human beings. This problem can also damage certain crops and can affect marine life and other life forms by affecting the food web.

Nuclear Warfare. The third indicator of a possible *pralaya* is the threat posed by nuclear arms and warfare. As almost everyone knows, the U.S. almost started a third world war when President Kennedy was in office as a result of the Cuban missile crisis. Information has come to light in the last few years regarding how serious the situation actually was. Russia was ready to back up Cuba and attack. Even though the hard-line communist government of Russia has been largely dismantled, there are still many nuclear arms experts and technicians whom the new Russian economy has not been able to employ, and there are weapons and materials that could all too easily find their way into dangerous hands.

Perhaps our government did not originally realize the danger of having these technicians on the loose. But now we have learned that terrorist organizations and governments have recruited some of them. Fear of this nuclear danger is certainly legitimate, especially when we put the situation in a historical context. It is rare in history for those in power to have weapons and not use them. Despite the fact that there are currently dozens of countries that have agreed to not fully develop or use nuclear weapons, there are also many countries with nuclear capabilities that have not made any such pledge of peace. It may only be a matter of time before history repeats itself and someone initiates a war.

If this occurs, we could be in serious trouble. The stakes have truly escalated because of the prevalence of terrorism and fanaticism. Terrorists can make nuclear bombs small enough to fit into a small suitcase yet powerful enough to kill tens of thousands of people. Many experts believe that it is only a matter of time before more politically motivated catastrophes occur.

In the past, most countries hesitated to attack others, fearing that opposing powers would counterattack. But present-day fanatics have no such concern. As we have seen in news reports, many terrorists are not afraid to lose their own lives. Because of their distorted mentality about salvation through the violent persecution of others, these terrorists will gladly sacrifice themselves if they can seriously damage those whom they perceive to be enemies.

Chemical and Biological Warfare. The fourth circumstance indicative of *pralaya* is chemical and biological warfare. Some of you may recall that only a few years ago, Israel invested in gas masks for the people as a protection against possible chemical warfare. The danger of chemical and biological warfare is that such an approach is infinitely cheaper, and therefore more widely accessible, than nuclear weaponry. Chemical weapons can quickly incapacitate and kill large populations, and biological weapons can cause the rapid spread of major catastrophic illnesses. Many informed people fear that biological warfare may soon get totally out of hand, causing all kinds of plagues and decimating the human family.

Pole Shifts. The fifth phenomenon is the possibility of a pole shift. A pole shift is an extremely dangerous event, because as the poles change position, the earth sphere moves in unpredictable ways, producing earthquakes, floods and other natural disasters. Archaeologists have discovered rock formations that suggest that such shifts have happened several times in the past. Many people believe that the poles are gradually shifting now and that a more sudden shift is imminent.

Comets

Comets can also portend a time of planetary upheaval. A comet is not simply a landmass or an inanimate object. It has a level of consciousness, as does everything else in the universe, because this is the nature of the Supreme Lord's energies. Many of us are consciously aware that the Earth is our mother—a living being. The Earth, the moon, the sun, and the galaxy itself are all living beings. Living entities have a certain presence, a certain consciousness. And so do comets.

In recent years, there has been increased attention given to the number of comets coming close to the earth, because of the threat that one of these comets might collide with the earth and cause tremendous destruction either by direct impact or by affecting our orbit. Of course, the sins that people have committed on this planet are sufficient in and of themselves to attract all kinds of disasters and misfortunes. We do not need a comet or harmful extraterrestrials to endanger us. Although many of these events are part of the necessary unfoldment at this time in history, they are not necessary to bring about our destruction. Consider it this way: If someone is afflicted with five deadly diseases and contracts another, it does not matter so much. For someone already on the verge of death, one more disease is basically inconsequential because the outcome is already certain.

All this notwithstanding, when comets do approach our planet, we should not be surprised that harmful events coincide with their arrival. Many of these comets and other planetary influences have an adverse effect on our consciousness and can bring out our worst conditioned responses. We have examples of this in everyday life: at the time of the full moon, sensitive beings can feel the influence. More crimes occur; animals howl. Comets, too, can intensify our propensities for good or for ill.

Extraterrestrial Contacts

In this time of global upheaval, many predictions exist about major extraterrestrial interventions, either to help save this planet or to hasten its devastation. The subject of extraterrestrial contact has always been a controversial one, yet many ancient scriptures emphasize the fact that higher beings have always existed. These beings travel throughout various universes and visit this planet as part of their itinerary. As we read the Vedas, the Bible, the Quar'an and the Torah, we find frequent mention of visits by angels and higher beings. The Bible also talks about sons of God marrying the daughters of man, and through all of the ancient oral traditions similar subjects have been discussed. Yogis and mystics who have been able to travel between different dimensions of God's creation have existed since time immemorial.

Many events that we now consider mythology were actually real. Because many of these experiences are no longer commonplace, and may even seem implausible, people are tempted to label them as mythology. Yet many of these occurrences most likely took place exactly as they have been reported. This becomes easy to understand if we remember that in those times people were more natural, had more reverence for God and were aware that they were not just a physical body.

This is no longer the case. People are the opposite now. Despite our persistent belief that we are an advanced civilization, we have actually become more primitive because we are force-fed by materialism. We tend to not look at the essence of things. Modern society is gradually finding more substitutes for God, and as a result we are losing our ability to appreciate divinity and our connections with higher dimensions of reality.

Therefore, to the modern mind, all these occurrences seem like myths. But whether we examine the traditions of the Egyptians, the Indians, the Celts, the ancient Druids, the Dogon or the Zulu, we find that all of these cultures had a vast knowledge of extraterrestrials, visitations, and communications with other realms.

Vedic scriptures constantly refer to the relationships among various universes and planets, and to the connections between human beings and other kinds of highly intelligent species. These texts suggest that powerful beings who are part of this galaxy have a major influence on events here on Earth. These ancient teachings, deliberately written down and preserved for thousands of years, serve to warn us of the upheavals that are occurring now.

Growing Public Interest in UFOs

Extraterrestrial beings have visited our planet for decades. Knowing that people were not ready to hear about UFOs, they found ways to infiltrate the media and literary fields to introduce ideas about extraterrestrial life to the general pubic. They inspired the production of books, television shows and films, knowing that when the information was released, even in the guise of fantasy, it would affect the collective consciousness and wake people up. Indeed, there has been a steady increase in the investigation and discussion of these subjects over the years.

The government has been aware of extraterrestrial contacts for quite some time and has actively attempted to cover up the situation or make the facts appear as fantasies or as the broodings of mentally unbalanced individuals. However, since the world is currently in such an unstable state of transition, governments are recognizing their inability to control future events. Consequently, officials are allowing more information to get out. They are hoping that if these unsettling realities are brought to the population's attention in a gradual way, there will be less fear and trauma when the realization dawns that governments and military forces can do little to protect them.

Unfortunately, people are so absorbed in material life that they do not realize how dangerous the situation is. Many of the negative occurrences in this world are results of the spiritual bankruptcy and low consciousness of the world's inhabitants. That is one reason why spiritual life is truly a matter of survival today—even physical survival—because a higher consciousness can change outer circumstances or, if it is too late for that, prepare us to face extreme adversity with serenity, skill and courage.

About twenty years ago, I was speaking about a variety of subjects on a radio program in Cleveland, Ohio. People were calling in, extremely enthusiastic and involved in what I was discussing. The program continued in this way for about an hour and a half. Then I made a few comments about UFOs—and all of a sudden people started calling in with their complaints: "Swami, your presentation was wonderful until you mentioned this nonsense."

I realized then that people were not ready to hear about extraterrestrials and UFOs. But the situation is changing rapidly now. These days, it is not unusual to hear about UFOs and alien abductions. For example, recently on the Oprah Winfrey show—one of the most popular television shows in America—a panel discussed UFOs, extraterrestrial phenomena and alien abductions.

One of the guests on this show was a psychiatrist with an active teaching position at Harvard University—one of the most famous and respected schools in the country. Just think about it: here was an expert from this great university speaking about phenomena far beyond the normal range of what we consider to be reality, viewed by millions on one of the most popular shows in the nation. This is just one example indicating that these kinds of topics are definitely being discussed more and more.

This psychiatrist, Dr. John Mack, said that our culture has consciously tried to avoid discussing such topics as alien abductions. Instead, he added, we have consciously put great effort into believing that people who report experiences with extraterrestrials are suffering from neurosis, psychosis or at the very least, hallucinations.

On this particular show several people reported that the abductions had continued for many years, and that only now were they able to "come out of the closet" to speak about their experiences. They felt more able to discuss them because so many books and articles have been written on the subject now and people have become more receptive to these ideas.

Those who talked about having UFO contacts usually described the same type of extraterrestrial—beings with unusually shaped heads, large eyes and a rather pale skin color. The abductees described the mission of these beings as a mission of survival. Abductees often talked about being sexually exploited, being operated on and having to endure severe pain. Some claimed to have held babies that seemed part human and part extraterrestrial—babies who were their own as a result of cross-breeding. In addition, some women reported being pregnant and then seemingly having a miscarriage. Later, when examined by a doctor, no trace of their pregnancy remained.

Many abductees were not able to make sense of their experience, and understandably they became upset and disturbed. If they went to a therapist for help, the therapist might not be aware that such phenomena were possible. Instead, the therapist would tend to diagnose the person as mentally unstable.

Dr. Mack claimed that these kinds of abductions have always been occurring, and that an interesting element of these abduction reports is that they demonstrate to many people there are connections and communications beyond what we normally see, feel, touch, hear, and taste. Indeed, in other cultures in the world, where there is more emphasis on the mystic or the metaphysical, it is not unusual for people to understand that there can be contacts beyond our material everyday consciousness.

There is nothing particularly astounding about the psychic or metaphysical realm. It is part of our reality if we attune ourselves to it. We have a physical body; in addition, there is a metaphysical or subtle presence and, of course, there is a soul. Many people initially move beyond the material level of reality as the result of a fascination with the psychic and the metaphysical. This helps them inquire more deeply about what is behind the many phenomena of life. Eventually, they begin to realize that there is more to human experience than what the senses normally show us.

Cloning

In his book *Genesis Revisited*, Zecharia Stitchin concludes that human beings were originally produced by genetic engineering. According to Stitchin and others, human beings today, and earlier ones in human history, may have deliberately been genetically engineered by extraterrestrial colonists to produce willing slaves. As the story goes, a comradeship developed between those big brothers and sisters and the little brothers and sisters on this planet. But initially, the relationships were not about comradeship or mutual sharing, but about creating an underclass of beings with low intelligence and great bodily strength who could perform hard physical labor.

If even some of this theory holds true, cloning is not at all a new concept. Rather, it is as old as human existence. Genesis 1:26.6 says, "Let us make man in our image." We must also wonder if the story of Eve being created from Adam's rib is more than a mere metaphor.

Increasing Turmoil

These discussions of extraterrestrials, comets, cloning and predictions of disaster have relevance to spiritual life. They demonstrate that our Earth planet is in great turmoil as a result of increasing violence and misuse of natural, financial and intellectual resources. We must remember that all systems have thresholds beyond which they lose their stability and produce an explosion or eruption. Just as water freezes at a certain temperature and boils at another temperature, the inhabitants of this planet can undergo positive transformation or be provoked into insane behavior by upcoming events.

Ancient Vedic scriptures predict that the situation will become so intense in the *Kali-yuga*—the Age of Quarrel in which we live—that citizens will flee to the forests to escape. These scriptures also predict that, as this age progresses, people will live a shorter lifespan, that most religion will turn into irreligion, and that there will be an inordinate rise in suicide. In certain places on this planet today, armed soldiers and police are attacking the citizens they are supposed to protect, and criminals are looting and assaulting victims with impunity. All over the world, "home" for many women, children and elderly people is a place where they are physically whipped, abused, intimidated or molested from morning until night. The list is endless of the ways in which we are abandoning our God-given responsibilities to love and serve each other and our planet.

Disasters Expose Our True Motivations

Disasters, when they occur, expose the real hearts and motivations of us all. Selfish persons simply remain part of the general negative atmosphere, trying to protect themselves and exacerbating the problems instead of helping to resolve them. But true spiritual warriors do not think in such a self-centered way. They do not seek to save themselves first. They are lovers of God who know that hurting or neglecting others will damage their relationship with the Divine, and they will do anything to avoid being estranged from the Supreme Spirit. After all, their every aspiration is to please the Supreme Lord and become worthy of divine association.

Wide Availability of Higher Knowledge

As we begin the twenty-first century, even those who are materialistic will have the opportunity to change their view of themselves and their reality. An important reason for this is that higher knowledge is now penetrating this culture as a result of mass entertainment. How many times a month is there a television show or a movie dealing with psychic phenomena,

UFOs, or life after death? Such topics are frequent themes these days.

It is the mercy of the Lord that makes such information more accessible. Such nonmaterial points of view can make us think more deeply and help us outgrow our self-indulgent habits and thought patterns. We do not necessarily have to participate in spiritual groups to learn about deeper aspects of reality. We can instead learn by keeping our eyes and ears open to our surroundings. We must keep in mind, though, that we are also being bombarded with a great deal of harmful information. Unless we manage to develop spiritual association with like-minded people, we will probably not take full advantage of the available information, or we will simply view the new ideas as irrelevant or impractical.

A Wake-up Call

We cannot emphasize enough that the present atmosphere of mass selfishness, greed and exploitation will continue to increase if we continue in our old habits, if we persist in ravaging the planet and if leaders allow their lower desires to dominate them. As such a negative situation continues, few of us will have a chance to enter into the twenty-first century with the spiritual security that we could have if we were more attuned to higher levels of existence. Is this the future we want for anyone?

Questions & Answers

Question: The Bhagavad-Gita predicts that the *Kali-yuga,* the Age of Quarrel, will last for 432,000 years, after which the material realm will be destroyed. How do all of these other predictions of calamities and earth changes correspond to this 432,000 year period?

Answer: In the *Brahama-Vaivarta Purana,* Krishna tells Ganga-devi that there will be a golden age within the *Kali-yuga* that will start about 5,000 years after the beginning of the age and last for 10,000 years. After that period, the full force of the Age of Quarrel will manifest on this planet. We are considered to be in the first phases of this golden age, during which some polarization and purification must take place. It is believed that the current shifts are a part of this transition.

Question: You have said that we are receiving direct chastisements from God. How can God be all good, all powerful and full of love, and yet be a punisher? If God were full of positives and devoid of negatives, why would He chastise people? Is this not a contradiction?

Answer: Actually, the opposite is the case. The Bible says, "Whom the Lord loveth, He chastiseth." So the discipline is for rectification, to help make the situation or person better. Parents who do not discipline their children are considered unhealthy, preoccupied and irresponsible. Chastisement is part of what curbs bad behavior in children. It is also true for adults. We see, for example, the extent of illicit sex life around the world has been one of the major causes for the spreading scourge of AIDS. If not checked soon, AIDS could nearly wipe out entire countries within the next 10 or 20 years. Experts predict that over one-third of the world population could be devastated—something similar to the Black Plague. Around the thirteenth century, the Black Plague decimated Europe, killing almost 30 million people out of a population of 75 million stretching from Italy to Switzerland in only four years.

Some powerful events can occur that are part of an amazing plan arranged by God to help us. While we are experiencing painful situations, we may not consider them as helpful, but we must take a long-range view. Eventually, to be truly happy, we must learn to live in accordance with God's laws. The ultimate result depends on us. If we are careful and begin to live in a righteous and just manner, we will stop receiving punitive reactions. Then we can begin to restore the planet and ourselves to a healthy state.

Question: You mentioned that during hypnosis, some people can learn about their previous lives. How can you authenticate this? Have there been any studies of people who have memories from a previous life to verify the accuracy of their reports?

Answer: One question we may want to investigate is: How do we know anything? We receive input from our senses, or we decide that something seems probable, but can we put our hypothesis to the test in various ways? If, under hypnosis, someone reports dying in a fire, we may notice that the person experiences a phobia of fire in the present life. This may make the report slightly more believable. To investigate further, we may have the opportunity to check certain court records or family records to corroborate reported events. We may find that a particular child did indeed live at the indicated time, that a specific accident happened, or that a certain journey took place. We may find out who the parents were. There are so many pieces that can fall into place. There are several careful studies that give solid proof; here are just two examples:

Dr. Ian Stevenson has written many books on this subject, two of which are *Children Who Remember* and *Twenty Cases Suggestive of Reincarnation*. Dr. Stevenson carefully documented the statements of thousands of children who claimed to remember a past life. He would then attempt to identify the deceased person the child remembered being and compare the facts of the deceased person's life to the memories of the child. His research method was strict and methodical, and allowed him to rule out all possible "normal" explanations for the memories the children had.

Another book, by therapist Carol Bowan, titled *Children's Past Lives: How Past Life Memories Affect Your Child*, stemmed from her own child's account of being a Civil War soldier. This account was so accurate that a historian was able to verify the events.

Chapter 3

The condition of society today

Most of us believe that the benefits of contemporary civilization are evidence of human progress, but there is another point of view. Rather than advancing to our present state, perhaps we have regressed from an earlier, more natural agrarian age. We have changed from an agriculturally based society into an industrial, scientific, and technological one—and now into an information culture. As this sequence has progressed, our civilization has become increasingly impersonal. We have placed commodities at the center of our existence, all the while minimizing community and our understanding of deep relationships, the soul and the spiritual dimensions of life. Western cosmology has become manipulative and exploitive, and it functions in a paradigm that does not consider the well-being of the whole. Is this progress?

Technology Is Not Neutral

Many thoughtful persons may ask, "But isn't technology

neutral?" The answer is both "yes" and "no." Technology may be neutral in and of itself, but its use is not, and its prevalence in any society is usually a symptom of underlying problems. Material technology generally becomes prominent in more degraded societies because people are mainly interested in sense gratification. Therefore, they are always eager for new thrills and conquests. As people abandon lives of spirituality, simplicity and serenity, they must find other outlets for their mental and physical energy.

Superficiality of Knowledge

Many young people today attend schools and universities where they expect to become more refined and learn how to cope better with the world. Modern universities and schools, both public and private, have instead become factories for creating a sophisticated animalistic mentality. A great number of students engage in drug-taking and promiscuity, and there is a widespread belief that all values, principles and truths are relative. Teachers must be extremely careful about mentioning subjects that hint of spirituality, because academia has little interest in spiritual truths and almost no understanding of anything beyond the senses, the mind and the intelligence.

Because academic pursuits today are mainly data-gathering activities rather than quests for real, eternal knowledge, they do not deal with the essence of every individual—the soul. Instead, by emphasizing relative values and objective knowledge, contemporary learning produces a great stimulus toward sense gratification, manipulation and exploitation.

Poor Quality of Life

Countless people are running around from place to place—on urgent business, or simply shuffling paper in a more sophisticated way. They have not had a home-cooked meal in years, and even that may have been microwaved. They sit under fluorescent lights, eat denatured food, work all day in windowless environments, and drive around on freeways inhaling toxic chemicals.

When evaluating the "progress" of a society, we must examine what that society has sacrificed to gain its supposed advantages. Modern society has sacrificed communities for commodities. We have sacrificed knowledge for information, and wisdom for propaganda. Further, we have sacrificed religion for politics and, most unfortunately, we have sacrificed love for lust.

The Extent of Human Need

We have sacrificed the welfare of billions of people on the altar of economic success for a relative few. More than half the people in the modern world go to bed hungry every night. One-fourth of the people on this planet are illiterate, and over half of the Earth's inhabitants do not have acceptable drinking water. Millions of people are homeless.

These problems are not restricted to any particular racial or sociological groups. Even America, the richest nation in the world, is riddled with malnutrition. In an age where we have the ability to relieve so many types of suffering, it is extremely saddening to discover that there is such a steep increase in the most basic human problems of survival.

One of the most staggering contemporary issues in all parts of the globe is the plight of refugees. Their situation is shocking. Millions of people have had to leave everything behind and run for their lives, or have had to migrate elsewhere in order to meet their fundamental needs for food, water and shelter. There are about 30 million refugees in the world today—more if we count those who cannot leave their countries, yet are unable to stay in their own homes safely.

Misguided Worship

Not only are we building shrines to money and the free enterprise system daily, we are worshiping many public personalities who are less than desirable role models. Modern culture has taken to deifying people with degraded values.

A few years ago, an English rock group staged a show in India that the Hindu public considered irreverent to one particular goddess. Well, God bless them, the Indian people protested with such vigor that the group was forced to leave the country. This is how dedicated many people in India are to keeping the purity of spiritual life.

But how do Americans react to lusty, half-naked, sacrilegious rock stars? Do we protest? Of course not. We deify them, imitate them, buy their records by the millions and make them a huge success. What do Americans do with a filthy-mouthed talk show host who can instigate all kinds of violence between different groups and display total irreverence for everything sacred? We revere him, make movies about him, give him greater spans of airtime, and reward him with a higher salary.

Entertainers who arouse our lust and desire for kinky sex have become the idols that many Americans worship. At the same time, banks, casinos and insurance companies are the buildings we enshrine as our places of worship. All these factors are helping to increase the decadence of modern culture.

It is commonplace for humans to engage in various forms of worship. In our culture, we worship entertainers, sportsmen, and even criminals. Television focuses on criminals to such an extent that the person committing the most violent act often becomes glorified. People seeing these role models are sometimes even subconsciously tempted to emulate them.

Improper Role Models

I recall one leading and extremely influential music group who stayed on the charts for decades. In the early days, this group delivered very powerful political and social messages. However, as time went on, the group began to send out increasingly degrading messages that were more subjugating than liberating. Members of the group had become known for their ingenious creativity. Over time, however, to maintain their outstanding prestige and popularity, they began to misdirect this creativity by using animal sounds and barking in their music. Over wonderfully elaborate and intoxicating rhythms, these human beings would make "woofing" sounds while singing lyrics that boasted of their doggish nature.

The group's stage show was even more degrading. In concert, these grown men would wear ridiculous wigs with outrageously colored hair, and one of the members was famous for wearing a baby diaper. Undoubtedly, because of their fame and influence, members of this group were targeted by more sinister powers who either forced, tricked or induced them into broadcasting such self-abasing messages and behavior.

In its early days, this group had the potential to be revolutionary. It was very popular at the time that African Americans were beginning to assert themselves strongly in American culture. Since many revolutionary-minded persons of all colors listened to them and identified with them, this group could have inspired people to bring about the changes required to build a more just society. Unfortunately, as this group and others began to degrade and regress in consciousness, it helped to dismantle any real attempts at revolution, the redistribution of wealth or the pursuit of political justice.

The bottom line is that many artists that the public thinks are "cool" have become completely absorbed in sense gratification. What kind of positive contribution does a publicly adulated womanizer stoned on drugs and earning millions a year make to the well-being of society? What sort of role models do people who bark like dogs offer?

From the perspective of higher knowledge, nothing could be more degrading to the human soul than to mimic animal behavior. This is not just a matter of aesthetics or refinement. The divine laws that govern this universe dictate that when one's body indulges in animalistic behavior, one's consciousness follows, and, of course, the reverse is also true. The divine mission of human beings is seriously defiled by regression to a lower level of development.

When human beings stoop to the level of copying animals, they have already succumbed to defeat. The most sacred knowledge on this planet tells us that all living entities have souls. The main difference between animals and humans is that humans have a sense of restraint, self-control, and conscience. It is for this reason that humans are given more latitude and dominion on Earth. We should never forget that, as human beings, we are accountable for our actions, while animals are under the jurisdiction of instinct and are therefore not responsible for their actions.

The Need for Real Leadership

Our contemporary governments and other institutions are sorely lacking powerful, responsible, selfless leaders. Do not mistakenly believe that the media is playing games when they expose leaders and unearth scandals. Their message is a serious one: we cannot trust most of our leaders. Why not? Because many of them are engaged in selfish sense gratification and manipulation to gain power.

The leaders of most countries are increasingly guiding people away from spiritual life, and many of their policies are officially encouraging massive immorality. For instance, many states are exploring how to legalize gambling because it is an effective way to build revenue. However, is this constructive for the people who are gambling? What about economic policies that further exacerbate the divisions between the world's rich and poor?

A serious situation arises when material illusions become so strong that sin is committed boldly and collectively, becoming a prominent part of the culture. I have personally observed the effects of this global delusion in my travels around the world.

Meanwhile, our other guardians are not proving themselves to be any better. For example, America has been uncovering many instances of disrespectful treatment, rape and abuse in mental health institutions and nursing homes. There have been numerous exposés in the media reporting the stories of helpless, bedridden, paralyzed patients who were raped in their wards by so-called health practitioners.

Corruption Is Commonplace

No matter where they live around the world, people in positions of power fall down or become corrupt for similar reasons. We see that when leaders are attached to their positions and the associated perks, they are unable to understand their roles as servants of God. Without a sense of detachment, they are unable to give to others effectively. They use their power to promote their own agendas rather than offering themselves in service to those they are supposed to lead.

Such leaders are master manipulators and will find ways to justify their actions by any means. They misuse their positions to sabotage everything of a higher nature. They take advantage of situations for their personal gain and betray the trust of those who place faith in them.

It is unspeakably sad that the president of the United States was recently investigated for serious moral and legal transgressions. Yet the world climate has become so permissive that people consider adultery and sexual misconduct commonplace and do not even bat an eye. This sends a terrible message. Citizens naturally become tempted to imitate this immoral behavior or to lust after positions in which they can exploit others with impunity.

When even our leaders resort to exploitation and abuse, fostering a culture of degradation rather than liberation, what hope is there for most of us ever to break free of the clutches of illusion?

Corrupt Police

In some nations, the police force—one of our supposed protective agencies—is so ineffectual that criminals boldly enter police stations and rob policemen of their weapons and uniforms. Sometimes criminals have sent out notices to warn victims of their intention of robbing their homes at a particular date and time. In such cases, the potential victims would be wise to vacate the premises.

In other parts of the world, police forces are so corrupt that some policemen double as criminals. I actually saw this in some developing countries in Africa. By day they would serve as uniformed policemen and by night they would become masked criminals. I also witnessed instances where policemen would rent their weapons to criminals—even to those that they had arrested. This kind of behavior is occurring all over the planet.

Short-Term Self-Interest

In many cases, our leaders are ineffectual because they have not trained themselves in the arts of self-discipline and austerity. In the pursuit of their own selfish interests, they use the same shortcuts and avenues of exploitation that criminals use. As a result, when they take charge, they sometimes make an even greater mess of things.

Let us look directly at the current world situation. It is not uncommon today to see rampant exploitation of the masses by politicians, government officials and other leaders. Certain third-world leaders have sold their own countries out by allowing the dumping of toxic waste in their homelands, just so they can deposit large sums of money into their Swiss bank accounts.

The self-centered, short-term thinking of our leaders can have devastating effects on the world for generations. For example, some nuclear reactors are being built to endure for only 50 years. Yet the nuclear pollution that they create can remain harmful for thousands of years. Are the tycoons who have created these poisons going to allow these toxic wastes to be stored in their own back yards? Of course not. They ship these wastes across the country, endangering the public, or they bury the toxic material at sea, or they put it on boats and send it to countries with leaders who will sell out their citizens for some temporary profits.

Ecological Devastation

People are well aware of the ecological degradation on this planet. As greedy fortune hunters, tycoons and speculators construct more factories, mine more minerals and dig more oil wells, they are literally rupturing the womb of Mother Earth. Their transgressions of dumping toxic waste, polluting the water and fouling the air will prove extremely devastating to the people on this planet in the near future.

When businesses and nations persist in engaging in exploitive behavior for short-term profit and power, without considering the ramifications of that conduct, then we are all put into extreme jeopardy. Mother Earth is reaching her limits in a great many areas. For example, the massive cutting down of trees is diminishing our oxygen supply. Our clean water supply has almost vanished in many parts of the world, and the provision of adequate amounts of water is fast becoming a worldwide problem. We are all responsible for this situation because we are all contributing to the depletion of our resources and the pollution of this planet.

Economic Exploitation

Economic exploitation is a particularly serious issue because those who control the economic system control other people, the environment, the nation and even the planet. This is the nature of the paradigm that views reality as material instead of spiritual.

This reveals the extent to which selfish interests can capture the minds and lifestyles of modern people. The current U.S. banking system is controlled by the Federal Reserve, which is not even a government agency. The Federal Reserve is a consortium of private bankers; in other words, it is a completely private business posing as a government agency, yet every dollar that is circulated in the U.S. economy is borrowed from the Federal Reserve.

A Debt-Driven Economy

America is one of many countries that can never get out of debt. Why? Because in order to pay off one debt, the American government has to borrow. This means that in order to pay off its current debt, the nation has to incur even more debt. As a result of the modern banking practice of fractional reserve lending, there is already many times more debt than money circulating. When you are in debt, then you are obligated to follow the rules the debtors are arranging. Incurring debt is a widely accepted practice today and an extremely effective way for certain elements of society to gain power and for others to lose it.

On another economic front, many people who are counting on insurance claims and social security stipends are going to be disappointed. Even now, as the world experiences increasing numbers of natural disasters, many insurance companies are having problems covering the losses. These agencies were never designed to be magnanimous and take care of their policyholders. Insurance companies were designed to make as much money as possible and to pay claims only when absolutely necessary. Consequently, they cover the costs of claims by raising their rates... It is obvious whose side they are on.

People become especially aggressive when they perceive a shortage of goods, services or necessities. Such scarcity seems to be pervasive in the world today. Actually, however, there is no real scarcity anywhere on this planet. There is only the scarcity created by the hoarding of the rich and powerful.

A small percentage of the people own a vast majority of the world's total wealth. The planet is divided into "haves" and "have-nots." As the "haves" grow wealthier, the suffering of the "have-nots" increases daily.

Houses of Worship in Decline

Even our places of worship are caught up in the general decline of morals. The mosques, temples, synagogues and churches are supposed to be places surcharged with spiritual energy. If a place is properly spiritualized almost anyone who walks by or enters can feel it. Sometimes even animals will become calmer and act in a more peaceful, gentle way.

Nowadays, however, when we go to the average place of worship, we often have to return home to find peace because of so much backbiting, political maneuvering and confusion. The failure of spiritual centers to uplift us creates an atmosphere of distrust and disappointment. When places of worship get caught up in the general turbulence of the world, people are not properly protected from the outer environment of contamination.

Frequently, members of religious denominations engage in prayer to fulfill their material desires, gain control over someone else or to take what does not belong to them. Many prayers are about manipulation instead of devotion and surrender to divine will. However, God is not an "order-taker" and does not cater to such prayers.

No Sacred Havens

At earlier times in history, people sought refuge from persecution or from criminals by entering churches, temples and mosques. Unfortunately, today that is often not the case. All too many modern churches cater to self-centeredness and spiritual impotence. They cannot provide any real shelter. It is only natural for people to run to their spiritual havens when they are suffering, but evil does not care where one goes to hide. In some countries I have visited, criminals and soldiers rape, abuse and murder people even within the church walls.

We have to look beneath the surface to see why this situation exists. These days, people see so much hypocrisy in their churches and temples that they easily lose faith in spiritual traditions and their practitioners. Otherwise, at least some climate of reverence would exist, and people passing by sacred places of worship would recognize them as abodes of God.

When a culture does not demonstrate sufficient love and respect for God, people will simply see religion as yet another form of exploitation. This is why all over this planet nuns, bishops and imams are being murdered.

Hypocrisy of Religious Leaders

On one of my visits to Nigeria, I appeared on a television program discussing the reasons for the robbery and murder of so many religious ministers in that country. I first suggested that perhaps the victims were not true ministers of God. Many of them were indeed wearing the garb and talking the talk, but we all know that such external appearances do not necessarily make one a minister.

Sometimes ministerial candidates go to schools where

they learn to quote verses, to speak with the right inflection and pause at the right moments. But unless there is a change in their own hearts and consciousness, they are simply learning to give a performance. The biggest sign of a positive change in one's own consciousness is the ability to uplift the consciousness of other people—a factor that is sorely lacking in many of today's religious institutions.

Atrocities in the Name of God

In some parts of the world we see Hindus and Muslims fighting each other. In Ireland the Catholics and Protestants have been at war for years, and in the Middle East Jews and Muslim Arabs have been attacking one another for decades. In what Bible, Quar'an, Torah, or Vedic scripture does it say to go out and murder those who have a different spiritual outlook? In what holy book is such violence recommended? These writings actually teach the exact opposite, emphasizing religious tolerance and compassion. In many different words, all these scriptures exhort us to love our neighbors as ourselves.

In the recent past, religion once claimed that women have no souls, and on this supposed "evidence" women were subjected to terrible abuse. The Inquisition and the witch burnings were appalling examples of the mistreatment of women and others who were considered outside the redemptive power of the church. Even more recently, women were not allowed to vote or own property.

In the modern world, popular culture often ridicules the value of religion and spirituality, implying that spiritual people are archaic, prudish and reactionary. This makes it easier for self-indulgent, atheistic agendas to gain prominence in our culture. However, as spiritual warriors, we are interested in the truth, and in living and sharing that truth with others. This means that we must not allow ourselves to be caught in the illusions that are so prominent in today's society.

Subtle Corruption

The church has its share of corruption. Sometimes, if a minister's sermon is a bit too truthful, a deacon sitting in the back of the church may give him a little sign to indicate that he is stepping on the toes of some congregation members. Later, in private, the deacon might even tell him: "You know that house you live in? We own it. That nice car you drive? We own that, too. If you're not careful, you could lose all of it." Then, suddenly, the reverend has second thoughts about what he said, realizing that he went a bit too far for his own good.

And what was his crime? Those of us who are preachers know the situation well. As we speak, we become filled with the holy spirit and want to help others make that leap of faith to be more accountable, to stand up a little taller, to walk a little more evenly and to resist the many temptations that surround them. It is our duty, after all, to redeem people by giving them potent truths that can make a difference in their lives—not truths that are watered down and powerless.

Just as schoolteachers have to point out defects in penmanship, punctuation or pronunciation so that students can correct themselves, preachers have to show others where they need to improve. However, most adults, far from appreciating real guidance, just want pleasant strokes and soothing words. They do not want to be challenged to look at their own shortcomings in order to discover where they are cutting corners and preventing themselves from getting the fullest divine mercy available.

Egocentricity in Excess

Everything we see tells us that the world situation is seriously out of control, and one of the greatest indicators is the degree to which people are becoming more egocentric. In this culture, even our children are permitted to display extreme levels of egocentricity. For example, while it was once common for students to wear uniforms or simple clothing to school, now little children try to distinguish themselves from their classmates by their outer attire—not by their character or performance.

School uniforms served multiple purposes: They made students more humble, more bonded and less distracted by the superficial aspects of existence. Rich and poor dressed alike. Now there is so much emphasis on appearance that people have become competitive, insecure and ultimately more self-centered. We have actually regressed in our development to increasingly infantile states.

We see the signs of this egocentricity wherever we go—in the ways that we shop, eat and try to enjoy ourselves. It is particularly true in the phenomenon of dance. Until a few decades ago, dance was a method of bonding and strengthening community. People danced in groups, squares or circles. Later, partners paired off in male and female couples to dance in a more isolated, yet still communicative, way.

Now, we see that a more freestyle dancing has become very popular, where participants "do their own thing" in an anarchical way. The dancers express their own independence and flair, without any effort to combine with others. Freestyle dancers are judged not by their ability to match, harmonize with or complement the group effort, but by their ability to separate themselves and show off their own individual prowess.

Of course, this is simply one expression of egocentricity among many. Our behavior in our homes is another indication of the same trend. Today, a person can sit in the house, order food, and watch videos by pressing a few buttons. But when we watch a show on a screen, we are merely observing without participating. There is nothing normal about this "couch potato" syndrome. It has a negative effect on our consciousness because we are depriving ourselves of opportunities to learn and love by interacting with others.

We grow and discover ourselves by interacting. By becoming mere spectators and observers of life, we are creating many unhealthy human disorders. Such a lifestyle creates inertia, insecurity, anger, frustration and possibly even acts of violence. It is not a pleasant way to live. Just think: when we want to punish a child for misbehavior, we give that child a "time out." The child is not allowed to interact with others and has to sit in one place. This can be excruciating for a child; even most adults would find it difficult. In essence though, watching television is the same kind of experience as a "time out." In this inactive state, one learns to be passive, self-centered and isolated.

Lost Children and Youth

Many of America's youth are lost souls. They walk around tattooed and stoned, with their body parts pierced, their eyes glazed, and their clothing resembling military or prison uniforms. Why is it that we can hardly recognize our children anymore? The answer is because, like most of us, they are feeling unappreciated and unloved. This is what happens when real love is not readily available.

Many kinds of healthy love exist, but they become virtually impossible to experience when people are constantly subjected to visual and audio stimuli that plant seeds of lust and violence in them. Our youth are being trained by sick-minded, lusty videos and music. In addition, our factory-like schools teach nothing about the soul and focus only upon the material dimensions of life. Our children have become lazy and arrogant in the face of luxuries and indulgences that fail to reveal any deep meaning in life. They are so empty inside that they feel worthless without some new conquest to give them a temporary lift.

From their earliest years, today's young people are raised on a constant diet of television. Besides the isolation and hypnotic state that television induces, another serious drawback is that viewers of American television are regularly subjected to violence. On the average, a ten-year-old child has already seen thousands of murders and acts of violence on television. Cartoons are often the worst offenders. Of course, while children are viewing these acts of violence, they are also learning disrespect, sarcasm, arrogance, rivalry and aggressive behavior. This stimulates an appetite for unhealthy behavior. Is it any wonder that our children are becoming so hostile and animalistic? These violent youths are the future of our nations!

Skewed Values

While so many human beings are suffering, some businesses are thriving. No enterprise on Earth makes more money than the pharmaceutical and illicit drug trades; combined, they form the number-one business in the world. The second largest industry is defense. In the final analysis, this means we have become a civilization that is perfecting our killing ability while simultaneously numbing ourselves with drugs.

World civilization is affected by these two major influences: intoxication and violence. Statistics show that in 1987, the worldwide pharmaceutical and illicit drug businesses brought in an estimated $71 trillion. This is comparable to the gross national product of the Soviet Union for that year. At the same time, the illicit drug business in America alone earned an estimated $300 million. Contrast that to General Motors, which in 1987 was the largest legal business in the country. It did not bring in even one-third of the amount that the illicit drug business earned.

The drug scene today is a Goliath! It is a very formidable enemy. In America, 80 percent of all people have taken some type of illicit drug by the time they reach the age of 21. Indeed, 50 percent of all illicit drugs in the world find their market in the United States. Unfortunately for the world at large, people around the globe are so desperate to imitate American values and lifestyles that they, too, are beginning to pollute themselves at an alarming rate.

In America, at least a third of all federal prisoners are incarcerated because of drug related problems. If, God forbid, the new drug-dealing countries actually manage to replicate the American nightmare correctly, they may also create a situation where a huge percentage of their population will be in prison, important components of their society will become liabilities rather than assets, and the prisons will become tremendous burdens to the taxpayers.

Looking at the situation around the world, we see that many countries today receive major revenues from the illicit drug business. We face a very grave problem, because countries such as Jamaica, Colombia, Peru and Bolivia, just to name a few, are alleged to derive their major income from helping to pollute and narcotize the world. In fact, it would appear that this income largely runs these nations.

We also may notice that some of the richest individuals in the world have some connection to the illicit drug business. Entrepreneurs, religious leaders and politicians throughout the world are often used as fronts for drug trafficking.

The Problem of Pharmaceuticals

Where do pharmaceutical drugs fit into the picture? Many stress-reducing prescriptions are addictive and subject to abuse. Often the drugs prescribed by a physician for a particular problem create another, sometimes more serious, problem. Various harmful and sometimes addictive elements are found in many prescriptions, and cause complications that do not show up for a while.

The harmful side-effects of pharmaceutical drugs can be tremendous. In the West, our senior citizens are walking pharmacies: the average senior citizen takes approximately 15 prescriptions each day. According to researchers at the University of Toronto, prescription medications cause more than 100,000 deaths and 2.1 million adverse reactions.

Any doctor will testify that these problems arise frequently. But what can an individual physician do? The drug-intensive medical philosophy of this culture is backed up by powerful organizations and social institutions. Many of these are designed to instill new doctors with a silent loyalty to the profession that makes them rarely question its procedures.

Dependency Is Widespread

Upon careful examination, we may notice that the differences between the illicit drug business and the pharmaceutical drug industry are not great. The two are similar in their encouragement of dependency. The fact is that in the modern world, many people need drugs to carry them through the day. We use pills, tablets and mood-enhancers to sleep, to awaken, to get energized or to relax.

The more we indulge in drug-taking, the more we increase our difficulties as a society. Of course, the problems are particularly severe now because certain powerful interests are manipulating society. Massive drug distribution is one of the major techniques these groups use to bring human civilization under their control. This is not some incidental occurrence; it is actually a fundamental step in a carefully prepared plan for the empowerment of these selfish groups.

War and a Weapons Culture

Humankind is in a very precarious situation on another front: that of the arms race. Not only are we extremely fragmented politically and religiously, but now more than ever the world community has also become a weapons culture. Human life is becoming less and less valued.

We are literally a culture of violence. Most governments spend more money on defense than they spend to educate their children. This is significant, because what a nation spends its money on reveals the collective consciousness of that country and its leaders. Obviously, our priorities are totally geared toward violence and aggression. Paradoxically, while countless peace talks and negotiations occur worldwide, there is also a continuous buildup of weaponry.

This is not meant to imply that there is something wrong with a society having a strong defense. Even in the ancient Vedic culture, which was spiritually oriented, the military played an important role. But when the major emphasis of a nation's leaders becomes developing ever more powerful weapons of destruction, this attitude will naturally filter down to the citizens.

In the same way, children imitate the role models established by adults. In our society, violence has unfortunately become the norm. As young people enter their careers, they are entering a global community that is founded on destructive, hurtful behaviors. They are entering an environment that fosters the idea that people should resolve conflicts by force. This means that they do not focus on cooperation, but on competition, dominance and destructive power.

Guns at Home and in Schools

Recently, as everyone knows, there has been a rash of juvenile homicides in America, including the fatal shooting of 15 high-school children by their teenage classmates at a school in Denver, Colorado. That atrocity was committed for thrills, and when the murderers were finished, they shot themselves. This later resulted in several copycat crimes by other youngsters around the country.

As a result, students at many schools must pass through metal detectors, just like passengers at airports. It is disturbing that environments designed for education, for improvement of character, and for developing a greater understanding of life have become the scenes of so much violence.

Violent crimes like this spurred a controversy in the U.S. Congress as to whether firearms should be sold "over the counter" or should be controlled by registration. Eventually, the issue was decided by one vote in favor of requiring gun customers to get permits—a process which takes merely two weeks. In this country, one out of three Americans has a handgun, and there is no country in the world that is more militarily equipped.

Widespread Crime

Unfortunately, we find in many places that criminals are more in control of the situation than the military, the police, the legislators and even the judicial branches of government. As we look closely at our environments, we may notice that criminals have taken over many of our neighborhoods and communities; in some cases they have seized whole nations. Recently, we saw that drug kingpins in Colombia and other South American nations actually proposed to pay off the national debt for their countries in return for being allowed to sell their illicit merchandise undisturbed.

All around the world, people are finding no shelter from the aggression of criminals, and privileged Americans should not continue to believe that these tragedies happen only in other parts of the world. People are attacking one another because they cannot postpone gratification even for a minute, and although these kinds of criminal behavior are somewhat less prevalent in America today, the overall violence could escalate at any time.

Unrestrained Lust

When sense gratification becomes our primary focus, the attitude toward all types of behavior becomes, "why not?" Persons who indulge in greedy and lusty behavior succumb to the allurements of profit, sensual pleasure and fame far more readily than pious people. We should remember that demonic energies capitalize on such conduct. If we are not careful, we can become prime targets for destructive forces that can manipulate us to cause harm in our environments as a result of unbridled appetites.

Many individuals who indulge in licentious behavior are simply small-time mischievous and misled troublemakers, such as the local drug pushers on the street. They are extremely selfish and of low consciousness, with hearty sensual appetites, and they are easily enticed to exploit others. Although they are not the masterminds behind our social decay, they are nonetheless important elements in it. Without their compliance, those who desire more broad-scale control for their own destructive ends would have little power.

Illicit Behavior is Self-Perpetuating

People who engage in illicit activities usually do not stop at any one point. Illicit activity is extremely hard to moderate. We have seen proof of this in the "war on drugs." Even government regulation has little effect on eliminating drug abuse and drug traffic, because these situations are the result of voracious appetites, powerful addictions and an intense desire for easy money. The potential for profits is so high that people are willing to risk their lives repeatedly to be involved with the drug trade.

Illicit sex is also difficult to regulate. Often those engaged in brief sexual encounters want to "get high" or drunk in the process, because subconsciously they know that their behavior is immoral and self-destructive. For example, when a man seeks the services of a prostitute, he may have difficulty doing so in normal consciousness. If he takes a drink or drug beforehand, he tends to feel less guilty, at least for a while. With his consciousness dulled, he is not as disturbed by his deviation from the higher principles of life.

Sometimes women do not help improve the sexually charged situation of modern culture. Many Western women nowadays dress like they just walked out of the shower! In some cases, their skirts barely cover their hips, yet they wonder why men become disturbed. By their body language and dress code, these women are announcing to others: "I'm available." A woman should cherish and care for the form God gave her, and not simply use it to attract a man. Any man she attracts on such grounds is not worth having anyway. As the world's mothers, women do not need relationships based solely upon physical attraction, because these will not have any sense of permanence.

Distorted Sexuality

In today's society, sexuality is gravely misunderstood. Many social ills can be traced back to a misuse of sexual energy. For example, we cannot discuss the spread of AIDS without dealing with the topic of illicit sex, because these two are inextricably linked. We also cannot talk about illicit sex without addressing rape, incest or child abuse. The social phenomenon of pornography and the crime of abortion must also be considered. All of these dehumanizing problems are interrelated.

Real love means selflessness, honesty and caring. It means that we live for one another's welfare. But these days most of us have forgotten how to love. We are more concerned with trying to impress, flatter and manipulate others. Instead of promoting our long-range best interests, and the long-range interests of those with whom we come in contact, we seek temporary pleasures that eventually lead to frustrated entanglements.

The notion that we are merely these physical bodies is at the root of all our social afflictions. It is part of our human condition to experience love—to give it and receive it. However, the modern personalities that we mimic and hold up as models do not promote loving relationships. We should ask ourselves if Hollywood ethics are really worth emulating. For example, many real-life Hollywood romances are extremely self-serving and lust-addicted, and Hollywood personalities engage in all varieties of deviant behavior. Because movie stars are encouraged to be vain and self-centered by all the adulation they receive, it is no surprise that many of them do not know how to relate in a deep and meaningful way. Is it any wonder that short-term, self-centered sexual encounters are so predominant in our society?

The Tragedy of AIDS

At the root of the AIDS problem, we find the unfortunate fact that the majority of people have lost an understanding of the glorious and sacred nature of the sexual act. The worldwide AIDS statistics are staggering. In less than 20 years, 40 percent of all African Americans in the United States will have AIDS. Two and a half million women in Africa now have AIDS, and 80 percent of all women in the world who have AIDS are in Africa.

Pornography around the World

Pornography is one of the biggest growth industries in the Western world, and now it has penetrated into Third World countries. Pornography increases the abuse of women and children, and it contributes to divorce, abandonment and general violence. This is because it tends to agitate our lowest nature and make us numb to ever-increasing levels of abuse and exploitation. Pornography is also believed to increase the incidence of rape, because false portrayals of violent sex on the screen may cause some men to feel that women want to be raped.

Rape and Violence

There was a time when people were far more reluctant to attempt rape than they are today. Nowadays, many abusers engage in such behavior with little concern for the consequences. They see the atrocities of rape and violence at the cinema, on television and in printed media constantly. Often, the nastier the behavior, the more it is applauded and the more attention it gets. This creates appetites in people for experiencing this kind of violence themselves.

Increasing Incest

Incest and child abuse are on the rise daily because, in this society, less actual love is being exchanged and more lust is being stimulated in peoples' hearts. It is of course proper and desirable for mothers and fathers to have loving feelings for their children. But when that love turns into lust, parents may pursue their own children for sexual gratification as a perverted expression of their love. This is abhorrent and abominable, but we must also realize that so many factors in our society, such as intoxicants and media stimulation, are strong aphrodisiacs that arouse the sex drive. When there are no healthy ways of expressing this drive, some weak people may look to their children to provide them with an outlet.

The Harm of Abortion

One of the worst violations of human rights is abortion. Abortion arises primarily because people want sense gratification without commitment. Abortion was first legalized in 1920 in Russia. China legalized abortion in 1950. Abortion became legal in England in 1960 and, finally in 1970, America legalized the procedure.

Why was abortion first legalized in Russia? Atheistic philosophy propounds that the human form is nothing more than a collection of organs and atoms. If we espouse such a view, what then is the problem with eliminating superfluous tissue? Millions of abortions are committed worldwide every year, and the karmic complications those parents may have to suffer for this crime are frightening to contemplate.

The practice of making all values relative has allowed millions of people to accept abortion and call it freedom. Yet, how can we ignore the fact that in just three weeks time, an embryo has a heartbeat? In seven weeks time, its brain is functioning. From the very beginning, all the chromosomes needed to produce a human are present.

Despite these realities, presidents, senators and other leaders will not put a stop to this crime because they are afraid of the power of pro-choice lobbyists to influence their elections. Even ministers and imams are afraid to challenge them, fearing they will be thrown out of their congregations.

The saddest aspect of the situation is that many young women resort to abortion without understanding that they have been blessed to be caretakers of a particular soul. Instead, these women are killing that soul's new body—the body of someone who may have been an intimate associate of theirs from another lifetime, or someone who may have had wonderful lessons and gifts to bestow upon them. But our present "civilization" says that it is permissible to kill an embryo that cannot speak up for itself.

Many souls are trying to come into this world to help make

it a better place, but they are being thwarted by the millions. The prime reason for this is that we have totally lost reverence for the sacred nature of sexuality. All too often, sex has become simply a matter of bodies rubbing together for pleasure.

Denial Does Not Help

The denial of unpleasant realities will never succeed in correcting the world's problems. Nor will the claim of being a spiritual person serve as a legitimate excuse for tuning out the present situation. If we study the lives of the most spiritual people history has to offer—from Jesus Christ to Harriet Tubman, from Dr. Martin Luther King, Jr. to Mahatma Gandhi, from Nelson Mandela to Mother Teresa—we will see that each of these people were extremely concerned about the world.

Something is wrong with the way we are living. We must ask ourselves why. In the face of so many resources, so much skill and intelligence, and such good intentions, why is there so much destruction and human suffering in today's world?

Questions & Answers

Question: Please explain in more detail how technology is not neutral.

Answer: As we discussed, technology may be seen to be neutral in and of itself, but its use is definitely not. The more degraded the user's consciousness is, the more dangerous technology can be in their hands. The dangers that come from a combination of big business and bad science can be a tremendous threat to humanity, and this is why many people fear some of the experiments going on now in biotechnology.

We normally think that a very advanced society is one that can manufacture many powerful external things, but in reality this is often a sign of people surrendering their power to machines and externals. A truly advanced civilization is one where people are not enslaved by external things, but have access to their inherent internal power to create and manifest what they need. There is a story in the Vedas where Arjuna saved the life of a demon named Mayadanava, who in turn wanted to repay Arjuna by teaching him the mystic science of *yantras*—the making of machines. Krishna however requested that Arjuna not study this science, explaining that it leads down a sinful path. History has indeed shown us that industrialization and scientific advancement in improper hands can create great destruction, and that technology in contact with weak-minded people can entrap them and lead them down a path of degradation.

Question: How do you reconcile our many difficulties with the fact that America is the headquarters of so many major spiritual organizations? There are so many strong spiritual and metaphysical groups in America, yet America is also full of destructive and antisocial behavior.

Answer: This is all because of duality. Duality is an essential component of the material world, just as water is an essential component of the ocean. The material world is inherently riddled with duality; everything good has some bad mixed in. Pure goodness exists only in the spiritual world. That is the difference between the absolute and duality. In the material world, whenever there is a highly positive force, a highly negative force exists also. The two go hand in hand in this realm.

Remember though, that power itself is neutral—whether it is economic power, mystic power or any other kind of power. Power can accompany both the forces of darkness and of light. So, just as Masons and other well-intentioned secret societies exist in America, so do secret societies with corrupt motives.

Not all secret societies are negative, but they are secretive in that their practices are not made available to the public. Their goals are often constructive. Many of these groups have become concentrated in America because of the role that this country is playing in the world at this particular time in history. Power naturally rotates in a systematic way. First one empire is given an opportunity to gain and sustain glory, but according to their use or misuse of their power, they may later lose their status on the world stage.

Many metaphysicians suggest that Africa was the world's center of knowledge and technology thousands of years ago. However, due to abuses of psychic knowledge, this continent lost its status as a beacon. Every culture has its chance. Karma unfolds in different ways, and it is no accident that some rise to power as others are falling. This happens with individuals as well as with nations. There may be lapses of time between the action and the reaction, during which God gives us an opportunity to correct ourselves, but at a certain point events can go too far, and the downfall is inevitable.

Just pause for a moment and consider history. Remember how America gained most of its landmass and its economic prominence. Most of the means were totally sinful—slavery, economic exploitation, and extermination of Native Americans, to give a few examples. Therefore the die has been cast. Reactions are setting in, and America will have to pay the price for building up an economy on blood and violence.

Much of the early American economy was built on the institution of slavery. In addition to the abomination of slavery, there was the Industrial Revolution, where people—both white and black—were essentially treated like slaves. In England, America's mother country, children worked for 12 to 15 hours a day, and America adopted very similar tactics. To make matters worse, America has constantly abused "weaker" nations and its own weaker citizens, rarely if ever compensating them adequately for their labor and services.

To put it bluntly, much of what has made America strong

has been demonic energy. America is not the only culprit—we are not trying to accuse any one nation. But we have learned from human history, in this current Age of Quarrel, that those in power tend to exploit their dependents rather than protect them.

The point is that we often look at "success" too superficially. We notice the short-term effects and ignore the rest. A sinful person may acquire something very quickly, but later the painful consequences will demonstrate that such shortcuts were not worthwhile. God-consciousness means to live within the laws of God and accept whatever quota is given us. Selfish, immoral people rebel and demand more, but inevitably suffer in the long run.

Look at the personal biographies of so many of the "super-rich." They are not all happy. Many have committed suicide or have died prematurely. Despite all the wealth and opulence of our society, mental illness is on the rise. Psychiatrists are in such great demand that just one building in Washington, D.C. houses more psychiatrists than exist in entire countries elsewhere. America has absolutely tragic levels of discontent and despair.

Other nations should take this as a warning. Rather than follow America's lead, they must be meticulous in discerning right from wrong. The healthiest step that the nations of the world can take for their own survival is to adopt a form of communalism suitable to their own culture. This has been a part of natural indigenous living since the beginning of time.

There must also be a natural reverence for hierarchy, and a recognition that this is God's plan. Democracy is often a farce, because nothing can be efficiently run by a mass of people. It is a ponderous process that actually retards progress. Further, during attacks or other crises, democracy is not a practical way of decision making. All that is needed for a society to function well is one trained and spiritually centered chief or one small nucleus of dedicated individuals with a few advisors. Indeed, indigenous people around the world have practiced this style of leadership for millennia.

The old ways must be re-embraced. We must show respect for elders, protect our children, and exhibit a natural reverence toward Mother Nature and God. Materialistic ideology has infiltrated our thinking to such an extent that we have minimized the basics. We have become so materialistic and individualistic that everyone is in danger. If we can adopt strong programs for self purification and if we can appreciate the great resources that Mother Nature has given us, we can do much to help ourselves and other parts of the world.

Chapter 4

What is behind it all?

One of the most dangerous phenomena on the planet at this time is a systematic effort to repress healthy culture in a deliberate attempt to destroy spirituality of any kind. The engineers of this attempt are using every tool at their disposal to create cultural erosion on both obvious and subtle levels. Their goal is to bring about a state of confusion by introducing lifestyles and habits opposed to the elevation of individual and collective consciousness. Beloved, surely some of your own problems are due to the influences of the spreading of sinful culture, however you will find solace and strength in the path of the spiritual warrior.

As spiritual warriors, we should understand that survival does not depend solely on our actions, but also on our response to the behavior of others. No one is an island. We must maintain a high level of consciousness in the face of the degraded values of society and transcend the negative influences that surround us. To accomplish this, we must first become aware of the true nature of the forces aligned against us.

Negative Forces Throughout the World

In Los Angeles, a *New Times Magazine* cover story titled "Soul Snatcher" stated, "In an abandoned Santa Monica building, Glen Mason worshiped Satan and mesmerized his teenage girlfriends. He needed a suitable victim to offer his god, and he found one in 14-year-old Shevawn Geoghegan." The abominable incident that followed is just one of many similar atrocities and illustrates the wave of negativity taking over the modern world. Materialistic culture is distorting the personalities of modern people. This dangerous phenomenon needs to be acknowledged and addressed.

What is Evil?

Evil has become entrenched in our society and its institutions. One may ask why we should direct our attention to this evil. Should we not simply focus on the good? The answer is that we must know our adversary to avoid becoming unwitting victims. By understanding evil, we become aware of the subtle inroads that such negativity makes in our society—and in our own psyches. Armed with this understanding, we become more vigilant and can prevent or neutralize the damage.

The word "evil" tends to evoke images of appalling crimes such as serial killings, child abuse, death camp operations in the Balkans or the horrendous conflict and impoverishment in areas like Sudan and Somalia. The term "evil" also reminds us of Hitler, Mussolini, Stalin and nameless others who were responsible for tremendous holocausts that annihilated millions of Jews, Europeans and Russians; tens of millions of Native Americans; and over 60 million Africans in the slave trade.

Evil has a far more insidious face as well, including a deliberate attempt to present the material world as the only valid reality. When we develop an attachment to sense gratification—a natural consequence of viewing the physical world as the ultimate truth—we become enslaved by our desires and easily susceptible to outside control. In our quest for more and more, we feel driven to compete with others because everyone becomes a potential threat to our pleasure. We become vulnerable when our sense of well-being is linked to the possession of objects and physical pleasures that can be easily stolen or diminished.

Because we tend to see in others the negativity we deny in ourselves, we believe that people will lie, manipulate and steal to acquire sense pleasure at our expense. The result is a world filled with fear, conflict and ignorance of the higher realities of life. A corollary of this is a world populated with human beings whose fear makes them extremely easy to manipulate and control.

The Historical View

The scriptures suggest that our universe was originally free from evil influences, and that purity and high consciousness reigned throughout. Later came a period when evil and righteousness were able to exist within the same universe and on the same planet. Still later came the time when evil and righteous individuals could take birth in the same clan or family. Today we have an even more challenging pattern, where evil and righteousness can actually coexist within the same individual. This means that there is a godly and a demonic side to all of us. Our individual responsibility, therefore, is to become aware of this personal inner reality and make the appropriate choices from moment to moment that will support higher consciousness.

This requires constant vigilance, because sin has many faces. However, we must be careful not to see evil where it does not exist. We must not succumb to stereotypes that encourage us to project the so-called evil "out there" to avoid our own self-doubts. We have all heard such generalizations as "All white people are selfish exploiters," "All black people are lazy," or "All women are temptresses." Many find it all too easy to believe that the "devil" is embodied in members of another race or culture, and many men believe that all women are dangerous, seductive sirens or witches.

It is not quite that simple. Such designations are never that "cut and dry." Our view of others depends upon the state of our consciousness and the condition of our hearts. Pure-hearted persons, even if provoked to be racist or sectarian by external pressures, will resist all such harmful influences because of their inner understanding and higher perceptions.

Conflict and Fragmentation

Demons love to create fragmentation and distract us from our internal consciousness of wholeness and connection to others. One method is to encourage prejudice, racism, sexism, a host of other "-isms" and sometimes even mass murder. In the face of such influences, we must always remember that we are brothers and sisters by consciousness, not by grade of hair, complexion, age or sex. Further, the person who sells drugs to our little cousin or puts our friend up to prostitution is not behaving like our brother or sister, regardless of racial or other common affiliations. If we accept such a person as a family member based on such superficial bases as skin color, age or dialect, then we have an extremely perverted vision and definition of family, and we will not survive long.

History also demonstrates the tendency for destructive persons to give greater importance to external differences than to similarities. For instance, everyone is aware of Hitler's emphasis on the differences between Jews and Gentiles and his twisted interpretation of the Vedic concept of an Aryan race. His doctrine of Aryan racial superiority was based upon a mistaken identification of Aryans with such external features as grade of hair, complexion and ancestry. However, the original meaning of "Aryan" refers to someone who understands the higher human values. It has no geographic or racial component. An Aryan is anyone who understands the human mission of returning to the kingdom of God through love and service.

Similar tactics were used to decimate other sub-groups like Africans and Native Americans. When Europeans first came to America, Native Americans were considered "savages," and this label was used to justify widespread genocide as Yankee settlers spread smallpox throughout the Native American population by giving them blankets infected with the virus. All this was acceptable because in the settlers' minds these persons were not quite human. Not so very long ago, African-Americans were also considered not quite human and categorized as chattel, similar to animals. Deprived of their human dignity in the eyes of white Americans, countless blacks were lynched, raped and denied many basic human and legal rights.

However, because superficial differences ultimately have no meaning, changing the race or ethnic group that is on top of the social ladder will not substantially alter anything. Once again, true change is a matter of consciousness. For example, we frequently hear black people claiming that the white man caused their problems, and that is why they are fighting now in the "motherland." This is all nonsense. Both black-on-black crime and white-on-white crime have existed throughout the material world for ages.

Just take a look at Ireland, where there has been so much civil unrest and religious strife. And do you think that most of the wars occurring in Africa are due to racism? As an example, let us take a recent issue. Nigeria's outspoken recording artist and political prisoner, Fela Anikulapo Kuti, was fighting against a black African oppressor from the 1970s until his death in the 1990s. Those black oppressors made several attempts to assassinate Fela and actually succeeded in killing his mother by burning her home to the ground. Color had nothing to do with it; again, it was a matter of consciousness.

In Nigeria alone, there have been over 250 religious wars since independence was won from colonial rule. Not one of these wars had anything to do with racism. Indeed, some of the greatest conflicts have originated between persons of the same color. In churches, the most intense conflicts are among practitioners of the same religion, just as the most severe problem any American policeman encounters is often domestic violence. The most serious threats and problems occur more frequently within the same family than with strangers.

When we are attached to the objects of sense gratification, we want to protect what we think we have gained. As a result, the world is filled with "in-groups" and "out-groups," implying that one group includes friends and the other group consists of enemies. The paradox is that, in the interests of safety and self-protection, we have created just the opposite: a culture filled with fear, conflict and danger. Around the globe, problems in ethnicity, tribalism, racism and genderism are proliferating. This is a clear sign of our collective ignorance of the true purpose of human life and of the urgent need for higher consciousness in all of us.

It is true that no two living entities are completely alike. We are like snowflakes, each with a unique design. Yet in our essence, we are all the same, just as all snowflakes are made of water. Demonic forces, in order to externalize our consciousness and keep us perpetually off balance, have persuaded us that there is profit in unduly distinguishing ourselves and competing against others. In this way, as we separate ourselves, they can more easily control us to carry out their self-serving plans. As we are weakened by our isolation and by our need to feel loved, they can more easily manipulate us to subdue and denature us as they see fit.

A Strategy of "Divide and Conquer"

Good and evil have never been just a matter of race or tribe. However, individuals of various groups are currently trying to inflame issues of race, nationality, tribe, social class or any other possible division among people in order to gain power and weaken their opposition. In this way, they seek to immobilize the forces of good by preventing them from coming together and recognizing their common threads. It is part of the demonic strategy to pit man against woman, race against race, nation against nation and tribe against tribe. Once the seeds of discord take root, we engage in useless tugs of war and become easily controlled by those who wish to manipulate us.

Naturally, evil-doing and evil-thinking people prefer an environment of confusion, because in such an atmosphere they can hide their motivations, steal whatever they wish and commit all kinds of undercover crimes. They facilitate their activities by veiling truths or distracting us from the secretive, surreptitious and ruthless behaviors they are engaging in. Such negative people are always looking for ways to pick our pockets, defile our purity and subtly contaminate our consciousness.

Demigods and Demons

We should use a holistic approach for analyzing everything. This means that first we try to observe and understand the human condition. God has deliberately made this earthly environment hostile to us because He does not want us to get comfortable here. He knows that being far from Him and covered in illusion is an extremely painful, dangerous experience that causes us a great deal of grief and suffering. He also knows that the contamination present in this environment causes us to invite even more suffering as we engage in sinful activities. But what exactly is the instrument of our suffering here? It is the demonic energy, presenting itself to us in innumerable alluring disguises.

As spiritual warriors, we must endeavor to embrace the positive and combat the negative. In doing so, we have to evaluate the differences between the demons and the angels or demigods. Many demons are empowered and possess mystic potencies, just as the demigods do. The difference between the two is the motivation and the results. Someone powerful and pious is uplifting for human civilization, whereas someone powerful yet impious directs energies toward destruction, degradation and annihilation. The powerful demons, just like the powerful spiritual beings, engage in various rituals. All rituals are designed to tap into fixed laws of the universe and to empower people to fulfill their various agendas, whether for good or for ill.

The Vedic scriptures explain that when a powerful demon takes birth, the entire atmosphere and ethers of the planet are often disturbed. The birth of these beings can cause hurricanes, droughts, earthquakes or tornadoes. Sometimes the skies grow black and lightning streaks across the heavens. Their birth causes these disturbances because such demons are vehemently opposed to the will of God.

The scriptures and other credible sources report that many powerful demons are not residents of this planet, and have great knowledge of the invisible realms. They are capable of using various powers and subtle energies to affect us on many levels. They have the means to affect matter as well as the human mind. These demons can actually transform matter and consciousness because they are expert at dealing with material and mental energies.

Both the demigods and the demons are mystically empowered, but demons by nature have some advantages, especially in the material realm. The demons' main advantage is that, unlike devotees of the Lord who are calm, content and detached, demons are extremely attached, aggressive and angry. This passion, upon which demons thrive, makes them extremely energetic and aggressive.

Notice, for instance, how demons have altered modern humanity's method of worship. Not long ago, a culture's most gorgeous architecture and palatial buildings were churches and cathedrals, temples, mosques and synagogues. Today, the most exquisite and impressive architecture is used for banks and casinos. In Las Vegas, the capital of gambling, many dazzling constructions are renovated every few years. This is a reflection of our modern value system.

We must remember that the prime goal of most people in the material universe is to feel a sense of power over others. In fact, this desire for "lording over others" is the very factor that brought us here to live on planet Earth. This is especially true for the demons. One of the methods that most readily gives them a sense of dominance and power is the torturing of other beings. Sometimes they even become leaders in spiritual organizations just to destroy the institutions or to exploit and even take the lives of hundreds of followers.

The sad fact is that demons actually despise God and want to replace Him. They are the very antithesis of God. Demons are always eager to engage in activities that enable them to feel like God, and they derive pleasure from being worshipped. In order to be worshipped, however, they need to gain more and more control and more and more power. They seek to make people their slaves so that humanity will be forced to depend on them for everything. Indeed, such is the demonic agenda for the twenty-first century. Let this serve as a reminder to us as spiritual warriors. We must be constantly vigilant about our behavior and motivations, and extremely discriminating about the music, movies and other influences to which we subject our minds. Only in this way will we escape contamination, degradation and unwitting slavery.

Who Are the Demons?

Demons are not simply some figment of the Hollywood imagination. Nor are they an invented class of entities that the "naïve" minds of the Middle Ages, or of non-Western cultures, accepted as real but that the modern mind can dismiss as mere superstition. Demons really do exist, and our materialistic, "scientific" culture's widespread belief that they do not only strengthens their power over us.

We often think of the scriptures as myths or, at best, inaccurate accounts of history. We forget that the scriptures also serve as telescopes into the future and windows into other dimensions. We fail to realize that the scriptures give us insight into what to expect here on Earth. For example, when we study the nature of demons in the scriptures, we find that, no matter where they are located, their behavior is always the same.

Further, demons are not confined to one type of being. Instead, many varieties of demonic entities exist. Some are human and some are of extraterrestrial origin. Just as this universe is filled with different races, tribes, countries and planets, so it is home to different types of demons who fit specific categories and perform actions based on their particular mission.

Who are the full-fledged demons? According to many of the world's scriptures, when people leave the body at physical death, and before they can enter into another physical existence, their previous lives are evaluated in terms of the sum total of their past actions. In their next stage of their evolution, they receive a body to house and accompany their souls based on their motivations and accumulated merits and demerits. Some beings have a strong desire for extremely sinful environments. They may become demons who then take birth in environments where they can be surrounded by the type of culture that allows them to perfect their demonic behavior and relish it.

The ancient Vedic scriptures alert us that demons are entities empowered for destruction. They are not simply small-time sinners making small-time plans. They are not merely normal human beings who have somehow been convinced to stray from the "straight and narrow" because of an interest in money or power. Instead, they are beings who have either been born for the explicit purpose of destruction and exploitation or who have been bred expressly for this purpose.

Very powerful demons are capable of affecting human consciousness on a massive scale. The Vedic scriptures also state that such demons engage in many rituals and enjoy eating human flesh—particularly those demons who try to undermine aspects of human society that are spiritual in nature. Indeed, most of the demons' rituals are the actual opposite of what enhances spiritual life. They defile the cross and abuse the scriptures. They create as much foulness as possible. As a result of their rituals, the human-flesh-eating demons are endowed with mystic powers to manipulate the material energies in all kinds of unusual ways.

A Real-life Example

Lest you think this is a melodramatic exaggeration, let me tell you an anecdote from my own experience. While I was a student at Princeton, I became friends with a powerful international professor. One day this professor told me in confidence that he was personally aware of places in the Caribbean and in Europe where wealthy multinational businessmen would gather to engage in rituals involving the eating of human flesh. When he told me this, I thought he was being overly dramatic, and the whole idea seemed completely ridiculous. However, as I read other accounts and studied the scriptures in depth, I could finally understand that the professor's account was highly feasible.

Indeed, in recent times there have been exposés of world

leaders who engage in eating human parts. These individuals, and those like them, are exerting an ever-greater dominance over society and have succeeded in propagating the *Kali Yuga* mentality, which is one of increasing degradation. For example, it is no accident that drugs are so widespread around the globe and that masses of people have become addicted. Drug distribution is a favorite activity of demons because, through drugs, people become enslaved, indiscriminate and prone to all sorts of criminal behavior.

Demonic rituals always involve selfish, individual gratification. This is why there are so many instances of demons turning on one another, breaking various pacts and betraying trusts. Demons are out for self. If they share something with others, it is only to maximize their own efforts to obtain what they desire. These demons sometimes exist here on Earth in disguise, as well as in more remote places from which they can influence our planet.

The Demonic Agenda

Demonic consciousness is far more widespread than we may think, and far more damaging than just isolated incidents of monstrous behavior. Terrible as these may be, the situation is actually much worse. Satanism has become embedded in the very fabric of our society, directing social movements, inciting global conflicts and manipulating political and economic systems behind the scenes on a grand scale. As each of us has been sleepwalking through life, focusing on our day-to-day bread-and-butter wants and needs, a demonic plan has been gradually implemented to corrupt the minds of our impressionable youth, fuel a general degradation in the population, and enslave the masses through drugs, mass media and economic exploitation. The intent is to stimulate our lower natures—arousing anger, fear, greed, depression and hatred—while simultaneously blocking our awareness of the higher realities of human existence.

At this time in history, there is a tremendous upsurge of demonic activity on the planet, in the form of a massive attempt to centralize power so that people will literally become robotic slaves. To understand this phenomenon, we must first gain an understanding of slavery and what slaves actually are.

Slaves are people who have no personal rights and who have lost control over their destiny. They can no longer exercise free will. Instead, slaves must work exclusively for the interests of an outside party. This outside party, or slave master, rarely, if ever, consults the slaves or allows them to share in the fruits of their labor. The freedom of slaves is, of course, extremely restrained by any number of means, because the curtailing of freedom is the very nature of slavery.

We tend to associate shackles with slavery, because in earlier times slave masters used physical means for confining people and restricting their freedoms. That is no longer the case. Most of today's shackles are mental and emotional, but they are just as effective—more so in fact, because, seduced by our comforts and a false sense of security, we no longer recognize our lack of freedom.

In a way similar to an average person's use of a remote control device to switch channels on a television set, many people in the modern world are being confined and manipulated by remote influence and control. For example, is there a choice if we are asked to select between two candidates, both of whom are pushing the same hidden agenda? In other words, the demon class has been practicing for a long time, and its members have gained invaluable experience in oppression, so that modern slavery has become much more sophisticated than in the past.

How it Works

For example, imagine that I have gained control of all your property so gradually that you hardly noticed it. Then imagine that I gave you an allowance of money, offering you the unlimited opportunity to spend these funds at any store you choose, all of which belong to me now. Suppose further that I create so many stresses for you that you are eager to purchase all the diversions that I am marketing to you.

The catch, of course, is that any money you spend will go right into my pocket. This is despite the fact that everything you buy has actually come from property that originally belonged to you as much as it does now to me. In other words, all of the merchandise I am selling to you comes from assets to which you should and would have free access, except for the fact that I have illegally claimed all of it for myself. Actually, I have only given you money so that you can boost my income, and I have only given you the appearance of freedom so that you will give this money to me more willingly.

Slave masters can have any number of profit motives and agendas. However, interestingly enough, today's new breed of slave master is different from any type who came before, because the modern slave master's objectives are primarily recreational. This new type of slave master is so utterly wealthy that the enslavement of others often occurs only for sport and recreation.

When the money game gets boring, these people have to find other means of stimulation. Because they cannot possibly spend all the money they have amassed, the next challenge for them becomes gaining power, control and manipulation. That is why some of the rich and super-rich are among the most perverted people on the planet.

Slaves become a means by which the slave masters can exert their manipulation and control. For example, one of the goals of today's slave masters is to find ways to employ cheap or free labor with which they can construct canals, roadways, railroad systems, factories or any other major instrument of supremacy and control. They also seek to dominate the political and economic arenas.

Enslavement Already Exists

On this planet many slaves already exist who appear to be normal, everyday human beings. These are people whose minds have been deliberately subverted by drugs, implants and other means. Some have actually escaped and published their stories, but in most cases these accounts are being circulated on a very small scale in limited underground circles, just to protect the former slaves from being destroyed altogether.

Yet, in addition to individuals specifically targeted for enslavement to carry out specific agendas, many of us on this planet are enslaved by physical desires: Drugs, the media and material comforts. What exactly enslaves us to our passions? It is simply our attachment to gross materialism. Who are the promoters of gross materialism? Guess who!

At this present juncture in history, the world is in a serious crisis because most people are already controlled. It is not that they are *about* to be controlled; they already *are* controlled. For example, how many people cannot go very long without a drink, a cigarette, a television show or a particular drug? Certain television addicts are so controlled that, if someone tries to tune out the commercials or a show they are watching, they will become furious because their dependence on that kind of stimulus is so great.

Take the example of drugs. When we desire something so strongly that we deny ourselves food, sex and companionship and lose all moral sense, even abusing, neglecting, or stealing from our families, this is no small-time criminal arrangement. The drugs that have given addicts their powerful "highs" are not concoctions that a few kids in a basement mixed up from household chemicals. These opiates and hallucinogens are often flown in from remote places around the globe. The worldwide enterprise is backed by serious money and masterminded by sophisticated kingpins and scientists who have conducted research for years while being supported by demons in extremely powerful positions.

The Pace of Modern Life

Average citizens are not using much of their free will. Indeed, how can they be considered free when so much of what they understand is being force-fed to them? So-called "normal people" are so completely overtaxed monetarily and energetically that they can hardly function. There are so many criteria to fulfill and so many hoops to jump through just to survive in the modern world that they have little or no time to actually think. They simply have to keep fulfilling their debts and meeting their obligations. All they can do is keep on the treadmill, like a hamster in a cage, and hope that nothing caves in beneath them. When they get home from work, they eat a little food, try to pay their bills, watch television and get some rest.

Where is the time to think and discern? There is none. In order to maintain the pretense and avoid total collapse, they resort to unhealthy alternatives like drugs, gambling and alcohol, just so they can make it through the week without a mental breakdown. Eventually something caves in—and most often it is their hearts or their harried minds.

These demanding material activities, masquerading as the "frenzied pace of modern life," are training people not to question the sources of such nonstop busy-ness, but, instead, just to accept noncritically whatever is made available. The intent is to prevent us from asking the larger questions of life, to keep us focused on the material challenges of daily living and to fan our desires for sense gratification as an easy escape from the pressures that beset us. Demons always want to arouse our longing for sensual pleasures so that we will neglect the deeper experiences of life and become preoccupied instead with trying to enjoy whatever titillates us. The ultimate goal is to centralize power throughout the world and control us all effortlessly and easily. Once this arrangement is in place, then we can be exploited and manipulated more directly.

Plans for Manipulation

Just as human beings make plans for business growth, new elaborate building projects or career development, demons make plans for promoting atheism, anarchy and mass enslavement. They devise specific campaigns for influencing countries, planets and entire universes.

Demons, particularly very powerful ones, are always extremely clear about who their adversaries are. It is their business to know what it takes to weaken, debilitate and destroy us. They know how to stimulate our lower passions, and they are expert in identifying our weaknesses and capitalizing on them.

Today, the demons have become so powerful that most of them are essentially saying, "So what?" and daring us to do something. They are saying, "That's right; we killed your JFK, your Malcolm X, your Dr. King. We killed your Gandhi, and if you are not careful, we will silence you."

It is in the nature of demons to arrange for financial exploitation, to manipulate ecology and to encourage genocide. Their program is also to establish corrupt dictatorships with totalitarian personalities as puppets. They seek control of our minds and hearts. All these activities, and many more, constitute "business as usual" for them because their whole agenda is one of power and domination.

Psychic Manipulation

One little-acknowledged method of demonic control is that of psychic manipulation. It is becoming increasingly apparent that many of the major world powers are dabbling in psychic research, which is tantamount to saying that many demonic beings are developing mystic powers. Just as sincere yogis use such methods to assist society, today many demons resort to similar methods to destroy society. Like a knife, the psychic methods themselves are neutral. In the hands of a surgeon a knife is a blessing, but in the hands of a criminal it is a curse.

Some people are no longer satisfied with considering paranormal phenomena as mere mythology. They want to know how to control it and understand it better in order to gain power over others. Therefore, countries such as the former Soviet Union and the United States have invested a tremendous amount of money in the investigation of psychic phenomena as a means to this end.

Domination through Propaganda

Because demonic elements are constantly seeking to destroy civilization, they use all means at their disposal to create damaging propaganda. These include modern-day mantras such as slogans, jingles and pop music to influence the general atmosphere and saturate it with negative energy. Many an apparently innocent advertisement produces an effect similar to that of a drug injection into our bloodstream. When we are subjected to such stimuli for a long time, we gradually become drained of our vital energy as we focus attention on our material senses in mundane, animalistic ways. The demons' game is to prevent us from accessing deeper levels of understanding so that we will be stripped of the mental and spiritual armor needed to avoid manipulation and control.

Do not mistakenly think that this situation is an accident. Elements in this world are deliberately using mind control and subliminal effects to take over our thought processes. All of these efforts are directed toward the goal of making us so confused and desperate that we will readily sell our souls for a little relief and serenity. The demons want us to be so on the edge that we will easily accept any kind of support from anywhere—even when such "support" is completely destructive.

Sometimes the media, under the direction of these harmful coalitions, uses implication and innuendo to manipulate public opinion and close our minds to inquiry. These negative forces want us to believe that all inquiries into metaphysics, spirituality, or extraterrestrial life are dangerous and cultic. For obvious reasons, they want to monopolize this sphere of knowledge so that they can maintain their control and keep the public ignorant, enslaved and powerless.

Drug Addiction to Control Society

We have already mentioned another phenomenon in the contemporary world that is no accident: drug addiction. What we are currently witnessing is a systematically planned initiative to deepen the already anesthetized state of human beings in today's civilization. Unbeknownst to a large part of the world's people, many of the world's governments are active in the drug trade. For example, in the United States, despite the "war on drugs," evidence has come to light in many quarters about the CIA's alleged involvement in drug-running activities.

Remember that drugs impair judgment, shorten our attention span and create disorientation and paranoia, making it almost impossible for us to identify our true enemies. At the very least, drugs are addictive, creating a dependency that makes users docile and easily subject to manipulation. The statistics are staggering. About 20 million people in America are addicted to marijuana. At the same time, in the United States alone, about eight million people are cocaine addicts and over one million are addicted to heroin.

The startling evidence is that, on the average, less than one-third of those addicted to a particular substance will ever get over that addiction. As a result, the moral fabric of all societies is weakening day by day. In time, fewer and fewer people will be able to conquer their addictions. In fact, many of their mentors and rehabilitators will themselves be addicts of some kind.

Interestingly enough, the influx of drugs in society often increases during certain periods—especially when there is a significant campaign for consciousness-raising. Further, when political uprisings are in the making, we frequently see a sudden flood of easily available drugs. This strategy, too, is part of the demonic attempt to capture and enslave us. When chaos and confusion reign at strategic times, our energy becomes diffused and we may begin to forget what the true problems are.

Deliberate Creation of Problems

What better way to strengthen power than to clandestinely create seemingly insurmountable problems and then, in response to public demand, develop drastic measures to resolve them? This is one technique negative forces use to maintain and increase their dominance, all with the full support and approval of the public.

For example, with the collusion of governments, large corporations can deliberately destroy agricultural self-sufficiency in a region and then sell seeds and agricultural supplies to the remaining farmers—thereby extending their centralized control. Wars have been started and ended, with the unstable peace monitored by "peacekeeping forces." Outbursts of gun violence in the United States have the public clamoring for "gun control." The process is all the more insidious, given that feeding the world's hungry, keeping the peace, or controlling gun violence are laudable goals in themselves. In this way, the clandestine forces always come out appearing to be our friends, when in fact they are doing nothing but using deception and immorality to leverage themselves into power.

Governments Have Betrayed Our Trust

It may come as no surprise that some elements of our governments do not have our best interests at heart. However, many of us are not aware of the extent to which we have been betrayed by those who claim to be our well-wishers. The truth, which will be revealed over time, is far more destructive than what we have learned to date through so many exposés in the media. Through these programs and articles, we have learned that what we had believed about our government, local leaders and school faculties is often the exact opposite of the reality. We have discovered that many of our supposedly dedicated public servants are total sell-outs and traitors, involved in lying, money laundering, seduction, manipulation, and even worse.

This is just a small tip of the iceberg. Instead of promoting the interests of the people, many of those in power seek to manipulate and exploit the masses. Shockingly enough to many of us, this is not only true of developing nations, whose abuses have often received wide publicity abroad. It is also true of the major world powers, in which, behind the scenes, many political figureheads and regimes are dedicated primarily to the destruction of the world economy and the re-introduction of the types of subtle slavery we have discussed here. All of this is a deliberately planned strategy that is part of the demonic agenda.

Secret Societies

The main reason for all the conflicts and confusion around the world is what I call the Big Lie. One of the biggest lies ever told to humankind is, "What you see is what you get." In reality, this is not the case. It is the root lie at the core of a whole series of smaller lies. Across the board—economically, politically and socially—innumerable scams and deceptions exist to fool the public. Almost nothing is actually as it appears.

As ancient scriptures have prophesied, the material world is currently managed and controlled by secret societies who form an "invisible government." In practically every division of life, groups, unions and fraternities exist to set specific plans and programs in motion. Secret societies are not only widespread in Europe and the United States; they thrive all over the world. The elected officials we see in the spotlight are seldom the ones who really manage affairs.

It is alleged that in the earlier history of the United States and other countries, secret societies were formed to preserve sacred information and knowledge for the benefit of humanity. Because of the ruthlessness of their opponents, many of those societies had to go underground to try to preserve ancient wisdom, universal knowledge and higher metaphysical understanding so that this knowledge could be saved and made available to others later.

Unfortunately, despite their honorable intentions, many of the societies that went underground to preserve sacred knowledge became heavily infiltrated by less constructive elements. As demons will, they spied on the activities of these societies, entered their membership, learned their techniques and used them to gain more leverage over the masses. Sad to say, many secret societies and groups that have some advanced understanding about the human condition and the cosmos have been infiltrated.

This is not to suggest that every secret society or power elite has a selfish, destructive orientation. However, it does remind us to exercise extreme vigilance and not to be fooled by appearances. The tendency is for those who have power, wealth and control to keep it for themselves, undermine the influence of competitors and deprive us all in any way they can.

The "Invisible Government"

These secret societies exert a powerful influence upon the "invisible government" that manipulates the course of world history. If we look carefully at worldwide events and the causes behind them, we are likely to discover that a few powerful individuals and organizations are actually dictating the order of things. Power elites and multinational bankers orchestrate much of what happens around the globe. In many corners of the world, isolated pieces of information are emerging about the invisible government that is controlling this planet, and about the possible links of this government to groups such as the Council on Foreign Relations, the International Monetary Fund and the Trilateral Commission.

Many believe that this invisible government is the directing force behind much of the destructive behavior currently afflicting this planet. This government is often viewed as maliciously motivated and politically and economically astute. For example, certain multinational bankers can determine whether a country experiences depression or recession, just by the structure of policies that are set into motion.

The members of this secret government are also aware of the non-physical realities that are deliberately hidden from the general public. As a result, some are in contact with powerful beings residing in other dimensions—beings empowered to carry out highly devastating actions on planet Earth.

Some Important Questions

We may wonder how an all-merciful God could allow such a situation to develop. Why are there so many satanic influences and powers amongst us? Can righteousness be victorious over evil? Have we been captured by demonic influences? And if this is the case, is it possible that the demonic element is superior to the divine?

These are questions we have to ask, because now it seems that the basic structures of our society promote more harmful behavior than acts of goodness. People have begun to accept sinful activity, rather than wholesome energy, as normal. What are the implications of this? Have the soldiers of righteousness lost the battle? Are they surrendering to more and more manipulation and control?

We must remember that this is a universe based on duality. All of the scriptures, such as the Bible, the Quar'an, the Torah and the Vedas, tell us about otherworldly personalities such as angels and archangels. And whenever there is one polarity, its opposite also exists. The balance between these polarities is often referred to as the "yin and the yang" or the masculine and the feminine. Wherever good exists in this universe, it is counterbalanced by evil.

On Earth, we see a constant warfare between the pious and the impious, arising from the aggression and criminality of the demons. This is an eternal aspect of the material environment, and a prime characteristic of this war is that demons are constantly trying to claim our minds and pollute us in order to tip the balance of power in their favor.

Relativity and Suppression of Higher Knowledge

Ancient systems of knowledge included specific customs and traditions that prevented evil from corrupting their fundamental, ageless principles. Today, this is no longer the case. Instead of a culture based upon a foundation of absolute truth, the modern world offers us a climate of relativity. Because modern civilization considers everything to be relative, destructive values can easily infiltrate the collective consciousness. Consequently, the predominating mindset of today is for each of us to do what we want, when we want, and however we want, regardless of the effect upon others. In our rush for self-gratification, we have lost our sense of community and of being our brothers' or sisters' keepers.

These days, many best-selling books on the market recommend that we "get in touch with our feelings," without considering the impact of our behavior on anyone else. We are encouraged to do as we please, free from any inhibitions. Unfortunately, this type of mentality is not far above the level of animal life. We should always remember that, as human beings, we are endowed with an internal conscience that gives us the means to practice self-restraint.

However, many of our media idols, therapists, psychoanalysts and in some cases, even preachers instruct us, in the name of self-fulfillment, to do just as we please and not repress our fantasies. Obviously, these imposters are just helping people to feel comfortable with their self-centered lives, without any sense of compunction or regret.

The situation has become one of the sick treating the sick. The greatest shortchange is that we have been coerced into believing that there are no absolutes and that all values are relative. This is modern nonsense.

Traditional systems have a structure that ensures that the purity of absolute values is preserved from generation to generation. For example, in Islam the Sheiks are entrusted with maintaining and transmitting sacred knowledge, as are gurus in India, lamas in Tibet and kings and chiefs in Africa. These individuals act as mediums for the divine influx. Moreover, if their behavior ever becomes incongruent with divine principles and violates their sacred task, assemblies of elders, priests and teachers ensure that these spiritual leaders either fulfill their duties or step down from their positions.

In other words, in traditional systems, priests, kings or chiefs are far from being autocrats exempt from any monitoring. Although these specially appointed individuals are intended to serve as conduits through which divine blessings can reach the community, they must still be accountable for their actions. Unfortunately, Western materialistic civilization teaches us that such traditional systems are archaic and irrelevant to modern life. Instead, we have become increasingly cultureless as we discard all the safeguards that would prevent us from being led astray by false values and incomplete knowledge.

When Western philosophy constructs its values upon the claim, "I think; therefore I am," or when experts advise us to "do our own thing," we would do well to run in the other direction. Such advice is detrimental and dangerous. Real existence is not about our own wants and desires and it does not revolve around our self-centered longing for personal fulfillment. Instead, it is about service to others within the context of our relationships with our families, our communities, our society and, ultimately, with God. In spite of this, the dominant Western paradigm suggests that the individual is the "be-all and end-all" of existence. Thus we are encouraged to compete against others to get as much as we can for ourselves regardless of the consequences. This, beloveds, is evil, and will never give us true solace or happiness.

A healthy, thriving culture has much broader concerns. In such a culture, each person exists as part of a whole. As mentioned earlier, a basic premise of Western thought is, "I think; therefore I am." Perhaps so, but what are we thinking about? We may be thinking about molesting a child, raping a woman or robbing an elder. It is the *quality* of our thoughts and our resulting actions that count, not simply the fact that we exist as separate, thinking egos. It is because we belong to a community—and are, in the final analysis, intimately related to the cosmos—that we have value. We cannot exist in isolation. As we interact in community, we become accountable to others for our actions and their consequences. This is what makes our existence important. Unfortunately, the emphasis on relative knowledge and values so prevalent in modern society encourages us to feel less accountable each day.

Many people today have become frustrated with relativity.

They are beginning to wonder why they should work themselves to death to learn a skill that is relative to the trends of the day, or to pursue a career that is also viewed as relative—all the while being expected to behave as if these were absolutes. How sad it is that our present paradigm does not encourage us to reflect on anything truly absolute and eternal. Instead, modern culture encourages us to dedicate ourselves solely to that which is functional without examining the greater questions of life. In these circumstances, we would be well advised to ask ourselves: "Functional for whom?" Who is benefiting from this exclusive focus on the practical, functional aspects of life at the expense of anything greater?

Modern society has indeed produced astounding scientific breakthroughs and technological innovations. In earlier times, as we know, many people thought the earth was flat. Our scientific knowledge has progressed to the point that we understand the error of this viewpoint. Today, we undoubtedly have a vast array of technologies to solve seemingly impossible problems. And yet in many ways, our culture is far more primitive than that of our predecessors. We have only superficial understanding of the true purpose of human life and we have lost our sense of community and accountability. To compound the problem, many of our so-called "technological advances" have only served to complicate our lives even further without addressing the fundamental human needs for meaning, service and love.

Despite its limited view on many subjects, modern materialistic culture generally understands that humans use only a small percentage of their brain capacity. So much of our consciousness remains dormant. We can gain tiny glimpses of the incredible potential of human beings when we observe people born with higher perceptions and faculties than we would consider "normal." Then we realize how little we really know. Further, science uses instruments that are biased and imperfect, and our scientific knowledge is ultimately derived from our senses, which are often relative and unreliable—as modern physics has shown us by demonstrating that the observer affects what is observed, or that light sometimes appears as a particle and sometimes as a wave.

One of the major goals of the demonic forces is to suppress spirituality in the modern world, Sometimes demons try to suppress our spiritual involvement directly, but if they do not succeed at this, then what is their next step? They try to corrupt religion and spirituality by subtly changing them to suit their own ends. In this way, people are misled into believing that they are engaging in genuine spiritual practices, when in reality they are subjecting themselves to harmful manipulation and control.

Another way that such forces work against spirituality is to attempt to discourage people who are in dire need. For example, they might ask hungry people, "What do you need: bread, money, food?" Then they might ridicule such people to pray to their God for these needs to be supplied.

This is of course a devastating blow for someone who does not have a certain level of spiritual maturity. When such individuals make prayers to God and do not get instant results, they become extremely disheartened. This is why spiritual maturity and strong faith are necessary. Spiritual warriors understand that God is not an order-taker. He is not an errand boy, running to the supermarket to fulfill our material desires. Spiritual warriors are very clear about many of the tricks and illusions constructed by the demonic class and are eager to avoid such traps while warning others of the dangers.

Question & Answers

Question: You are presenting a great deal of detail about some very unusual topics. Why isn't this knowledge more available to the average person?

Answer: This knowledge is available to everyone, but

What Is Behind It All? 121

many people prefer to not see certain unpleasant realities. As we mentioned previously, there is no shortage of individuals anxious to take advantage of those who follow blindly. We often hear about the very real dangers of blindly following religious leaders without proper scrutiny, but what about the dangers of blindly buying into this materialistic culture? We are constantly accepting data as knowledge and propaganda as wisdom.

A story in the Vedic teachings illustrates this nicely. Once there was a king's washerman who kept a donkey to help him carry his heavy loads. He was very attached to this donkey—he would sing to him, feed him nicely and thought of him every day. The donkey, named Sunanda-Gandharva, was his closest associate, up until the sad day that Sunanda-Gandharva died. At that time, it was common practice to shave one's head when a family member or other important person died. The washerman, stricken with grief over the loss of his friend, decided to shave his head. As he traveled to the palace, the King's priest saw him and asked him why he had shaved. The washerman replied, "My dear Sunanda-Gandharva died today." The priest assumed that a very special person had died, and so he also went into mourning, shaved his head and took a bath in the sacred river. The Kings' minister saw the priest and the washerman, and asked why they had shaved their heads. The King's priest replied, "Don't you know? Sunanda-Ghandarva died today." So naturally the minister also shaved his head and bathed in the river. The King saw his priest, minister and washerman with shaved heads and asked the same question. Wanting to support one of his loyal subjects, he shaved his head and bathed in the river as well.

The queen saw that the washerman, the priest, the minister, and her beloved king had all shaved their heads, and asked her husband why. When the King replied that a great personality named Sunanda-Ghandarva had died, the queen then inquired, "Exactly who was this Ghandarva?" The king had no answer, and asked her to wait while he asked the minister. When he asked the minister, the minister replied that he would have to ask the priest. When the minister asked the priest, the priest replied that he would have to ask the washerman.

When the priest approached the washerman and asked, "Exactly who was this Sunanda-Ghandarva?" The washerman immediately burst into tears, explaining how wonderful Sunanda was; how they had so much love for each other; and that his life would never be the same now that his great associate had departed. The priest more persistently requested, "I'm sorry, but I have no recollection of him, who exactly was this person?" Finally, in an even more tearful state and choked up voice, the washerman exclaimed that Sunanda-Ghandarva was his ass.

This story illustrates the hazards of accepting and acting on information without genuine understanding. In Sanskrit this is referred to as *gaddalika* or "like a sheep." When one sheep jumps into a ditch, the whole flock follows.

Question: Do you think that your message can actually penetrate deeply enough to reform people and make them more God-conscious, to the extent that they will behave in the constructive manner you describe?

Answer: This depends on many factors. It depends on how well the message is disseminated and how quickly it is implemented. Normally, the message of God and His ambassadors is only heard and accepted by a small number of people. This message, which the prophet Muhammad, Lord Jesus, the Buddha and so many other great teachers brought to the world, is a universal message of love and peaceful coexistence. They taught that we should not be overly attached to this temporary existence. But despite the fact that such powerful personalities imparted divine knowledge and inspiration, the majority of the citizens did not take advantage of such gifts in their time. However, God is so merciful that, time and time again, He empowers teachers with various levels of commission to walk among us, teach the higher truths of human existence and remind us of what is right.

Question: Being an aware and informed person, how do you reconcile the idea that religion is the opiate of the masses with your commitment to being religious?

Answer: I am spiritual rather than religious, and I lecture constantly about the need to go beyond religion. We have to realize that many religions have nothing to do with a belief in God. For example, many people have made a religion out of drug-taking, out of rock-and-roll or out of watching sports. I am not being facetious. The problem with religion is that it tends to create divisions, and divisions always complicate matters. When we examine most of the major conflicts in the world at this time, we notice that many of them are the result of religious sectarianism. There is an urgent need in today's world for people to go beyond religion and turn it into spirituality.

All too often, religions content themselves with ritual, form and external differences. But as we go more deeply into any bona fide religious tradition, we begin to touch upon universal truths that are common to all religions. Part of the problem is that people have become so absorbed in external practices, sentimentality, emotionalism and escapism that they use religion for business, politics and a sense of belonging, instead of really exploring themselves and discovering the possibility of more profound conscious experiences. Many of these sectarian feelings play right into the demonic agenda.

If we delve deeply within ourselves we will discover the universality at the root of all religions. Once upon a time, scholars had to know many languages, as well as history, biology, philosophy, and a host of other subjects. But now, in this age of specialization, we are encouraged to focus on the most minute areas. We might even get a degree in how ants move their legs when they die, how roaches crawl or how butterflies mate. We study the most outrageous topics. Of course, this is necessary to a certain degree in today's scientific society, but sometimes we become experts in the most insignificant areas only to be imbecilic in many other aspects of life.

Knowledge is really interdisciplinary. As we explore any discipline thoroughly, we will eventually see how it connects to other disciplines. Instead of learning to say of ourselves: "I am a mathematician," or "I am paleontologist," we should learn how to improve the quality of life for others. This requires us to see the interrelationships among all forms of knowledge.

Question: How can we protect ourselves from evil influences?

Answer: When you act as the great spiritual teachers of history have acted, you are under an umbrella of protection. If you behave differently, you are a ripe candidate for disaster. Therefore, we should act as spiritual warriors. As warriors, we should take a closer look at the spiritual knowledge that has been given. We must take a closer at look to see how the Lord, who brought you this far, is trying to now take you even further.

What are some specific ways to recapture that spiritual attunement? One important step we can all take is to focus on the collective power of calling on the names of God. This is a powerful tool of deliverance. Using whatever name of God you feel comfortable with, call on that name with feeling and conviction.

Most religious systems now have given up the idea of calling on God's name. Or if they do call, they just do so to deliver a shopping list: "I need a new car"; "I need a new house"; "I need a raise;" "—and don't forget my boyfriend."

Do you think the Lord is happy about such an approach?

He wants to see how we are genuinely changing and becoming like a child ready to receive a parent's love. When we call on the names of God, we are invoking the Lord, so we must be ready to receive. If we start calling, if we start praying, if we start meditating, if we start toning, if we start chanting and we are not ready to receive the Lord, we are going to be confused. This is because we are not going to be either materialists or spiritualists, but something vague in between.

If we are out-and-out atheists, at least we can be good atheists. But if we are uncommitted spiritualists, we are in a "no-man's land," because we know the higher teachings and are not following them. If we do not live by what we know, our inner nature knows the truth and our hypocrisy chokes us. And while we are smiling and speaking to others, inwardly we are feeling something totally different. This is because our mind is under siege and the soul is crying out, asking for a real sense of freedom and liberation.

In summary, what we have to do is take a close look at ourselves. We have to bring ourselves back into balance, into our natural state. We have to stop overly emphasizing the material and the external. We must always remember that we are spiritual beings who happen to have material bodies, and that our real existence is as spirit souls.

Chapter 5

We are easy victims

Despite the fact that destructive forces on this planet have been able to create mass confusion, they are not entirely to blame for our difficulties. Actually, our greatest enemy is not some outside devil, but our own weak constitutions. In other words, negative powers can exert control over us only to the degree that we open ourselves up to their influence.

The actions of a society are the aggregate of the activities of the individuals within that society. Therefore, when we find fault with the behavior of society, when we observe a general breakdown of values within our communities, our first response should be to look inward. We must scrutinize our own behavior and values, and take a serious look at the quality of our relationships with the people around us. We cannot address the decline of modern society without examining how we each, through our daily actions, allow ourselves to be part of the problem.

Mind Control

One of the greatest weapons in the battle to destroy a civilization is the ability to direct the thought patterns and perceptions of the population. Anyone who can do this can influence the values and behavior of a society, because all actions begin in the mind. Thus, mind control has become a powerful means for manipulating and enslaving others.

As technologies become increasingly sophisticated, mind control will surely pose one of the greatest problems in the twenty-first century. Using increasingly subtle and pervasive methods, scientists will continue to devise ingenious ways to harness our mental energy without our even knowing it. Governments have devoted vast resources to researching and mastering techniques of mind control, and they apply the results of their experiments in public and private settings from military bases to shopping malls. While not every advertisement reflects a conscious effort to deceive or control the public, such phenomena as piped-in background music in stores, subliminal suggestions in advertisements and appeals to sexual desire throughout the culture have become tools for many determined, well-organized and maliciously motivated groups.

Manipulative Techniques

Today, several programs exist to train ministers, lawyers and public speakers in subtle mind control techniques. Under the guise of "effective public speaking," they learn to control their tone, meter and gestures and arrange carefully orchestrated settings to create a desired mindset in their audience. These techniques are based on detailed studies of individual and group psychology, and use knowledge gained from a careful analysis of current trends and attitudes. Those who lack a strong spiritual discipline, or who cannot separate themselves from the "herd" mentality, are likely to be repeatedly victimized by these types of mind intrusion to the point of accepting the opinions of others as their own. As we build up our spiritual strength and understand more about who we actually are, we become shielded against such invasion.

Psychic Control

Some extremely high-level negotiations at the UN and other places often deliberately plant psychics in the audience to try to influence the minds of the people in attendance. This is not so unusual when you really think about it. Whenever a new advance in technology becomes available, self-centered people will inevitably find ways to use it to manipulate others. Just as psychics have been used to find lost children or help in some other constructive endeavor, these quite real capabilities can also be used to influence peoples' minds in negative ways. As the world falls increasingly under the sway of evil influences, we must actively protect ourselves not only from gross aberrations but also from subtle manipulation and control.

I was once asked to give a presentation to a "meditation club" at the Pentagon. Of course, spiritual warriors are willing to go anywhere and everywhere to impart higher knowledge and attack that which is devastating to the human condition. We soon realized, however, that some members of this club simply wanted to learn the practices of various progressive people in order to explore new systems of mind control and psychic phenomena as a means of exploitation.

Manipulation by the Media

Members of modern society are in a constant state of mental and psychological warfare as a result of relentless bombardment by the media and advertisements that assail us every day and persuade us to think that we are merely physical bodies in a physical universe.

For example, many popular songs are designed to influence peoples' subconscious in a negative way and encourage them gradually to become more and more degraded. Music that increases our lust enslaves us. While our bodies sit in one place and our minds get stupefied and groggy, our desires run wild, fantasizing about any number of exciting sensual pleasures.

Television is also enslaving and hypnotizing us. That "idiot box" is one of the major contemporary forces causing humanity to become more and more illiterate, anesthetized and immoral. For many of us, the process of watching the news, major sporting events and other popular TV programs has become the modern equivalent of being "well read." As we can all observe, popular opinion and the general topics of conversation are dominated by the prior evening's programming. The danger is that this places producers of popular television shows and commercials in an extremely powerful position to manipulate public opinions and perceptions. Is it so difficult to believe that some of these people recognize this power and use it to their advantage?

Psychologists define four general states of awareness, based on the type of electronic signals that are dominant in the human brain as measured by an electroencephalogram, or EEG. The beta state is the state of normal waking consciousness, when we are awake and attuned to our surroundings. The alpha state is associated with deep meditation, hypnosis, daydreaming and REM (rapid eye movement) sleep. Subjects tend to fixate on one particular point of concentration, and can be up to twenty-five percent more susceptible to suggestion in the alpha state than when in the beta state. The theta and delta states are progressively deeper levels of unconsciousness that generally occur only during deep sleep or under anesthesia.

As we sit in our nice, secure, climate-controlled homes, in our favorite armchairs, enjoying our favorite snacks, watching hours of television, we tend to enter an alpha state—to varying degrees—without even realizing it. We are literally hypnotized—so tuned-in to a program that it is difficult to break away. We do not process what we see and hear with the same caution we would use in normal conversation.

The Influence of Advertisements

Advertisers take full and deliberate advantage of this situation, employing leading psychiatrists, psychotherapists and trained hypnotists to program us to buy their products. We are constantly receiving implants in our consciousness, to the point that we may have difficulty distinguishing between our own thoughts and those that have been implanted by post-hypnotic suggestions. We can actually become disoriented, losing our judgement and discretion as the lines blur between what is real and enduring and what is false and temporary.

Much of this relates to the extremely high cost of advertising. Television stations charge advertisers thousands of dollars for every second of airtime. Surely, these advertisers intend to make their investments pay off for them, and to do so most of them will use any advantage that modern science makes available.

The prohibitive prices of these commercials also tend to prevent many good and positive messages from getting through. It is not our well-wishing friends and compatriots who produce most of these advertisements. Who can afford to pay that kind of money? Our local health food store owner? No! The same people who are trying to control the masses and dictate the new world order are planning our recreational diets. We must ask ourselves honestly: Do such people really intend to give us the secrets of success? Of course not! They are running their own self-serving agendas.

What they pump into our minds constantly is their own information designed for their own specific goals. "Buy this." "Wear that." "Eat this." In other words: "Put money in my pocket and, if possible, get so completely absorbed in my agenda that you altogether forget your own purpose and simply do my bidding." Have you noticed which products are advertised during the Super Bowl or the World Series? Educational or life-enriching products? We are much more likely to see endless commercials for fast food, fast cars and fast "highs."

Another phenomenon we may notice while watching TV is that the volume gets louder during commercials. Further, the rhythm of the speaker's voice during these advertisements is often metered in such a way that it has a subliminal effect on the viewer's consciousness. As a psychology student at Princeton, I did quite a bit of research into hypnosis, and I have always been shocked by the degree to which we can be literally hypnotized without even knowing it.

Television's Power

Even more troubling is the content of the television programs we devote our attention to. With rare exceptions, most of the episodes we see on television are fear-producing and adrenaline-arousing. They can cause us to feel exhausted even though we have not left our seats, and continued exposure can leave us feeling burned-out in our daily lives, as if we had been subjected to genuine traumatic experiences.

By the time children in America are 18 years old, they have witnessed hundreds of thousands of violent crimes on television. It is no wonder that violent youth crimes are on the rise. Even when we listen to children playing in a schoolyard, we frequently hear them exclaiming, "I'm gonna kill you!" They even brandish toy weapons and act out violent scenarios.

We are often lulled into a false sense of security because of our belief that what we see on television is "not real." This attitude is extremely dangerous, however, because television images do leave real impressions in our minds. They can cause us to feel anxiety and agitation; they can even encourage some people to act out similar scenarios in real life. Watching television agitates our lustful propensities to the point that many individuals are now like time-bombs, ready to explode with all the violence they have viewed since childhood.

Most of us, especially if we are spiritually oriented, would never allow the events that we see on television to occur in our homes. Yet, unfortunately, we are unaware that the energy of these occurrences enters our atmosphere almost as deeply when we watch them on television as if they had actually happened in our lives.

Obsession with the Body

Most television viewing amounts to an endless campaign for bodily comfort. This is because the backers of most television programs manufacture products that cater to our bodily comforts. This in turn produces an obsessive interest in concerns of the body, and an extreme distraction from matters of the soul. This focus is utterly counterproductive to human progress. Nevertheless, every day, we unwittingly continue to subject ourselves to influences that most profoundly arouse this obsession with the body at the expense of our souls.

Because of all the negative thoughts and images that are constantly bombarding us, those who are not dedicated to elevating consciousness will find themselves totally unable to think freely. If we are not engaged in some practice of spiritual rejuvenation, or of prayer and purification, we will just get swept up in the current of self-centeredness, competition, hatred and eventually violence.

This is not to say that television itself is bad or evil. It is only our total absorption in the diversions offered by television that creates a problem. Such absorption tends to distract us from the real self-affirming acts of loving others and inquiring into our higher nature. And when we are not aware of the higher purpose of life, or when we feel isolated and out of touch with other human beings, we respond either by numbing ourselves, distracting ourselves, or becoming depressed and even suicidal.

Glorification of Suicide

The desire to take one's own life is more likely to arise when members of society and their leaders fail to acknowledge the spiritual dimensions of existence, focusing instead on the material aspects of human experience or metaphysical paths that do not delve deeply into the true meaning of life. If we do not have sufficient connections to the transcendental realm, we can easily be swept up in a great wave of apathy and depression. When people commit suicide, they can open an avenue for other individuals and groups to do the same, because we are all social creatures who tend to be susceptible to the trends around us.

It is interesting to note that those who seem to "have it all" from a material perspective seem to commit suicide more than people in any other social group. Further, some of the most intelligent members of society advocate views that tend to encourage a negative attitude toward human life. For example, the philosophy of existentialism, which influenced an entire generation, came from the highest intellects—so-called great minds such as Albert Camus and Jean Paul Sartre. *The New Columbia Encyclopedia* says that Sartre's existentialist writings "examine man as a responsible but lonely being, burdened with a terrifying freedom to choose and set adrift in a meaningless universe."

These thinkers were of course extremely materially intelligent, but because they were atheistic and only recognized material phenomena, their analyses of history and the human condition led them to draw conclusions of futility and hopelessness. Many of those exposed to this philosophy inevitably ended up asking themselves, "What is the use of living if we are only born to struggle and then die?" They have been led by the tenets of existentialism to make perverted interpretations of the freedom it implies. In their view, given that life has no transcendent meaning, suicide becomes a permissible and justifiable act.

Sylvia Plath is another example of the glorification of suicide. She was a popular female author and poet whose poems and novels are admired and taught in many contemporary English literature courses. Both she and another contemporary writer, Virginia Woolf, have become almost legendary pop heroines, partly because of their rejection of the demands of life, which in both cases ultimately led to suicide. Plath asphyxiated herself by putting her head in an oven, while Woolf tied heavy rocks to herself and then hurled herself into a body of water.

These suicides are of course tragic, but another great tragedy today is that these women have been almost deified by academia. This makes their choice all the more attractive and acceptable. When they are honored as great authors, they become role models for other frustrated intellectuals. Then it becomes easier for them to proclaim that the act of acknowledging their misery by taking a pill or shooting themselves is an honest and courageous achievement.

Collective Suicide

Sometimes, the glorification of suicide occurs in a collective setting. There are increasing numbers of suicides, homicides, and holy wars in which groups of people willingly follow some charismatic crackpot to an early grave. For example, in 1997, thirty-nine adult males of mostly upper middle-class backgrounds committed suicide using a combination of barbiturates, vodka and suffocation. This tragedy took place in Rancho Santa Fe, California, under the direction of a self-proclaimed religious leader named Marshall Applewhite. The unfortunate group of misguided individuals called themselves the Heaven's Gate adherents, and each believed that by suicide they could join the Hale-Bopp comet as spirit beings and pass through the doorway of the physical kingdom into the spiritual world.

At the heart of these types of seemingly impossible events is the fact that the majority of the people involved have abandoned the exciting, universal adventure of life. Life's greatest adventures are self-discovery, self-actualization and love. All three of these aspects are intimately related, because if we genuinely discover ourselves we will also attain self-actualization and find that we are eternally, constitutionally loving creatures. The beauty of love is that it works both ways: truly loving ourselves requires that we love others, and, conversely, if we love ourselves enough, we naturally love others because loving others fulfills a primal need in ourselves.

One-Dimensional Thinking

We must not allow ourselves to be influenced by a societal climate that accepts any form of suicide. According to all bona fide spiritual teachings, the truth of the matter is that suicide is not an acceptable way to end suffering and does not assure entry into the spiritual kingdom. We are here on Earth for a purpose, and death is not an alternative lifestyle. Suicide is an extremely pitiful and cowardly act, prompted by a simplistic and one-dimensional understanding of life.

Unfortunately, many people are afraid to have their belief systems challenged and are frightened of releasing their habitual ways of thinking when faced with other perspectives on life. They are reluctant to investigate ancient wisdom, because they are terrified of what such wisdom might require of them. Then too, many persons become subject to the three modes of material nature known in the ancient Vedic scriptures as *sattva, rajas* and *tamas*. These translate roughly to the modes of goodness, passion and ignorance. Nowadays, the modes of passion and ignorance are extremely widespread around the world—especially the mode of ignorance.

The mode of ignorance is characterized by laziness and dull-mindedness. People in this mode are inclined to intoxication and delusion. Under the influence of the mode of ignorance, individuals have great difficulty understanding anything beyond the familiar material realm. When the higher light of spirituality is denied to a soul, whether by the soul's own actions or by the actions of another, that soul cannot grasp the subtler issues of life and may eventually become extremely depressed. Indeed, persons in the mode of ignorance often become atheists, wondering, "Why is God allowing so many millions of people to suffer?" or "Why does a loving God allow genocide, holocausts and natural disasters?"

Frequently, these people do not understand the "rules of the game" of life, failing to recognize the essential justice of each and every event. Therefore, they have little incentive to continue living when confronted with apparently arbitrary, random cosmic "injustices." Think about it. If we believe that we have no control over our destiny—if no higher authority is empowered to impose justice or if that higher authority has no love for us—then it can easily follow that the most sane and viable solution is to end everything as quickly and painlessly as possible.

Of course, as spiritual warriors we know that we are not the ultimate owners of our bodies. Instead, we understand that God is the proprietor of everything, including these bodies, and that to destroy someone else's property is a violation. We also know that a specific period is allotted to each of us to spend in our particular bodies. If we prematurely interrupt any particular life span, we may be forced to live out our assigned term in another—possibly much worse—environment. Genuine spiritual warriors will have nothing to do with suicide.

The Failure of Our System

When we realize that we are not our bodies, but rather souls residing in a body, we gain an important key to our happiness and sanity. Indeed, unless we understand that we are eternally pure spirit souls, we will not remain peaceful, happy or fulfilled for very long—even with great wealth. If we are unwilling to take sufficient time to discover and confirm our eternal nature, we cannot avoid anxiety and depression. We will simply be riddled with fear, sadness and anger, worried about protecting what we have and afraid of losing everything.

There is a Vedic axiom that we can judge a tree by the fruit it bears. If this is a valid measure, then three strong contemporary indicators reveal that our way of life is a failure: widespread suicide, drug use and mental illness. All these factors point to a similar conclusion: maybe material success is not sufficient on its own. Perhaps the accumulation of tangible commodities and the ability to manipulate personal assets are not sufficient guarantees of happiness. And, quite possibly, the knowledge gained from academic and empirical investigation may not be adequate by itself to ensure that our lives have meaning. These are relative and subjective phenomena, pleasing us one moment and disappointing us the next. They cannot bring us lasting fulfillment.

In addition to its almost exclusive emphasis on material satisfactions, modern society seems designed to isolate us from one another. Yet, ultimately, we are all interrelated—everyone affects others, and the environment, in countless ways. When we are selfishly individualistic instead of dedicated to the collective welfare, we all suffer because we ultimately hurt ourselves when we undermine others. At our core, we all identify ourselves by other people's perceptions of us—by the kind of contributions we make and by the ways in which these are accepted or rejected. When we feel useless and dispensable, or incompetent to perform our functions, we grow sorrowful, apathetic and possibly suicidal.

Ecstasy is an innate human need and a natural human state. Every living entity desires a peak experience or an effortless "high." It is normal for us to look for deeper levels of happiness—especially in these times when people talk *at* each other instead of *to* each other, and when so few of us can say that we truly love someone or that someone genuinely loves us. Is it really so surprising that suicide is so widespread in our society? Suicide says emphatically, "I am deeply unhappy. I don't love myself, and I don't love you enough to live for you either!" It even goes further to declare, "I don't feel enough love from anyone to make my life worth living."

Poor Relationships

It is a sad irony that while so many sophisticated methods of communication exist in the world, mutual intelligibility—the ability of people to understand and know each other at a deep level—is at its lowest ebb.

As relationships become more superficial and cosmetic, we are not required to think or interact profoundly. We are not held accountable for our actions, and we are not compelled to express ourselves honestly. At the end of the day, however, such a shallow mode of relating tends to leave us bored, dry and unfulfilled. We then engage in extracurricular activities in an effort to fill the void, or we may turn to addictive substances as a way to minimize our suffering, or at least suffer peacefully.

Nowadays, many avenues are easily available for us to enjoy ourselves blindly, with little requirement for genuine interaction and communication. People are suffering greatly because of empty or abusive relationships. They are being disappointed and exploited by their mothers, fathers, boyfriends, girlfriends, husbands, wives, children and even ministers or politicians.

Such relationships can hurt us deeply because these are the

people who are most dear to us. We depend on them to give us the greatest love, attention and assistance. Nobody can hurt us more than those whom we truly love. Of course, these same people can also give us the greatest happiness, protection and satisfaction.

Obstacles to Loving Interactions

One of the main reasons for this sad state of affairs is the Hollywood conception of relationships. Because of the harmful examples that are being force-fed to them, couples are having serious trouble with loving relationships, children do not know how to be respectful to their parents and parents do not understand how to care for their children properly. Even when we recognize that something is wrong, we cannot pinpoint the cause because we are unaware of the profound effects that negative role models in the media can have on our consciousness.

Decline of Families and Community

The term "community" means communion. It indicates cooperation and communication. But in the present world order, genuine communities are rare. Instead, we have countless pseudo-communities. Too many of the institutions, groups and families that surround us lack real intimacy or communication. But love and intimacy are essential to life. Just as love heals, lack of love can kill.

Anyone who lives in a community that places great priority on material assets—a community in which people work much harder to acquire wealth than to create intimacy—is bound to fall prey to despair, just as their peers, colleagues and mentors do. Such is the case with modern civilization.

Strong, loving communities are particularly important

for raising healthy, happy children. Children are especially wounded if those who are meant to protect them hurt, ignore or attack them instead. They are particularly injured if those who are supposed to provide for them only do the bare minimum on their behalf or even worse, arrange for their exploitation.

The Mental Health Crisis

More than anyone, therapists, counselors and ministers recognize the severity of the problems associated with poor communication and lack of community in this society. Because of insufficient connections and fractured relationships, countless individuals feel lonely, gloomy, depressed and frustrated, and many are losing their desire to function effectively in the normal arenas of existence. Many lead lives of "quiet desperation," while others turn to violent and destructive behavior.

As we have discussed earlier, the World Health Organization has stated that one of the greatest health crises facing the global community over the next twenty years will be mental illness. Various forms of mental illness are already approaching epidemic levels, as vast numbers of people around the world experience the deterioration of their family relationships and face profound disappointments in life.

The subject of mental health is intimately linked to politics and oppression, as it has been throughout human history. Now more than ever, the mental health of the world's people is at the mercy of influences they cannot control. Overt abuse and tyranny have been the rule in the past, and certainly continue today. Yet subtle manipulation and control through the media have become new, powerful weapons in the hands of the elite, with devastating consequences. When outside forces manipulate our minds, our degradation and enslavement can become catastrophic.

As we have seen, the media encourages its audience to

focus on the material aspects of existence at the expense of higher consciousness. At the root of the current increases in mental illness, violence, homicide and suicide is the fact that, despite the overindulgence of our material appetites, most people are spiritually starving.

We all have an inherent, natural desire for love and deep connections with others. In direct opposition to the requirements of our individual natures, however, society is evolving more and more toward reliance on the mechanical and the superficial. As a result of wishful—actually delusional—thinking, people are taking refuge in material consciousness and resorting to ever more sophisticated forms of sense gratification. Many of us just live from day to day like rabbits chasing dangling carrots without understanding how precarious our situation is. When we follow the dictates of our fallible minds and senses, we make ourselves vulnerable to the inevitable consequences that arise when immediate gratification is no longer available to us.

We must go beyond the orthodox approaches to mental health in order to remedy the situation. It is obvious that the traditional approaches of psychiatry, psychology and counseling have not been sufficient to avert the widespread human tragedies that are occurring around the world. These problems cannot be resolved on the level at which they present themselves; instead, they must be addressed from a spiritual, holistic platform where we view our difficulties in a far greater context than the immediate preoccupations of daily life.

One of the characteristics that make us human is our free will. Without a developed will, we easily fall prey to forces that we cannot control. This is why spiritual practice is important, because the source of genuine free will is a higher state of consciousness. If we do not regularly engage in a serious spiritual discipline but instead focus our total attention on material pleasures, we will have little access to this free will. We will be captured by the modes of material nature and allow ourselves to be manipulated by the clever tyrants who have already convinced us to worship money, prestige and material acquisitions.

A Challenge to Psychiatrists

Some years ago, I gave a lecture to a group of psychiatrists at a university in Michigan. My primary point, presented in a tactful way, was that psychiatrists are basically cheaters. I felt compelled to challenge my audience in this way in order to bring their attention to the untenable assumptions that form the basis of their work.

Psychiatrists are among the world's most highly paid professionals, and they benefit from the implicit trust of those in their care. Indeed, the lives of many people are profoundly affected by psychiatric evaluations. Whether the issue is accountability for a crime, commitment to a mental institution, suitability for employment or the interpretation and treatment of specific deviations from "normal" behavior, the assessments of psychiatric professionals carry great weight.

Having studied psychotherapy at Princeton, I reminded the psychiatrists that neither they nor the psychologists have been able to agree as to what "the mind" actually is. Yet members of these professions address issues of the mind every day, acting as experts despite the fact that they have no clear understanding of what they are doing. To complicate matters even further, these professionals also lack any clear consensus about what is considered "normal."

How can professionals who deal with the mind and treat abnormal behavior actually have no clear definition of what is "normal"? What's more, how can psychiatrists and psychologists address the emotional lives of their patients when no psychological or psychiatric textbook offers any clear definition of an emotion? In other words, these professionals may charge their patients over $100 an hour to offer "treatment" for issues that the psychiatrists and psychologists themselves do not fully understand.

Physician, Heal Thyself!

In Western culture, those who profess to heal others are often in dire need of healing themselves. Psychiatrists are not the only ones standing on shaky ground. Physicians of all types are experiencing difficulty in their lives. If we are to heal the individual, the community and the planet, we must give particular attention to the state of our healers. Unfortunately, a great number of physicians are suffering from various degrees of dysfunction and depression—even to the point of committing suicide. As a rule, Western physicians have the worst health of any other professional group, and life spans at least ten years shorter. In addition to high suicide rates, statistics show that physicians have extremely high divorce rates and serious levels of drug abuse. Surely these problems do not stem from a lack of scientific knowledge, nor from any material or financial deficits. More often, they arise because of an inner spiritual bankruptcy.

If physicians are to be effective leaders and spiritual warriors—as they should be—they must maintain a healthy balance between the material and the spiritual, and understand the spiritual principles that support the physical sciences. Physicians should base their practices upon a strong integration of spiritual awareness and scientifically based skills. They should also have a great desire, backed up by deliberate action, to make positive contributions to their communities.

At least 2,500 years ago, Hippocrates, one of the founders of the medical profession, said, "Thy food will be thy remedy." He also stated that everyone has a doctor within. However, modern medicine's current mode of practice has strayed far from this paradigm. Indeed, all too frequently, modern medicine has deviated from platforms that truly work to heal the individual. Awareness of this situation may help us challenge our basic approaches to health and healing. Changing our point of view about medical treatment is extremely important, because our enthusiastic embrace of drugs, symptom suppression and purely physical remedies has been responsible for a vast amount of human suffering and misery.

Fortunately, many medical professionals today have begun to explore areas of metaphysical, paranormal and spiritual knowledge. They are recognizing the intimate relationship between the mind and the body. Some are even considering the possibility that we are in fact much more than our bodies and minds. As physicians and other medical practitioners shift their perspective away from a strict reductionistic approach, they have started viewing patients and diseases more holistically. Hopefully, this development will lead them to understand more deeply the subtle factors that have a bearing on the origin and treatment of disease.

Examples of new developments include discoveries in the burgeoning field of psychoneuroimmunology, which validates the close connection between mind and body; and in writings by physician Larry Dossey about the reality of the "nonlocal mind" and its implications for medical practice. Further, one medical journal recently summarized a Harvard research project by saying: "The conclusion that we find in the Harvard working group on new and resurgent diseases reports...disease cannot be understood in isolation from the social, ecological, epidemiological and evolutionary context in which it emerges and spreads."

The Importance of Role Models

How can physicians heal themselves? They can do so by recognizing the higher truths of life and by becoming accountable to others in the most selfless way possible. Their great responsibility, power and influence give them the capacity to become some of society's most important spiritual warriors. To accomplish this they must learn to integrate their minds, bodies and souls in a unified purpose. Indeed, this integration and sense of purpose are the marks of true spiritual warriors and genuinely spiritual persons. Someone true to these commitments will strive to live a congruent life in which words and actions are in alignment with each other.

Much of the world's future is in the hands of the medical community. Physicians and others in prominent positions in society—whether they like it or not—serve as role models. Therefore, it is extremely important that such people work toward balance and health in their own lives. As role models, they influence the entire society. More than anyone, health professionals must display to the world the possibility of whole, integrated personhood that addresses the concerns of both body and soul. The ancient *Bhagavad-gita* supports this view in verse 3.21: "Whatever action a great man performs, common men follow; and whatever standards he sets by exemplary acts, all the world pursues." Leaders must demonstrate healthy living by their own examples.

Not only do doctors possess great responsibility and high potential, but they also have an extremely strong impetus to change their views and behavior. This is because, as mentioned earlier, physicians have some of the shortest and most stressful lives. It is consequently beneficial to the doctors themselves, as well as to society, for them to broaden their medical perspectives and investigate holistic health. In this way, they can heal themselves and thus be of greater benefit to others.

These admonitions apply to all of us—not just to physicians. As we make inquiries and change our perspectives on life, at some point we will realize that we are not merely engaging in an intellectual exercise. As spiritual warriors, we learn to recognize and accept our responsibility to others. There are innocent people all over the world counting on us to be earnest and vigorous in our search for solutions that will address the real physical and mental issues we all face.

Truth Must Not Be Distorted

One of the problems of Western culture is that it refuses to respect the attainments of earlier civilizations, or of contemporary non-Western societies. This is a serious mistake. There is much we could learn from traditional systems of knowledge. Instead, we reserve our esteem for "original" thinkers and those who question the attainments of the past. Not all cultures adopt this approach to knowledge.

In the Vedic scriptures, a mildly disparaging term refers to a type of philosopher known as a *muni*. *Munis* are known for altering the ideas of their predecessor philosophers in an effort to win name and fame for themselves. Genuine truth-lovers in Vedic culture consider the practice of such *munis* to be a serious disservice to society because it is based on pride and lack of respect rather than on a humble appreciation for the original unadulterated teachings.

Another category of philosopher, held in much higher esteem, is one who learns the truth through humble direct reception from authoritative sources. Such a philosopher, while remaining faithful to the original teachings, then expounds upon what has been transmitted with new examples, analogies and personal insights. In this way, an individual's creativity and skills are used to defend, analyze and illuminate the truths learned from trusted sources. In Vedic times, this was considered an acceptable way to utilize genius because there was a great reverence for tradition and a healthy suspicion of arbitrary conjecture.

The opposite practice—simply disputing previously declared truths in order promote one's own status—was considered unconscionable, producing nothing but arrogance and confusion. This is the extent to which Vedic sages felt protective of the truth. Indeed, we could learn much from them. The truth is worthy of protection. That is not to say that the truth is fragile. On the contrary, it is we who are fragile, and when we protect the truth, we actually protect ourselves by avoiding faulty behavior. In this day and age, our ignorance and lack of respect for ancient teachings are causing us profound suffering.

Need for Positive Examples

Not only do we fail to honor the wisdom of traditional cultures, but we also revere the wrong people. In the modern world, we have far too many faulty role models. We cannot overemphasize the fact that "like attracts like." Wherever immoral behavior is rampant, more of such behavior is bound to occur. There is a Confucian saying that if you commit a sin twice, it will not seem a sin to you at all. Modern people have become so numb to the consequences of their harmful behavior that they are indeed misbehaving at every step without the slightest compunction or hesitation.

We must avoid making excuses for our weaknesses. If someone's behavior bothers us, it is not the fault of the other person. Instead, it is because we are on shaky ground. We must develop enough inner strength to prevent other people's nonsense from making us nonsensical ourselves. If we succumb to weakness, it is because we do not have sufficient resolve. We should stop making scapegoats of others and do what is necessary to strengthen ourselves.

Despite some notable exceptions, the era of "super-bad" hustlers and "macho" Hollywood screen idols is in decline. Some of those "heroes" smoked too many cigarettes, and a few years after their deaths, their faces have appeared on billboards begging youngsters not to be as foolish as they were. As spiritual law-breakers disappear from the scene, nature is making a way for spiritual warriors to prevail and reestablish divine order. But if we stay stuck in the rut of materialism, who knows what will become of us? We must all take a deep look at ourselves. If we waste our time boasting of how fierce or "bad" we are, we may become candidates for the planet's endangered species list. We are destined for a better fate, but it is up to us to make the right choices.

It is no accident that today, when illicit activity is commonplace around the planet, problems of disease and addiction are on the rise. In many cases, people actually believe they will get away with their self-serving, materialistic behavior. This is a result of ignorance. The fact is that when we turn to artificial stimuli for pleasure, we miss the chance to experience the genuine thrills that accompany high spirituality. The more we understand how much bliss is accessible to us when we harmonize our thoughts and actions with Divine will, the more we will want to escape this confusion and move into the light of truth. However, to realize this requires spiritual maturity, which brings the necessary tolerance and flexibility to open our minds.

Our Link to Collective Consciousness

As members of "modern civilization," we are so anesthetized by our addictions—and by our lust, illusions and fixations on the temporary—that we are easy victims for whatever games others may wish to play with our consciousness. Consequently, humankind is becoming increasingly enslaved to vicious urges—perhaps the most vicious that this planet has ever seen. For example, drug addicts have no friends, because friendship may interfere with their primary goal of obtaining the next "fix." The addiction becomes their sole fixation and drive, and they will stop at nothing to get what they need. Drugs become their very lifeline.

Everyone's thoughts are part of the collective consciousness of their culture, their nation and the planet. These collective thoughts, desires and actions bombard us constantly and produce extremely powerful effects. Most people are docile and tend to follow the latest fads and the normal everyday patterns of those around them. However, what we need today is the strength of character to think for ourselves and to remain unaffected by the negative energies all around us. We must always remember that God is watching us, and that our actions and attitudes influence others and contribute to the collective atmosphere in either a constructive or destructive way.

Misusing the Mind

Our entire problem can be summarized in one word: consciousness. The problem of consciousness is intimately related to the mind. From a spiritual perspective, our consciousness is based on faith, and faith depends on the potency of the mind. The quality and capacity of our mind determine our realizations, experiences, perceptions and interpretations of what happens to us. Ultimately, it is our mind that decides the meaning of our lives. Our mind can assist us or harm us. It can delve beneath appearances to help us discover the truths of existence, or it can skim the surface of phenomena, enslaving us in self-centered illusions.

We must stress again that no external technology perpetuates our illusions more than that of the almighty television set. Not all television programming is useless or harmful, but its subtle effects can be quite dangerous. Some people's whole sphere of existence consists of a supermarket, a shopping mall, a little office cubicle, and a comfortable chair in front of the television set. Because they watch the "idiot box" constantly, they believe themselves to be great adventurers, valiant law enforcers, mighty wrestlers, secret agents, famous detectives, daring criminals, great lovers or pioneering space explorers. They can fulfill their fantasies with their eyes glued to the flickering screen while their lives just slip away.

Fantasizing has two inherent problems. First, fantasizing can feel so much like the real experience that it creates an artificial sense of satisfaction and removes the motivation for us to achieve what we really want. The second problem concerns the subject matter. Because we can be swayed in various directions by the content of our fantasies, if we focus on base and immoral models, we tend to resemble what we imagine. In other words, fantasy has a great potential to create lethargy or licentious behavior.

Of course, many people do not merely fantasize about the shows they watch on television. Some of them take things a step further and actually act out these fantasies by imitating their television heroes. The only problem here is that many of these heroes are in fact fakes themselves. This means that in many cases people are imitating imitations.

Certainly, the roles played in TV dramas do exist in real life: there are law enforcers, detectives, lawyers, doctors, nurses and high-paid fashion models. However, in our everyday world, many of these peoples' personal lives are not working, and few of them are as fulfilled as television may make it appear. The television screen shows only half the story. It portrays characters having a thrill a minute as they solve crimes and handcuff criminals. It tends to overlook the equally accurate fact that many of these people are disillusioned, disenchanted, divorced, lonely, alcoholic, drugged, overstressed or suicidal.

Self-destructive Patterns

In addition to fantasy, the mind has several other mechanisms that can lead us astray. The main activities with which the mind sabotages us are dullness, dwelling, rationalization and attachment.

A dull mind is never our friend because it will not use its powers of recall and analysis to recognize why we are in a particular predicament. Such a mind is not interested in finding a solution to problems; indeed, it may not even have detected what those problems are. This type of mind is trapped in the mode of ignorance, which is characterized by laziness, sleep and inertia. This is why a dull mind is so slow to diagnose its actual status. According to ancient scriptures, "foolishness, madness and illusion" are the children of this ignorant mode of living. So we should be extremely careful to avoid mental dullness and try to purify our minds by spiritual practices.

The tendency of the mind to hang on to past impressions and thoughts—even unwelcome ones—is what we call "dwelling." We have all had the experience of a commercial jingle replaying in our brain until it becomes almost unbearable. Although we may not like the song, the lyrics or the product being advertised, our mind mercilessly repeats the melody in our head—over and over again. Unless redirected in a positive way, this tendency of the mind to linger on habitual, unwanted thoughts or impressions is a great impediment to spiritual advancement. Spiritual advancement depends to a large extent on consciously guiding the mind in constructive, divine directions.

Rationalization is another important obstacle to our own growth. The religious author Marilyn Hickey writes, "Rationalization is a dead-end street, and many are they who find it." Rationalization is a serious affliction of the mind. Sometimes the mind fears and avoids maturation because it does not know what is around the corner waiting. We are apprehensive about what will be demanded of us after we move into a new sphere of thought and action, and our insecurity causes us to resist and subconsciously make our own growth almost impossible.

Rationalization prevents us from seeing faults in ourselves. Instead, it makes us shift all blame for our imperfections to others. When we rationalize, we have the tendency justify ourselves by saying, "I did the best that could possibly be done under the circumstances." We fail to see that others in the same situation might have produced a far better outcome by applying themselves with more humility, more enthusiasm, more determination, or more sincerity. Rationalization minimizes our capacity for growth and effort by convincing us that we are already perfect or the best we can be. This is not an attitude conducive to spiritual advancement. No one achieves optimal results with this approach. To avoid this trap, spiritual warriors should be strict with themselves and lenient with others.

This state of consciousness usually accompanies mental dullness, because it generally attacks those who are lazy. Even if our intellect is strong, if the mind refuses to engage in self-analysis with humility and honesty, we may act foolishly and destructively because of this tendency to rationalize. Put another way, the person who constantly rationalizes is like a muscle builder who exercises only one muscle in one direction and never attains any useful goal.

Attachment is the habit of dwelling on the past to great excess. Attachment generally arises when we do not adequately feed our minds with new and positive stimuli. Just as those who are underfed tend to dream constantly about their last good meal, an underfed mind tends to focus on its fondest memories and place undue importance on them.

Attachment is a natural aspect of our being. However, when our attachment is misdirected toward mundane subjects, the mind can never find total satisfaction. Instead, it wanders like an orphan searching for its parents. For us to attain genuine happiness, we should direct our attachments toward the spiritual realm. Unless the mind absorbs enough divine knowledge to become attached to its proper spiritual objects, changing our mental habits remains almost impossible. Therefore, we should not expect our minds to cooperate unless we are willing to develop the necessary mental discipline to direct our thoughts properly.

We Can Make a Difference

Fortunately, today increasing numbers of people understand the necessity for a complete change of mind—a revolution in consciousness—to ensure a viable future for humanity and the world. Superficial changes are insufficient. We require far more than "action plans," however well conceived, or a series of quick and comfortable "fixes." What we urgently need is a profound shift in the worldview that underlies all our behavior. The old patterns of thought, which created this predicament in the first place, must give way to something new.

Given this situation, we must each realize how essential we are to the future of life on this planet. The participation of each one of us is vital. We should make a firm commitment to raise the level of our consciousness, day-by-day, moment-by-moment. We all have the capacity to become spiritual warriors if we are willing to make the choice and embrace its consequences. These consequences include pursuing truth in earnest and doing our utmost to create healthier modes of living founded on accountability, maturity and ultimately purity. Purity protects us—and our world—because when we are honest and "above-board," no one can cheat us and we cannot do harm to others. So let us all make integrity our insurance policy and do what we must to heal this planet.

Questions & Answers

Question: It seems that this particular society thrives on the ignorance of people when it comes to spirituality. For example, it seems that there are individuals who know the powerful positive influence that regulated spiritual practice can have, and actually want to keep the people at large in the dark about it.

Answer: Imagine sitting down in a restaurant and not understanding the language of the menu or knowing what any of the dishes are. If you order something arbitrarily, you may get something you like or you may not. Many people actually live their lives in a similar way, making whimsical choices based on what feels good at the moment. They hope that material nature will give them something good in return. Sometimes they are pleased with what they get, and sometimes not. Not until we make an in-depth study of the rules that govern material nature can we make decisions that consistently benefit everyone.

When we understand the rules of this material prison, we also feel a sense of responsibility for our actions and for the effects we have on others. That is a major reason for our fear of knowing the truth of our situation. We are afraid to break out of our easy, customary patterns because we dread the unknown. We have become comfortable within our illusions, which do not require us to think. If and when we do start "thinking too much," we often numb ourselves with intoxicants in order to return to the apparent safety of a more familiar situation.

There is no shortage of individuals willing to exploit and profit from the ignorance and fear of others. When these people gain positions of influence and power, terrible abuses become possible. It is for this reason that, while we work to protect ourselves, we must also make a determined effort to assist those who are struggling on this battlefield of human consciousness.

Question: People often claim that society simply is what it is. They say, "This is how it has always been and this is how it will always be." They claim that our very nature binds us to a cyclical alternation between positive and negative, and that we are naïve to believe that we can change anything.

Answer: In warfare, leaders often use propaganda to try to make the other side lose hope. They send such messages as, "You are already defeated," or, "Our side is so much more powerful; we're going to wipe you out." The hope is that the enemy will become demoralized and quickly surrender. This is to be expected in spiritual warfare, too. Here, the propaganda is much subtler, encouraging people to think, "It's no problem; it's nothing. I'll just go on with my regular sense gratification, because it feels so good." In other words, the enemy is manipulating others to continue being slaves and to suppress any qualms.

We should not allow ourselves to be discouraged by the degraded culture that surrounds us. We must recognize that our positive actions add to the collective atmosphere just as the negative actions of others do. Our devotion and intensity go far beyond our immediate environment. Though confusion and negativity may surround us, we must do our part to help raise consciousness. Each of us has our own propensities and gifts, our own strengths and weaknesses. We should use our talents in every way that we can to make a difference in the collective consciousness of the planet.

Chapter 6

A spiritual warrior's view of the world

There are only two categories of happy people in the material world: fools and transcendentalists. Fools are so oblivious that they manage to convince themselves they are happy in this material prison. Transcendentalists are happy because they can see above the material dualities, and know that their parole is at hand. Everyone else is essentially miserable. This is because calamity in the material world cannot be avoided, just as water cannot be avoided in the ocean.

The material world is impermanent and constantly changing. One of the first skills we must develop as spiritual warriors is equipoise in the face of constant change and apparent chaos. We must not become overly proud in a moment of happiness, or overly fearful in a moment of distress. Happiness and distress will come to us of their own accord for as long as we reside in this realm.

In our quest to become strong spiritual warriors, we must keep in mind the difference between religion and spirituality. Religion is frequently bound to superficial differences of doctrine and institutional structure. Although religion can play an important role in our development of spiritual understanding, it can also promote divisions and sectarianism. In contrast, true spiritual pursuits are unifying, because they seek the common ground among all approaches to the divine. We can develop a genuine spiritual understanding by a careful study and practice of the deeper teachings in the traditions of ancient wisdom available to us.

We Are Not the Body

A fundamental premise of spiritual teachings around the world is that we are not the physical body. In the Bible, 1 Corinthians chapter 15 tells us that both celestial and terrestrial realities exist, and that we humans have both aspects within us. This scripture reminds us that while we are in the terrestrial, or physical, state we are away from the Father. Being accustomed to material existence, we can easily perceive the physical aspects of our being, while our celestial parts are less easy to perceive. However, despite this perceptual difficulty, we must constantly remember that we are not physical beings. Instead, we are fundamentally spiritual, transcendental, antimaterial entities who are simply using these physical bodies as vehicles. Each body is like a garment, a ventriloquist's dummy. Without the spiritual spark within, our flesh is absolutely lifeless.

Consider the example of a little boy being fatally hit by a car. His mother runs out and cries, "My son Ahmed is gone!" To whom is she referring? The physical body is still there, but we know for a fact that the real "Ahmed" is gone. What she means is that Ahmed's life force, his spiritual essence, has now departed. The real "him" has moved on.

Although we can lose an arm or a leg—or even have a heart transplant—we still remain the same person. We are clearly not these physical organs. Sometimes these limbs, organs and body parts disappoint us and sometimes they give us pleasure. But they do not constitute our identity. There have been numerous cases of people reporting, after major traumas, literally floating above their bodies and watching the doctors work to resuscitate them. Clearly, these circumstances demonstrate a separation from their physical forms.

Not only do we exist separately from our bodies, but also we cannot rely upon our physical senses for accurate knowledge. Our senses are unreliable. For example, our eyes are lying to us every single moment. As we look into a cup, our eyes may tell us that it is empty. However, careful scrutiny with a microscope would reveal all kinds of germs and microbes. Our ears are so dull that we cannot even hear what is going on two rooms away and we are deaf to the high-pitched sounds that a dog may hear. When we put on clothing, very often our senses are so dull that they are not even aware of the feel of the fabric on our skin. Our sense of taste often leads us to eat too much and desire foods that are not healthy for the body.

Overall, our senses are extremely dull and mislead us constantly. Yet, in all of the modern sciences, we continue to claim to have made definitive observations, knowing full well that all of our tools are flawed. It is crucial for us as spiritual warriors to understand that we have a non-physical essence that is eternal, has a mission and is looking for ways to love and serve.

The Search for Ecstasy

One of the fundamental premises in almost all spiritual paths is that human beings seek a deep experience of ecstasy. Everyone wants pleasure; we all want a natural "high." If we have not experienced the joys of a higher taste, we tune in to a lower one, but we are never quite content with such a solution because the senses are insatiable.

Instead, we simply become more and more locked into the

cycle of desire. The more drugs we take, the more we need for the same stimulation. The more sex we engage in, the more we want; rather than quelling our desires, excessive sexual activity agitates the senses to the point where normal sex will not do. Under proper circumstances, however, even a sexual encounter can be highly spiritualized. If we want lasting pleasure, we should consciously check our lower impulses and seek the highest pleasures of all: Genuine loving relationships that are caring and God-centered.

Naturally, we are all searching for ecstasy. We have an innate desire to feel such ecstasy because, like the Lord, we are pleasure seekers. If we do not experience these higher pleasures through spiritual activities and spiritual absorption, we will inevitably turn to artificial means. This turning to artificial means requires that we break the laws of God that have been conveyed by the great prophets. In so doing, we incur various individual and collective karmic reactions. We also deprive ourselves of genuine, lasting fulfillment.

Sublime ecstasy is the birthright of all human beings who seek divinity. However, we must make an effort to discover this ecstasy by releasing the attachments and desires of our limited egos. "Seek and ye shall find" is a well-known phrase that refers to this search, but we must always remember that the goal of the search has nothing to do with temporary, material treasures. Jesus said that we should build our riches in the kingdom of heaven. Even Benjamin Franklin said, "Those who seek temporary shelter above their basic liberties deserve neither." If we want to actualize the fullest potential of our species—a species that was given dominion over everything on this plane—we must trust in and act on the words of the Lord and His representatives, or we do ourselves a great injustice.

True Liberation

Human beings have an innate longing for freedom—for liberation from the constraints and limitations that keep us bound to suffering. We also have a deep hunger for community and loving relationships. Yet the global increase in homicide, suicide and ecocide can be traced to the fact that we have lost the understanding of how to coexist with one another on this planet. In our unguided quest for freedom, we have forgotten what this freedom actually means. Freedom is not just a matter of dominating nature and forcefully extracting riches from her. Freedom is a matter of living in harmony with other living beings and with Mother Nature, because when she is pleased with us, her trees are laden with fruit and she bestows a wealth of plants, edibles, foliage and healing herbs.

Our true liberation will not come through domination of the earth. Nor will it come through social reform. It is not a matter of replacing one material system with another, of valuing one race over another race, of affiliating with one political party over another. What we must alter is the tendency in each of us to dominate, manipulate and exploit, and we must also check our attempts to hoard and to trick nature by grabbing more than our proper share.

Ultimately, we must aim at purifying our own hearts and consciousness so that we can in turn purify the atmosphere around us. Then—and only then—can we leave the realm of limitations and re-enter the eternal reality: The kingdom of Mother-Father God.

A specific spiritual science exists for us to transfer ourselves out of this prison and attain liberation. This science involves purification and reform of our character, the acquisition of relevant knowledge and, finally, realignment with divine will through service and action so that we may reestablish a loving relationship with the Supreme.

Materialists who lack this knowledge are at a serious disadvantage. Without an understanding of the laws of karma—of action and concomitant reaction—people make short-sighted choices based on immediate gratification that later serve to further entangle them in the material realm.

Basically, wherever we look in the material sphere, we find living entities trying to play God in different capacities. The constant theme of material existence is that of trying to dominate and lord over others in order to establish an imagined supremacy. Yet the ultimate happiness of human life is to offer oneself fully in loving service to the Lord, relinquishing all desires for domination and control.

The Deluding Qualities of Material Nature

In these hedonistic, self-gratifying times, most people do not want to hear that the material world is a place for tests and for lessons. The kaleidoscopic aspects of this world pique our curiosity, and most people simply want to sample and enjoy all the temptations nature has to offer. Yet so many of these so-called "pleasures" truly endanger us once we have tasted them.

Different spiritual traditions represent these material temptations in various ways. While we find reference in the Bible to "Satan" as a personification of evil, opposed to the Lord and determined to capture souls into his service, the Vedic scriptures refer to "Maya" as a personification of the material illusion. Rather than opposing the Lord, she is a servant whose thankless task is to offer the conditioned souls all kinds of sugar-coated poisons to test and ultimately reform us—teaching us the hard way until we develop the good judgment and discrimination not to stray from the path of true happiness.

Just as a soldier must learn to identify the uniforms and equipment of the enemy and become familiar with the enemy's tactics, the spiritual warrior must learn to discern the attacks of harmful and degrading influences in all circumstances. We should, of course, not become paranoid or allow our fears to rule us. On the other hand, if we are not attuned to the devastating power of our adversary, we may not resist intensely enough to be victorious.

Maya first tries to get everyone actively engaged in destructive, harmful activities. For those who cannot be captivated so easily, Maya tries to make individuals feel overwhelmed, isolated and hopeless—to the point of believing that it is impossible to make a change, or pointless to try. In this way, even those who are not grossly materialistic are still kept in check.

Everyone residing in a material body is a target. Before we become too angry with Maya, though, as honest spiritual warriors we must accept the fact that we have gotten ourselves into this predicament. The very fact that we are in material bodies means that we, at some point, ran away from God's love. We have rejected our natural state as loving servants of the Lord, choosing instead the confines of the material realm. In this realm, we can forget for a while that we are not equal to God, and we can pretend to own, create, dominate and destroy as we please. Although this choice is literally our God-given right, the unavoidable consequence is that we must be confined to the material world and compete for dominance with others of the same degraded, delusional mindset.

Instead of viewing Maya as an evil opponent bent on our destruction, we can then begin to see her more as a warden of this material prison, charged with keeping us contained until we decide we have had enough of this realm of shadows. She can then teach and challenge us until we prove beyond a doubt that our only desire is to return to our natural position in service to the Lord.

We have been provided with ample help along the way. The religious scriptures of the world have not been given to us for entertainment value. They are literally instruction manuals to help us make the most of our human existence and attain our "parole" back to the spiritual world. Their lessons are designed to teach us the rules of the material and spiritual worlds and provide us with the tools to begin making better decisions. Having received these tools, each of us individually must make a conscious choice to employ them to conquer our self-centered desires and pass Maya's tests as they come.

Three Modes of Material Nature

The *Bhagavad-gita* deals in minute detail with the manifestation of matter, and analyzes material activities based on three basic modes: *sattva, rajas* and *tamas,* which translate roughly to the modes of goodness, passion and ignorance.

According to the *Gita*, those situated in the mode of goodness develop a sense of happiness and well-being through selfless service and the pursuit of knowledge. As they continue to mature spiritually, they gradually prepare themselves for the platform of transcendence. The mode of passion is born of lustful desires. People in this mode spend lifetime after lifetime in an endless cycle of pursuing the fulfillment of these voracious desires, only to replace them with new ones. In the mode of ignorance, living entities are ruled by sloth and inertia, and act with no consideration of the consequences of their selfish actions. People who live in this way tend to spiral downward into deeper and deeper levels of despair, intoxication and delusion.

The *Gita* gives numerous examples of the effects of various activities performed in different modes. Generally speaking, actions performed out of duty and for the benefit of others are considered to be in the mode of goodness. Actions performed out of desire for distinction, profit or personal gratification are in the mode of passion, and actions performed whimsically with no regard to their effects are in the mode of ignorance.

We can use these descriptions to better evaluate our own situations. For example, if we find ourselves feeling frustrated and dissatisfied with our lives, as if we are always chasing after something we cannot reach, we can see this as a symptom of the mode of passion. If we look honestly at ourselves, we will most likely find that the majority of our daily activities revolve around our own glorification and sense gratification.

Similarly, if we find ourselves feeling hopeless and believe that life is unfair and constantly dealing us undeserved misfortunes, we may discover that we have been acting in the mode of ignorance. We may find ourselves concerned only with what feels good at the moment and without any plan or regard for the long-term consequences of our actions.

On the other hand, those who act in the mode of goodness fill their lives with selfless service to others, experiencing a profound sense of joy, fulfillment and progress through the sacrifices they make, despite obstacles and difficulties along the way.

Generally speaking, most of us are dominated by different modes at different times, depending on the quality of our consciousness. This works both ways, however, and the *Bhagavad-gita* suggests that, as we elevate our activities from the lower modes of ignorance and passion to the mode of goodness, our consciousness becomes purified and we qualify ourselves to begin the journey of transcending the material realm altogether.

Reincarnation: Fact or Fiction?

Many, if not most, of the spiritual traditions of the world accept reincarnation as a fact. Ancient African cultures, American Indian cultures, Hinduism, Buddhism, Taoism and mystic Christianity all recognize the validity of reincarnation. It is only the "modern" world that has been slow to acknowledge this idea.

There is overwhelming evidence of reincarnation in both modern and ancient times. In modern Western culture, for example, methods such as hypnotic regression evoke apparent memories of past lives. People under hypnosis may speak languages they have never heard before or recite detailed, verifiable memories of periods long before their current birth.

The Vedic tradition confirms the reality of reincarnation. For example, the *Bhagavad-gita* (2.13) explains the transmigration of the soul, saying, "As the embodied soul continuously passes in this body from childhood to youth to old age, the soul similarly passes into another body at Death. A sober person is not bewildered by such a change."

In Bhagavad-gita 8.16 it explains: "From the highest planet in the material world down to the lowest, all are places of misery wherein repeated birth and death take place." Meaning that, not only do we have to die once, but we must perish over and over again as long as we are in the material dimension, falling victim to such misfortunes as accident, disease, manslaughter or some other grievous ill.

The Quar'an (2.28) states: "How do you deny Allah and you were dead and He gave you life? Again He will cause you to die and again bring you to life, then you shall be brought back to Him."

Modern reductionist thinking, however, combined with the economic incentive to keep us bound to material desires, propounds that we are no more than collections of physical organs and chemical reactions. This outlook tends to support the "you only live once" attitude, with no incentive to act responsibly in this lifetime.

In contrast, mature individuals are ready to be responsible and accountable. Only immature people are not interested in accountability. Much of the fast-paced and impersonal culture currently being embraced influences people around the world to become less and less accountable and simply function impulsively based on satisfaction of the senses. This of course makes them very easy to manipulate, exploit and control.

Even in the West, the idea of reincarnation was originally part of the Christian outlook. For example, early Church Fathers such as Justin Martyr (100-165 AD), St. Clement of Alexandria (150-220 AD) and Origen (185-254 AD) taught aspects of reincarnation. The belief in reincarnation remained in certain currents of Christianity until the sixth century, when the emperor Justinian, seeking to unify his empire, outlawed the belief. Members of the priestly class also began to realize that the Church could gain power and exploit the masses more easily if the general public did not have access to higher spiritual knowledge and believed that they only lived once.

Our Karmic Patterns

Spiritual warriors must examine this idea of reincarnation as deeply as possible, because our present situation is inextricably linked to our previous lifetimes. Given that we are eternal and that our real identity exists on a continuum, our future lives will be shaped by the sum total of everything we are presently doing and thinking. Ultimately, it is our interactions with the cosmic laws of God that are especially relevant to the next life we are preparing. Our thoughts and actions now shape what we will become.

Our current life—combined with the residue from previous lives—will determine our future karma. Karma is the principle that every action produces a reaction, and somehow affects every living entity in God's creation. The effects we cause will eventually be reflected back to us. The way others view and behave toward us is directly affected by how we view and behave toward God and our fellow beings. Not only must we sometimes experience various miseries based on our accumulated karma, but we must also realize that the accompanying degree of pain, fear or suffering we experience is a measure of the extent of our karma.

With so many of us acting whimsically without regard for the karmic pollution we may be producing, the resulting environment can become extremely complex. We may begin to believe that events are happening by accident, without rhyme or reason. However, this is not the case. Many of the calamities happening on the planet today are directly related to humanity's collective karma for the levels of disturbance that have been generated in the past. As we develop a greater understanding of karma and how it acts upon us, we begin to realize that there are no accidents. When the twists and turns of fate become less mysterious and less frightening, we begin to accept responsibility for the future we are creating, and endure our present difficulties as necessary purification. This is a crucial step in our maturation process.

Some examples are more obvious than others. The super-rich members of the leisure class who boarded the Titanic were out to prove their mastery of one of the Creator's most unconquerable elements—the ocean. At the height of their arrogance, the ship sank, drowning many of the passengers after reducing many of them to a state of utter dread, desperation and helplessness.

Not all karma is negative. We also carry with us the positive reactions for those activities we have performed in the mode of goodness. We can even carry certain useful abilities and understandings with us from lifetime to lifetime. "Instinct" is a modern term for knowledge or ability that seems innate, with apparently no previously learned pattern. What we call instinct, however, may be in direct correlation with learning in previous lives.

The scriptures can help us avoid negative karmic reactions by prescribing lifestyles that help us steer clear of trouble. For example, many scriptures recommend a vegetarian lifestyle. By refusing to inflict cruelty on our fellow living entities, we can also avoid the harsh ramifications that such institutionalized cruelty brings to our society: violence, hunger, suffering and a wide array of health problems, among others.

Sense Control

As human beings, we are naturally servants. We are always

serving someone or something. Given this fact, we will either dovetail our efforts to the service of Mother-Father God and their devotees, or we will find ourselves serving our senses. Unfortunately, the frenzy to satisfy the unrelenting demands of the senses tends to leave us steeped in the modes of passion and ignorance.

Uncontrolled senses lead us to exploit others and our environment, whereas controlled senses help us to serve others. A proper spiritual atmosphere reinforces positive, healthy activities and relationships and helps us manage our senses. As a result, we may find it easier to remain focused on serving one another.

The more we live a life of degradation, the easier it is for us to be dominated by forces that seem beyond our control. As long as we succumb to the powers of the senses, we will remain entrapped in the prison house of sense gratification, manipulation and exploitation. But whenever we "just say no" to uncontrolled sense gratification, we qualify ourselves to become genuine spiritual warriors—principle-centered people with highly accelerated divinity. The choice is always ours, even when we feel victimized and helpless.

Each of us has a lower and higher self. We must exercise vigilance if we are to avoid those temptations that arouse the "impatient disobedience" of our lower nature. When we find ourselves overly absorbed in experiences of a relative or temporary nature, which provide no lasting sense of fulfillment, then we are choosing to serve our lower nature.

When we indulge in activities that cause us to minimize community, reject family and set one gender or one race against another, we are backsliding toward a negative, self-destructive mindset. When we accept the notion that life is only about giving pleasure to our material senses, we are embracing the culture of destruction for which we will sooner or later pay the price.

Cheaters want results without paying a price. Criminals and manipulators want to get as much as they can while giving nothing; what's more, they even want to grab what belongs to others. If we pursue life in this way, the quick and temporary solutions we may obtain will be cosmetic at best.

Humans have been equipped for higher reasoning and for displaying compassion, humanity and, ultimately, divinity. Only animal life is designed to center on survival and sensuality. Animals are allowed to indulge in gross materialism because they are not capable of anything else. Gross materialism at the human level pits individuals against individuals, tribes against tribes, gender against gender and reduces humans to a regressed, animalistic state of consciousness far beneath our capacity.

The Kingdom of God

The kingdom of God is not mythic. All ancient systems reveal that a spiritual realm exists beyond the material world. As for why we do not know about the spiritual kingdom, there are many possible responses. Most notably, we tend to use disbelief as justification for our absorption in immediate pleasures and our disinterest in God and His kingdom. Another cause of our disinterest, as mentioned earlier, is that we ourselves opted to leave God's kingdom. Thus, to varying degrees, we have little or no desire to return there because we are caught up in our own envy of God's power and our lack of surrender.

But paradise does exist. All ancient systems speak about it. However, these discussions are especially meant for the welfare of surrendered, or surrendering, souls who have accumulated a sufficient amount of spiritual merit to appreciate the glory of the Lord's kingdom and to recognize the futility of pursuing the pleasures of the material world.

Have all these religions lied to us? Have they just created a sham? Have they formed a coalition to dupe us? Of course not. They are giving us an essential teaching, and our spiritual progress is based on how attuned we are to that message.

A Personal Approach

Most philosophies concerning the "meaning of life" fall into four basic categories: materialism, voidism, impersonalism and personalism. Materialistic philosophies, such as behaviorism and empiricism, emphasize the primacy of physical reality and the nonexistence of anything called a "soul." To behaviorists, we are essentially a collection of conditioned responses, and for empiricists, only what is physically tangible and objectively measurable is considered a valid subject of knowledge. These philosophies tend to overlook the more subtle aspects of our existence.

In contrast to materialism, voidist philosophies attempt to explore our existence beyond the gross physical level. Voidists believe that interaction with the physical world simply brings pain and disappointment, and therefore they endeavor to go beyond the physical world and become absorbed in a cosmic "oneness." In this vast emptiness, all activity ceases and all individuals merge into a single unified consciousness. In this union—free from desire, activity and even identity—voidists believe that they will experience fulfillment.

The philosophy of impersonalism resolves the emptiness of voidism by accepting that a distinct creative force has given rise to the universe. Impersonalism emphasizes the idea that everything is connected with everything else so that, beyond immediate physical experiences, we can discover a universal oneness—the ultimate reality—flowing throughout creation and present within ourselves. By continuous study and meditation, impersonalists endeavor to reach a state of *samadhi* wherein they can merge with this "universal consciousness."

Personalists believe that all aspects of the spiritual and material worlds have been meticulously created by an omnipotent and loving Supreme Godhead, who takes a personal interest in every aspect of His creation. Those who embrace this approach dedicate themselves in loving service to God with the goal, ultimately, of gaining His eternal association.

As we keep this approach in the forefront of our minds, our otherwise ordinary pastimes of working, sleeping, caring for our families, and serving others begin to dovetail with our eternal mission of reconnecting with the Supreme. This is the key to what the *Bhagavad-gita* refers to as *bhakti yoga*, the spiritual science of overcoming our material desires and redeveloping our thirst for pure devotional service to the Lord.

In all actions, spiritual warriors remain focused on the most important questions: How do we get back in touch with Mother-Father God? How can we transform this "take" society into a wholesome, loving culture conducive to spiritual growth, spiritual exchanges and spiritual activity? How do we dedicate our earthly experience to what is most important: returning back home to the kingdom of God?

Questions & Answers

Question: The concepts of shame, guilt and atonement exist in all religions. As we enter the "new age," emphasis on these attitudes is starting to wane. Instead, people are endorsing total self-acceptance. Still, it seems that guilty feelings often naturally arise without any prompting. What is the value of shame and guilt, and are they actually useful in our efforts to progress along the path

Answer: This is a very relevant question. Shame and guilt can help us, but we must use them purposefully. First, people should not fake these feelings. In full honesty, they should look closely at their own lives and embrace genuine guilt if it is warranted. At the same time, they should not become paralyzed by such guilt, but instead employ it as a catalyst for action. Think of it as a boil or pimple on the body. A boil or a pimple indicates the presence of toxicity, but we should not just look at the blemish and say, "Okay, my body has toxins in it." Rather, our recognition of the toxicity should call us to action. We must remedy the situation by taking the appropriate herbs, going to saunas or changing our diet.

The same is true for spirituality. When we recognize that we have toxic thoughts, we can alter them by improving our lifestyle, our perspective and the quality of our speech, friendships and pastimes. For example, we can read more spiritual literature, avoid trashy movies and listen to less mundane music. We can begin a regular spiritual practice such as chanting, reading, praying or service work. In that way, we utilize our guilt and shame properly as stimuli to remedial action. But simply dwelling on guilt and shame in a melancholy way without producing positive action is counterproductive.

Question: We know that many great scientific discoveries have resulted more from inspiration than from scholarly research. What is the connection between inspiration and the mind?

Answer: The ability of the mind to dive more deeply into the reservoir of the higher self lies dormant within us. Most of us are unaware of this potential. Yet it is available to many, and apparently miraculous breakthroughs have come from mulling over a particular problem and later receiving an inspiration, especially in sleep. When we put the physical body to rest, other aspects of our consciousness become more accessible and allow us to connect with inner, subjective levels of reality.

We are all touched by subtler realms to a certain extent. For example, sometimes several people have the same dream, or a dream may turn out to be a premonition that actually comes true. In other dreams, we may experience apparent contact with other life forms or other dimensions. Even when we are awake, we can sometimes know what others are thinking or get an internal message that someone close to us is in distress. These subtle communications are always occurring at a certain level. It is just a matter of how much we notice them.

Question: Why do we sometimes hear that God has only one son?

Answer: Many people say that Jesus is God's only son. Indeed, he was a powerful son. He came to earth and accomplished a great deal in only 33 years. However, by claiming that God can have only one son, these people minimize God's ability to act according to His own independent will. Such believers are really concerned with religious sectarianism although they hide behind a facade of spirituality.

These individuals have failed to grasp the immensity of God. In this world, many are so envious of God that they try indirectly to discredit Him—even while claiming deep religiosity. A God with only one son is a limited God. We do not worship a God with one son—any more than we devote ourselves to a God of one city, one religion, one nation, one planet, one galaxy, or even of one universe.

Let Christ speak for himself. He said in John 14:12, "He that believeth on me, the works that I do shall he do also; and greater works than these shall he do; because I go unto my Father." He also said in John 6:38.19, "For I came down from heaven, not to do mine own will, but the will of Him that sent me." There have always been great personalities like the Prophet Muhammad, Christ, Buddha and others who deliver messages that are universal, if we look at the essence. It is their followers who have created sectarian divisions. The philosophy of mystical Christianity is not greatly different than that of Sufism. Mystic Islam is not profoundly different from the teachings of Buddhism or Hinduism. These various spiritual traditions are simply different vehicles to take us to a particular destination, and just as with an automobile or an airplane, once you reach the destination, the means of transport is no longer relevant.

Every religion has "exoteric" and "esoteric" practices and teachings. Exoteric practitioners are involved in rituals, scriptures and the outward appearances. Because these practitioners look at the superficial, material aspects of their traditions, where differences are easily perceptible, they tend to be the ones who fight with others of differing persuasions. Those who are involved in the esoteric aspects focus more on the essence. They direct their energies to consciousness-raising and self-realization, delving beyond appearances into a direct experience of the divine. If we study any bona-fide spiritual process deeply enough, we will uncover the ancient timeless wisdom that is universal to humankind.

We must demand that our churches stop telling us absurd lies, claiming that God appears in only one way and has only one son. If this were the case, why would Jesus say, "In my Father's house there are many mansions"? Let us stop making our own interpretations and allow the prophets to speak for themselves. Why have we created dozens of different versions of the Bible? Why, when we read the Qu'ran, do others give their own opinions, saying "It doesn't mean that; it couldn't have meant that—and even if it did, it doesn't apply now"? This behavior is nonsense, whether it applies to Vedic, Christian, Ba'hai, or mystery school teachings. In all times and circumstances, great teachers have come to show by their example what is necessary and what is possible in spiritual life.

Question: In light of all that you said earlier about karma and our reaping enjoyment or suffering based on that karma, I am wondering about divine intervention. In our relationship with God, is there ever a justification for making specific requests? Can we ask God in prayer for whatever we consider necessary and desirable, or should we just be content with the situation and allow Him to intervene as He wills?

Answer: We should always pray for something, but we should pray intelligently. This means that we should always pray for the highest. The highest is connected with the understanding that God is eternally our greatest well-wisher. The more we realize that God knows what we need and want, the more genuinely can we utter the prayer, "Thy will be done." Then we can pray like this: "Please use me as You see fit. I don't understand all the contamination in my consciousness that has resulted from improper choices in this life and previous lives. I am not fully aware of what awaits me as a result of what I have put into motion. All I can do is beg You to let me be Your humble servant."

When we find ourselves praying for a particular outcome, which can happen, we should pray with a sense of regret that we have to focus on something other than better opportunities for service. Praying to the Lord to become a better servant automatically includes having our internal obstacles removed. Such prayers are more, not less, inclusive than prayers focused on a specific result, and the responses may include whatever we need but do not even know to ask for.

In His great mercy, the Lord wants to help us even more than we want to be helped. If we do not take advantage of God's love and empowerment when they come through to us, we simply become an embarrassment. The spectacle we create can even influence others to become atheistic.

But in order to accept divine help, we have to appreciate that we are a little crazy—quite crazy, actually—and that we are extremely clever at finding ways to run from God's love. When we begin to realize this, we can choose to stop fleeing and allow ourselves to fall back in love with the Lord.

Question: As spiritual warriors, how do we avoid becoming distracted from our goals?

Answer: There is a Vedic story about a great warrior and teacher by the name of Dronacarya. Once while training some of his best archery students, he placed a fish-shaped target high in a tree and asked them to shoot an arrow through the small eyehole. As his first student, Yudisthira, arched his bow, Dronacarya stopped him and asked, "What do you see? Do you see the tree? The leaves? The fish?" Yudisthira replied that he saw all of these things. Dronacarya said that Yudhistira would not make the shot, and asked him to sit down. He called up each of his students and asked a similar question before they shot. Each of them responded that they could clearly see the tree, the leaves and the fish, yet each was denied the opportunity to shoot.

He called on Arjuna, who was his very special student, and asked him, "Do you see the tree?" Arjuna replied, "No." Do you see the leaves?" Arjuna again replied, "No." "Do you see the whole fish?" "No." "Do you see the head of the fish?" "No." Dronacarya then asked, "What do you see?" Without taking his gaze from the target, Arjuna replied, "I see only the eye." Dronacarya allowed Arjuna to shoot, and the arrow struck its target.

This is a good example of the concentration and focus necessary for a spiritual warrior. There will surely be distracting elements in our environment—there will always be setbacks and problems to distract and slow us down—but spiritual warriors do not let such things stagnate us.

Question: How can we as scientists develop a deeper appreciation for that which is really non-scientific?

Answer: You can begin by being honest and questioning what is really scientific. In other words, is something scientific because of statistics? Is something scientific if it is based on relative cultural patterns or perceptions? In certain cultures, a particular activity may be accepted, while in another part of the world that same action may be condemned. We all know that we are affected by heredity and environmental factors, which determine how we codify our surroundings.

In this culture, we call "scientific" whatever is the best

of what we know empirically at a particular time. We accept the current knowledge and use it because, of course, we have to be functional. On the other hand, those who believe that they have acquired all possible knowledge in any area are not scientists or scholars, especially today. Is it not true that the more we learn the more we realize how much there is to learn? Only someone who has little knowledge will say, "Okay, I've mastered that; now I know everything about it."

Science and spirituality can complement each other. The point of "spiritual technology" is to apply the scientific method of observation, experimentation and proof to the knowledge contained in the scriptures. As we apply these ancient principles in our lives and discover the wisdom behind them, we develop strong faith based on our own experiences.

These are not the days for sentimentality. These are not the days for closed-mindedness. These are not the days for allowing ourselves to be cheated. Do not cheat yourself by thinking only of the physical model, and do not dupe yourself by embracing excessively dogmatic religion that undermines the universality of God. Put the scriptures to the test. Try them, use them, and enjoy them—and, most of all, learn to be more loving toward others. Love will become an extremely powerful weapon as you become increasingly selfless. When we become more loving, we receive all kinds of empowerment as we attract more and more love to ourselves. Each of us must put these teachings to the test and judge by the results.

Chapter 7

12 qualities of a spiritual warrior

Spiritual Warriorship

On first hearing, some gentle souls are put off by the notion of spiritual warfare. The phrase seems contradictory. Can a true spiritualist be violent? Spiritual warfare is rarely violent in the literal sense, but spiritualists must consciously resist the aggressive attacks and covert influences that want to warp their identity. A true spiritualist must engage in battle, if only to avoid being consumed by the avalanche of ever-increasing impiety and materialism that is quickly engulfing the world. True spiritualists must engage in battle or be cheated of our spiritual inheritance.

Our real identity is that we are eternal beings, and it is important to think and act as eternal beings. We must remember that each person plays a part in the universal energy of the planet. We can choose to do something positive and make some serious changes in the world, or we can sit back waiting, becoming a product of the increasing aggression and violence of this material world.

To live a truly non-violent life, we must understand and imbibe the characteristics of a spiritual warrior. If you are going to embark on a spiritual mission, especially in this age of quarrel and hypocrisy, you must hone the arts of the spiritual warrior through sincere study and application.

Our goal is to give you the tools you need to prepare yourself for the twenty-first century. If you feel the tools are for you, then use them; make them yours. If you feel the tools are not for you, file them away, but please realize that humankind is in a precarious situation.

We must realize that we are in a warlike situation and learn how to protect ourselves. We must know how to improve our resistance and how to combat negative influences or we will become susceptible to attacks.

If you are ready to integrate all your departments of knowledge into one single force for righteousness, then you have heard the call to warriorship. If you are not yet ready to carry the torch of full-time spiritual warriorship, we wish you success in all your encounters and know the tools we are giving will still greatly benefit you.

Spiritual Warrior Checklist

Consider the following list to be your official spiritual warrior checklist, and do not leave home without it. This list supplies attributes you can aspire to, and a barometer to measure your progress. Use this checklist to see where you stand in your spiritual warriorship. Pay close attention to each item, and honestly evaluate your mastery of them.

Vigilant application of spiritual warfare may prove to be our very lifeline as our planet is gradually overtaken by negative forces. Each item is critical to the success of your endeavors; so by all means, do not take this checklist too lightly, because as with any battle, the unarmed opponent is bound to meet with destruction. After a preliminary listing, each of the items will be discussed in greater detail.

1. Sense control and mastery of the mind
2. Humility
3. Fearlessness
4. Truthfulness
5. Compassion and pridelessness
6. Material exhaustion and disinterest in material rewards
7. No idle time
8. Patience and selflessness
9. Firm faith
10. Perseverance
11. Curiosity and enthusiasm to learn and grow
12. Surrender to divine will

Sense Control and Mastery of the Mind

The first tool is controlling the senses and mastering the mind. A spiritual warrior needs a sense of regulation and focus in order to excel. We must be able to regulate our minds. If our minds are scattered, going from one philosophy to another, one religion to another, one job to another, one mate to another, then we need to look inside ourselves. We need to perform self-examinations to see where we are weak, because the areas where we are weak are where we will be tested the most. Regulation of the mind and senses cuts down the areas in which we can be attacked.

The mind is extremely powerful and can be our greatest friend or it can be our greatest enemy. The mind knows all our secrets, and all our weaknesses. There is truth to the phrase, "An idle mind is the devil's workshop." An active, progressive, devotional mind is a place where the Lord can focus and radiate transcendental messages and understanding. The Lord is in everyone's heart just waiting to come out, but the mind can block that relationship. Spiritual warriors allow their mind to open the door that will allow the Lord to work through them. The mind has a natural, original focus, just as the bee is naturally drawn to honey. The mind's most important and natural purpose is contemplation of Mother-Father God and service to Them. Unfortunately, the mind has lost its original purpose and has been diverted by the distractions of material life.

A materially conditioned mind is like a machine that has limited programming with which to respond to events and people in its environment. Like any machine confronted with situations outside its preprogrammed purpose, a conditioned mind will rebel and reject stimuli that are beyond its immediate conscious realm. The mind has many sabotaging qualities and will attempt to rationalize, argue and put up barriers to ensure that higher cosmic messages do not sneak past and reach the soul. Our conditioned minds hate change, and have a deep fear of being abandoned. That is why the mind does not want the soul to take over.

Spiritual warriors must first discover what their mind's habits are, and determine whether their mind is acting as a friend or enemy. If you discover your mind is acting as an enemy, as most people do, please do not feel discouraged, beloved. Rather, begin to work on gradually coaxing your mind into realizing that its conditioned tendencies are bringing no real satisfaction and explain to your mind that true peace will come from cooperating with God and our soul's agenda.

In addition to this "self dialog," help your mind adjust to not being in charge. So many people in this age are ruled by their senses. So many people are spending their lives running after things that are not real—that will disappear or fall apart. It is easy to get caught up in mundane patterns. Most people's lives revolve only around eating, sleeping, mating and defending. That is an animal's consciousness! We are divine spirit souls! We need to cultivate our higher faculties and experience the sublime ecstasy that is every person's right. Controlling our senses and regulating our minds will lay the foundation for being alert spiritual warriors, otherwise we are committing violence against ourselves and cannot be of help to others.

This is certainly not easy. By deciding to not engage in the animal's consciousness you are making a strong statement that you are not going to play into the degradation of this material world. You are making a statement that you are not going to become controlled by your lower senses and give in to whatever appeals to them. This is a strong, brave stand to take beloved, and as you move more toward a higher consciousness you will receive help.

The first step in regulating our senses and our minds is to look at the quality of our associations. Take a close look at the people you spend your time with. Do they make it easy for you to give in to your senses, perhaps even encourage you to follow your lower senses? The saying, "You can tell the character of a man by the company he keeps" is quite true. Spiritual warriors must either elevate the conscious of the people we associate with, or look for new contacts with people who value God consciousness as much as we do. If a person is an alcoholic, they avoid spending time with people who drink and avoid going to places where alcohol is. People say, "Of course that makes sense—that is wise." The principle is the same for spiritual things. If you do not want to live a life where you are ruled by what your senses require, then it is wise to not spend your time with people who are simply serving their senses. This does not mean you have to become an elitist and cut all ties with family and friends. We are simply suggesting that you take a close look at your associations. If they are keeping you locked into a lower consciousness, you need to seriously evaluate the relationship. Sometimes just fully realizing the damage these relationships are doing can make it possible for you to maintain some level of contact with the person, yet protect yourself from being influenced by their lower consciousness. As you continue to elevate your consciousness those people will have to make their own choice to elevate their consciousness or get away from you. It will happen naturally.

The second step in regulating our senses and our minds is to provide alternatives. For example, when someone stops smoking it is usually best to find a healthy alternative. Some people will chew gum when they want a cigarette, some people will go for a jog; whatever works best for that individual until they reach the point where just the thought of a cigarette disgusts them. This is how a spiritual warrior needs to approach regulating their senses. Do not simply try to cut out all the things that you see are harming you physically, mentally or spiritually. We need to find alternatives to these things. For example, if you are hanging out with a group of friends and you realize they are simply intoxicating themselves and turning off to higher things, this does not mean you have to cut them out of your life and turn into a loner. Seek out new friends, go to a spiritual community and immerse yourself in higher association. Find people with interests along the same line as yours, with goals similar to yours.

The final step is to be accountable to your true self. Do not look away when your own actions are destructive to your spiritual self. Be aware of what you think, what you say, what you do, how you interact with people, how you act alone. Constantly evaluate where you are on your spiritual path and where you want to go. The quality of your thoughts and lifestyle will dictate how effective the attack of an intruder will be. If our vibrations are of a higher caliber and we can think lovingly of even our enemies, then we become a fortress and no one will find an avenue to intrude. Being regulated will also provide security against the enemy within ourselves, which we already identified as our materially conditioned mind. Regulation allows us to persevere in good or bad times, and allows us to almost spontaneously do what is necessary. Please try to organize your life so that it is simpler and regulated and supported by higher consciousness. This will fortify you to survive spiritual emergencies.

Humility

The second tool is humility. In this age people view humility as a sign of weakness, but the reality is that humility is a powerful weapon. Society considers humility as the position of the conquered towards the conqueror instead of seeing it as a position of power. We must rediscover the pure strength of humility.

The Bible says the pure in heart shall see God, and the meek shall inherit the earth. This is the opposite of society's opinion; society views a meek person as someone who gets abused, exploited and denied because they do not push their case. We must realize the Bible emphasizes that the meek shall be victorious. It does not say the foolish or the naïve, but the meek. In meekness or humility there is strength, focus and some idea of a mission or purpose. We pursue that mission or purpose with determination—without ego, without distraction, without any obfuscation.

Too many things in the environment will distract a person when there is excessive ego. Something in the environment will cause a state of imbalance and the person will feel they have to act to rectify the situation. So much of a person's energy is drained in this way. A lack of humility inevitably causes undue or excessive responses to situations around you. These are easy things to talk about, but it can be difficult to change because in this age we are conditioned to respond quickly to whatever someone says or does. Take a moment to reflect back on your past week. How many times did you over-react to a situation, or put yourself in a conflict that brought you down to the other person's level, or allowed someone to involve you in a situation that you did not want to be a part of? We often get wrapped up in a situation only to realize later that we wasted so much valuable time.

The spiritual warrior never overreacts to fame, success or position, for while dealing with the many he does not overlook the one. He or she is always concerned about each person's highest welfare. Humility means knowing there is so much we do not know, so much we still need to learn. Humility means knowing there is a higher part of ourselves, and being eager to awaken that part. Humility means knowing that we are servants of the Supreme, children of God. Unless we become like the child who is lost and confused and calling out to their father, knowing everything will be fine when daddy appears, we cannot enter into the Kingdom of God. Children are dependent on the fact that their parents are in control of their well-being; this is humility. Humility means recognizing who is doing the controlling and being dependent on that actual controller. As individuals we must move aside, let the Lord drive and become as dependent as that child crying for mommy and daddy. Deliberate and voluntary surrender to the Lord requires great trust, and the next tool helps bring about this surrender.

Fearlessness

The third tool is fearlessness. A spiritual warrior is naturally fearless. What need is there to shuffle our feet when we are backed up by a Supreme power? How can we be intimidated when our actual origin is divine? When we realize these things, there are no reasons to hold onto various crutches because there is no cause for insecurity.

A spiritual warrior is able to act with true fearlessness and confidence by continuously validating their conclusions through a threefold check and balance system of spiritual mentors, saints and holy scriptures. With this system there is no ambiguity or confusion. There is confidence that the spiritual program we have chosen is valid, because we can verify the words of our teachers and prophets with the ancient scriptures, and our present day teachers can help to protect and accurately convey the original message. When something is not fully in accord with this system, the spiritual warrior will then look to ascertain the nature of the distortion or deviation, knowing this to be a sign of some adverse infiltration. We expect precision in material affairs, so there is no reason to not expect the same level of precision in spirituality. When someone has pneumonia or hepatitis, for instance, there are certain distinct symptoms that will enable the doctor to make a diagnosis. A good doctor can evaluate your symptoms and let you know exactly what you are suffering from, what your status is and what the cure will be. In this material world we often reserve strict scrutiny for only material subjects, and base our spiritual conclusions on things like sentiment.

Choosing our spiritual path based on how it pleases our senses or how much we like the way the choir sings, may lead us to a big letdown if we do not receive the necessary knowledge to get us back to the spiritual world. We will know when we are properly engaged and committed to a strong spiritual life because we will begin to feel a certain detachment from the mundane world. We will become channels for the Lord and will begin to acquire causeless knowledge. We will have nothing to fear, because the Lord will actually begin to express Himself through us. We will then be a puppet for the Lord and will reap all the rewards, thrills and benefits of being an instrument of the Supreme Lord's will.

Truthfulness

The fourth tool is truthfulness. We should be so fixed and steady in our realization of the Supreme, and in our love and our compassion for others, that we can speak the truth even to an enemy. Spirituality is a realm of its own, thus, the spiritualist functions under different laws than the materialist. For instance, the law of spiritual mathematics. This law dictates that the more we give away, the more we will receive. Rather than depleting our supply of spiritual merits, if we give our spiritual thoughts and deeds away, we actually increase our supply. This is especially true in aligning ourselves with truth. The more we speak, behave and live truthfully, the more truth will enter into our existence.

However, we should not become self-righteous or demeaning in our delivery. We should also try to give the truth in a way that will elevate whomever hears it. That is real warfare, because as we come down to someone else's lower level, we allow ourselves to be defeated. When we engage in proper spiritual combat, we are not only trying to avoid becoming a casualty, but we also want to do something that will help elevate others. In that way, more souls have a chance to become free and move on.

Today, the world community is severely depleted of wisdom. One reason for this is that people do not compete with a sense of honor or a sense of respect for themselves and their opponents; they constantly cheat in combat—whether this is in the mental or physical arena. Few people fight fairly, and even if someone does defeat another fairly, the defeated party wants to bribe the judge, challenge the decision, or discredit the opponent.

This behavior actually reduces the collective storehouse of knowledge and respect. Rather than exchanging techniques and wisdom with one another, we have become petty and unscrupulous, bringing about an overall stagnation in world progress. This is very unfortunate. The best antidote for this problem is truthfulness coupled with humility. We should truly admit defeat if defeated, then earnestly work to better ourselves. We should give credit where it is due and sincerely try to help others in all circumstances. This will restore truth to the planet and create an environment of mutual trust and progress. The next tool is important in developing that mood of truly helping others.

Compassion and Pridelessness

The fifth tool is compassion and pridelessness. Constantly looking for a pat on the back and for people to like us will overshadow our concern for what is right and proper, causing us to lose our higher principles. It is better to be right than it is to be honored.

When we have real love, we will not only inconvenience ourselves for another, but it becomes a joy to do this for someone we truly love. It should give us pleasure to put ourselves out to do something nice for someone we care about. The spiritual warrior takes this attitude of selfless love and broadens the field of affection to include all individuals. The spiritual warrior takes loving compassion to a whole other level and is literally prepared to suffer for others.

One story from the Vedic scriptures beautifully illustrates this. There was a young holy person named Ramanujacharya, the disciple of a great mystic teacher who was instructing him in sacred mantras. One day the teacher gave Ramanujacharya a special mantra which he claimed was extremely powerful, because he was pleased with Ramanujacharya's progress. The teacher then stressed that this mantra should remain a secret at all costs, and should not be given to anyone. When Ramanujacharya asked him why, he explained that the sacred sound vibration had the power to immediately deliver anyone who spoke it back to the spiritual realm, but that there were consequences for its misuse.

Ramanujacharya immediately thanked his spiritual teacher, pondered the situation for a moment, and then ran to the top of the tallest building and started shouting out the mantra at the top of his lungs. The teacher heard his student shouting and came out and harshly scolded Ramanujachayra. "You fool!" he cried. "I gave you this sacred mantra for discrete distribution, and you have shouted it from the top of the tallest building to all kinds of unqualified people!"

The teacher expected Ramanujacharya to deny the accusation or at least apologize, but instead Ramanujacharya replied: "You said that anyone who uses this mantra can gain God-consciousness. I saw all these townspeople suffering for lack of knowledge, so I decided to give them the key to liberation. If there is some penalty for this act of mercy, then let me go to hell immediately. I am prepared to suffer on their behalf, to let all of them go free."

That is spiritual warriorship! Of course, we may not be as qualified as people in the age of Ramanujacharya. However, when one is determined to benefit others, and when they are prepared to endure all kinds of austerities to keep the mind, body and consciousness fixed for warfare, despite whatever temptations, anxieties and emotions may arise, one has qualified himself for advanced spiritual warriorship. A spiritual warrior becomes fixed and focused on the idea that whatever it takes to be successful in raising people's consciousness is not too much to ask. It can never be too much to see that there is ultimate liberation and unmotivated spiritual service to the Lord.

This was the position of Jesus, and of many saints and teachers, who were literally prepared to absorb the collective universal karma of the citizens so those souls could have less weight holding them back from launching ahead in their spiritual quest. Such a warrior is a general. In these situations the Lord is so satisfied by their actions, He not only helps the souls they are trying to connect with, but He also gives those generals more empowerment to represent the higher scheme of reality.

Love is the greatest weapon—its greatest enemies are lust and greed. When there is proper love and compassion, these things will not distract us. If we are true loving beings, then our love will extinguish all things unnatural and hostile because we will vibrate with such intense energy. If we are carriers of such empowered love then everyone must either join us at that level or get away from us. We then become role models for others to see what spiritual life can achieve.

Material Exhaustion and Disinterest in Material Rewards

The sixth tool is material exhaustion and disinterest in

material rewards. We cannot become God conscious if we think material life is the all in all. As long as we think life is just a process of manipulating various people and material elements, we will continue to be slaves to matter. We will continue to make different plans and adjustments, which may give us temporary relief, but will certainly lead to more frustration at a later time. We must realize that there is much more waiting for us beyond this plane.

For this reason, the Lord sometimes arranges setbacks for a sincere spiritualist. It can be a blessing for us to become *materially* bankrupt. There is a difference between material bankruptcy and financial bankruptcy. A person can have wealth and prestige, but their mind and consciousness may feel empty. That empty feeling is sometimes the destitution and desperation we need to move beyond temporary things into spheres of the sublime.

We need to literally reach complete disgust with day-to-day life because if we are fixed in the mundane it is a sign that we are prisoners and will continue to be prisoners. If we are no longer feeling satisfaction with the mundane then we will be in the proper position to become free from the prison of this material world. Moreover, if we continue on this path, the universe will be obliged to accommodate our growth in consciousness and provide us with a road that leads to more service and fulfillment, and eventually an avenue for escape.

Our present thoughts and actions are producing our futures. If we maintain desires and activities in full agreement with the atmosphere of the material culture, we will find ourselves repeatedly returning to the material world in slightly different bodies and circumstances. A person who maintains a criminal mentality and resorts back to criminal behavior will be brought back for imprisonment again and again. On the other hand, a prisoner who has genuinely changed his mentality and activities becomes eligible for parole and eventually full freedom. If there is too much complacency with the prison lifestyle, we will not have the proper incentive to work on our escape to true freedom.

No Idle Time

The seventh tool is realizing that there is no idle time. A spiritual warrior does as much as possible in the time given, because they fully understand that many wars in the past have been lost due to procrastination and a lack of sensitivity to the fact that every moment must be used to its full potential. The alert soldier takes every moment of life seriously. We must constantly employ strategies that will deliver the greatest blow to the enemy in the shortest time available. This will bring about a greater chance to destroy the opposition and bring truly positive changes to this world.

To truly realize how important time is, we must first understand that it is not healthy to think of time as your own. It is God's time! What does that mean? If something belongs to someone whom you really love and care for, or whom you respect, you are more conscious about how you use it than if it belonged to you. Our time belongs to God. He provided it to us and we are therefore held accountable to the Supreme Lord for how we spend that time.

Part of being accountable to God for how we manage our time includes also being accountable to humanity. Spiritual warriors are interested in the upliftment of all people, so we also must remember that our time belongs to the people in our environment as well. Sometimes in my correspondence and consultations with different leaders and diplomats, I often warn them that a leader who abuses an hour must multiply that by all his constituents, because it is actually their time. He is the representative for all those people. Therefore, if he has five million people in his country, he has wasted five million hours. If you are taking care of your family, of your office, group or community, any time wasted, whether one hour or five hours, means that you have wasted an amount of time equivalent to your level of responsibility.

A strong spiritual warrior realizes the importance of using time wisely. We must remember that every encounter, every moment, is an opportunity to be uplifted or to uplift someone else. Every moment is a chance to be an example of divinity. Every moment is a chance to learn a new lesson or further develop an old lesson. Every moment has a purpose, and a spiritual warrior will make each moment work for the Supreme Lord, who has so mercifully given us these moments to move closer and closer to Him.

Patience and Selflessness

The eighth tool is to be patient and selfless. Actually, we need a combination of patience and impatience. Patience can be harmful to spiritual life, yet at the same time it is important to spiritual life. This may seem like a contradiction at first glance. We cannot over indulge in patience, because we must realize we are in an emergency time on an emergency mission.

We are at war! We must realize that whatever it will take to be God-conscious, we want it, we must have it now! We cannot wait another lifetime! When we have an impatient desire to be God-conscious we will remember there is no time to be inattentive or apathetic.

At the same time, patience is important because even though we need that fervor and desire to become God-conscious now, we must realize that we are not worthy in our present state. We must be prepared to surrender to whatever the Lord's plan and timetable for us is. We must reach the level where we can sincerely say, "God's will be done." We must reach the level where we can say, "This mind, this intelligence, these senses and this will is for You, Lord." When we reach that level and truly mean it, then we can become empowered.

When we have truly made the Lord's will our priority, instead of our selfish priorities, we will be under a higher shelter. All holy scriptures state that we are not to put anything before the Lord, and that we are to love Mother-Father God with all our heart and soul. When we take this commandment to heart, we will become incredibly mystically connected. We must endeavor to reach that level, but it will not be easy. Spiritual life is full of challenges, tests and wars. A strong spiritual warrior realizes that there must be a combination of patience and impatience coupled with a mood of selflessness.

Firm Faith

The ninth tool is having firm faith. Faith is necessary in everything. It is not a matter of being Presbyterian, Episcopalian, Muslim or Buddhist, it is a matter of how much we are following the laws of God and how much faith we have in God's potency.

There is a story about a brahman (a Vedic priest), a cobbler, and a mystic sage. The mystic sage had the ability to come and go between the higher kingdoms and actually visit with the Lord. One day the sage was making a trip to visit the Lord, so the brahman and the cobbler both requested that the sage ask the Lord how long it would take for them to join Him.

When the sage met with the Lord he asked how long it would be before the brahman and the cobbler could join Him. The Lord said, "The brahman who is doing all the rituals, austerities and reading all the scriptures, will live many lifetimes before he will join me, but the simple cobbler will come to me in his next life." The sage was surprised by the Lord's answer and asked for further explanation. The Lord said, "When they ask you what I was doing, tell them I was threading an elephant through the eye of a needle. You will understand my answer when you hear their replies."

When the sage returned, he met with the brahman and told him the Lord said he will live many lifetimes before joining the Lord. The brahman was shocked and said, "That's nonsense! I have done everything ethical and moral that I need to do, and everyone knows it!" The brahman began to wonder if the sage really did visit the Lord, so he asked the sage what the Lord was doing. The sage told him the Lord was threading an elephant through the eye of a needle. The brahman laughed and said the sage had not really seen the Lord.

Then the sage met with the cobbler and told him the Lord said he would go to Him in his next life. The cobbler gratefully accepted this answer and asked, "What was my Lord doing?" The sage gave him the same answer as he gave to the brahman and the cobbler accepted this answer as well. The sage was puzzled so he asked the cobbler if he truly believed that the Lord was threading an elephant through the eye of a needle. The cobbler answered, "If my Lord can take a tiny seed and make fruits, vegetables and huge trees grow from it, then what difficulty is there for Him to do other unusual things?"

The cobbler's faith was not based on rituals, externals, or what he thought he was or what he thought the Lord owed him. The cobbler's faith was based on how he saw the Lord's hand in everything from the simplest things to the most complicated. The sage realized the cobber had deep faith and a truly spiritual consciousness. We need to purify our consciousness so we can develop that deep faith.

Perseverance

The tenth tool is perseverance. A true warrior never wants the war to end. A true warrior is relentless and always ready to continue. We must be prepared to continually evaluate ourselves, regroup and adopt strategies to help us move beyond what may seem to be defeat.

The true test of warriors is how they act when wounded. The real spiritual warrior bounces back immediately in the face of defeat. Rather than caving in, the warrior learns from the encounter, imbibes it, owns it, and becomes stronger from the experience. There will always be temporary setbacks in spiritual life, but the real test is how we continue to move ahead. Even though spiritual warfare is seldom an easy path, the joy and love that we receive serve as the spiritual warrior's "rations." Further, our joy and love creates positive energy that brings more joy and love, and the cycle will continue and intensify as we persevere.

There is joy in spiritual combat because it creates a tremendous vibration of purification. We have to remember that our spiritual activities are not confined within our consciousness, our family or our immediate environment. Spiritual energy has an extremely powerful way of permeating and affecting the environment. People are uplifted and rejuvenated by the positive energy of a spiritual warrior's association. We must endeavor to keep moving forward and not be detained, and constantly renew our commitment to serving the Lord on the battlefield of consciousness-raising.

Curiosity and Enthusiasm to Learn and Grow

The eleventh tool is being curious and having enthusiasm about learning and growth. We must start each day curious about what tests we will encounter, what lessons we will learn, what lives we will connect with. We must take each day as a fresh new experience and another chance to serve the Lord better.

We cannot think that we will automatically be successful today simply because we were successful last week. Thinking this way will cause us to drop our guard and go into battle without our weapons. Our previous victories will not carry us through our present obstacles. God does not forget our service, but our enemies do not forget us either. If we leave ourselves open for attack, we will surely be ambushed. The easiest way to become vulnerable is to gloat over our former successes.

We must remember that sin is constantly increasing in

intensity. Breaking out of the material prison requires constant dedication in devotional service. If we are still using yesterday's weapons, yesterday's realizations, yesterday's techniques, yesterday's considerations, we will become today's casualties. We must take each day as another chance to serve the Lord better and accelerate our growth. Make a game of your challenges and compete against yourself to surpass yesterday's performance.

Surrender to Divine Will

The twelfth tool is to surrender to divine will. All of the previous tools help to prepare the spiritual warrior for this very important step. For a spiritual warrior, surrender is actually a victory, as long as we are surrendering to God. We see amazing results when we truly put God's will and mission before our own. We simply have to pay close attention to what God is telling and showing us. The Lord is active in our heart—we are simply blinded by the material coverings of this world and often do not see the help He constantly offers us through His arrangements. Spiritual warriors realize the Lord will guide them, and they remain on the lookout for help and the lessons to be learned.

As we sincerely try to live a spiritual life and better ourselves, God will reciprocate tenfold. Often when we are trying to resolve a particular problem or we are consumed with our difficulties, the Lord will arrange for us to meet someone who can help, or will give us a hint of where the answer is. It is not a coincidence that we find the answer to the problem because we looked at some old notes, listened to a lecture or read a particular book; that is the Lord assisting us. The help is always there, but sometimes we put up walls that do not allow this guidance into our heart.

Other times we are wide open, begging for help. When we are distraught and seeking, we become eager to receive the

Lord's help. That is why many times the transcendental system will arrange for us to feel desperate and frustrated. Sometimes the Lord arranges to make us sick, give us this problem or that, or take something away—so we can become intensified in consciousness and open to receive the Lord's help. When we are frustrated, really frustrated, we think, "HELP, Lord!" Then our barriers go down and we see how the Lord has been offering us assistance all along.

Living a spiritual life means living a natural life. Our natural state is to be surrendered to God's will, but we cannot surrender to God's will without developing the tools of the spiritual warrior. Working with these tools automatically puts us in a different consciousness. Simply reading about the tools puts us in a higher consciousness. We need to evaluate our relationship with God and constantly take inventory to see whether we are catering to our material self, or if we are acting in accordance with our understanding of God's will for us. This is not easy to do, but spiritual warriors try their best and always look for ways to do better each day, each situation, each moment.

Questions & Answers

Question: How does one develop the consciousness of being totally dependent on the Lord? Sometimes people think they have that consciousness but then something happens and they realize they are really not in that consciousness. How do you move beyond the false presumption that you are totally dependent on the Lord, and actually become totally dependent?

Answer: The Lord will give you many tests to qualify that dependency. We do not have to artificially feel humble, or force ourselves to be humble, we simply have to look honestly at what little control we really have. If, thinking we have control, we decide not to eat any food for a month, we will see how weak the body becomes. If we decide not to drink water we will surely die. We are dependent on such little things. We have to rest the body, we have to take the body to the toilet, so many things.

No matter how much money or power we have, sickness and death are still there. If we are honest, it is not difficult to feel humble or dependent. We just have to look at how we are controlled by higher forces, and what little power we have over such things. We sometimes talk about hurricanes, floods and earth changes. People spend thousands and sometimes millions of dollars on their businesses and estates, yet with one disaster everything is gone. People will be in good health, follow a good diet and exercise, but then one day have a heart attack. It happens every day. Every day, someone who is rich goes bankrupt. Every day, someone discovers that they have a chronic disease: AIDS, hepatitis, cancer, heart failure—so many maladies—every single day. Every minute somebody is dying.

We are not in control, but obviously someone is, because there is order to the universe. Trying to become more God-conscious puts us in harmony with that order. When somebody has all the power and all the control, we want to be their friend and be close to them. That is wise. To be an enemy of that person, or work against that person, is foolish. It is just a matter of realizing how little control we have and then seeing the need to be protected and cared for. We must realize the necessity of being under the care of the Lord.

Question: I understand the need for controlling the mind, but sometimes my mind loses the battle against negativity. I do not like to admit it, but sometimes my best is not good enough. Is all of spiritual life like an arm-wrestling match? Is grace one of the ingredients in getting back to God's kingdom?

Answer: By all means! In every bona fide faith, the grace of God is integral, not only to our deliverance, but to our very existence. We should not forget that our stomachs digest food by the grace of God, our eyes see by the grace of God, our vocal chords work by the grace of God. Of course, grace is key, particularly in our re-entry to the spiritual kingdom. But God's grace comes in numerous ways, and very often it comes to us as a formula. God gives us the recipe for success, and then waits to see how intensely we work to apply it and feel gratitude for it.

The Divine Couple is the witness of all activities. They specifically watch how we treat others and ourselves. It is said that the female aspect of God is so humble and compassionate that She frequently recommends souls to the male aspect, who is more of a natural disciplinarian, asking Him to give His favor.

Mother-Father God are amazingly merciful, but They do not want us to be miserly with ourselves and only look to our temporary interests with no thought to our eternal situation. Nor do they want us to hurt others with our arrogance, sarcasm or abuse.

We have to come up to a certain level where the grace of God can shower upon us. The Supreme Personality of Godhead's mercy is actually greater than His law. The laws are there and we should obey them, but God's mercy is even greater. That mercy is usually manifested through bona fide agents of the Lord. The prophets are carriers, just like a postman delivers a package. If a postman brings you a million dollar check, you may hug him out of spontaneous gratitude, and to a large extent this is valid. After all, that postman had to cover a lot of ground. He also had to qualify himself and pass certain exams to become entrusted with your personal mail. This is even more true for the carrier of God's message.

Everyone is actually a carrier, but some of us are not yet aware of the treasures we have access to. The prophets are generally those who have woken up a little earlier. When we are asleep, it is like being tied up. It is not easy to untangle ourselves when we are bound with ropes. It is the duty of the Lord's messengers to wake others up on the Lord's behalf. We should never feel that we have the ability to escape this prison on our own, because we will tend to rely too much on our own limited knowledge and intelligence. Every major world scripture emphasizes that God helps those who help themselves. We should therefore try to get the grace of God by qualifying ourselves according to the formulas He has provided.

This means treating others cordially. It also entails being non-violent in the truest sense of the word, and this means sharing whatever higher knowledge we have with others who are ready for it. Self-restraint is also a factor because every major scripture urges us to be humble, serene and equipoised. We do not need to be docile or give up our individuality; we should develop enough strength to tolerate things. The person who masters tolerance can actually convert negative energy and elevate it, because it takes real strength to avoid becoming aggressive when met with aggression. It takes strength to refrain from being obnoxious or getting angry and following suit when someone attacks you. It takes even more strength to maintain loving consciousness when you are under attack. That kind of strength invokes great mercy and blessings from the Supreme Lord.

Question: In my work environment I am frequently caught-up in conversations that do not revolve around spirituality. In fact, it would be frowned upon. I try to model, at some level, humility and patience. I try to emanate good feelings, but as you were talking I was thinking about a conversation I was caught up in at the end of last week. Someone was carrying on about some completely mundane activity and I could not hang up, walk out or disappear. In that type of situation, is the mindfulness just in my own self to be clear about God consciousness or is there something more that I can do to protect myself and to convey to the other person there is another way of being?

Answer: Mindfulness does not mean to be rude, instead it means to not commit violence or have violence committed against you. When people are throwing harsh words at you or around you, this is violence. When you accept that, you are supporting that violence. If somebody we love and care about—and we want to care about everyone—engages in violent, destructive activities, we should try to do something to help. If they speak harshly about someone, we can just turn the conversation around by asking, "Yes, and how do you think we can help? What can we do to make a difference?" You have not been rude or condescending, you have taken the conversation to another level, and changed the atmosphere. Body language has an effect also. When people are speaking some kind of nonsense and they see that you are hanging on their every word, you are going to get more and more. You are feeding them. On the other hand, when they realize that you are really not into it, but simply smiling and tolerating their nonsense, you are letting them know, "I have to go."

It is very important that we be careful about how we use our time and how we interact with others. It is our duty to be our brother and sister's keeper. It is our duty to love our neighbors as we love ourselves. It is our duty to do things that will constantly make a difference and that will help the well-being of that person. It is unfortunate when someone does not try to help when there is a chance to elevate the people they have contact with. We must remember that helping people does not involve lowering ourselves to whatever level they are on. That is violence to ourselves and also to them, and helps no one. Spiritual warriors are always engaged in strategies of trying to genuinely help as many people as possible while keeping ourselves fit and equipped.

Chapter 8

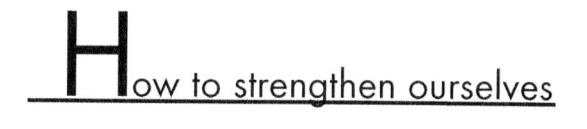

How to strengthen ourselves

Spiritual Life is Challenging

The path of a spiritual warrior is not an easy one. As we strive for the spiritual maturity to become effective spiritual warriors, we inevitably encounter numerous obstacles. Anyone expecting an undemanding, trouble-free ride should think twice before making a commitment to spiritual life. Once we have committed ourselves, all sorts of difficult challenges arise for us to overcome.

These challenges serve as qualifying tests, to see if we are serious about entering the spiritual kingdom. The process is similar to school, where our teachers regularly gave us tests designed not to defeat us, but to determine how well we had absorbed the knowledge and could apply it. Ultimately, we learned from our test results what material we understood and what material we still needed to study.

Maya, or the illusion of this material world, acts as a teacher for God. *Maya* arranges difficulties, temptations and obstacles to test the strength of our longing for the spiritual kingdom. Our reactions to these challenges indicate the extent to which we genuinely want what is available.

Many people do not understand why the Lord allows obstacles to appear along our spiritual path. Why does God test us? We must remember that in this material world we are in an unnatural position similar to that of prisoners. The burden is on the prisoners to prove by their actions that they are ready for parole and can be safely re-integrated into normal society. Humankind is in a similar incarcerated state. To obtain our release, we must prove that we are ready to reclaim our spiritual heritage and align ourselves with natural living.

At this point, we may respond, "OK. Now I understand why God tests me. But why are my tests so much harder than those of my neighbors?" The answer is simple. Children in elementary school do not receive the same tests as students working on a doctorate. Obviously, those studying for a PhD can expect more arduous tests because they are expected to be more qualified.

The opportunity for elevation is always available to us. If we are not serious about spiritual life, tests and obstacles will curtail our advancement. On the other hand, each time we pass a test, our qualifications increase and we are one step closer to becoming our natural, spiritual selves. That is why the tests are more difficult and more frequent at this stage: they are arranged to match the higher level we claim to have reached.

A true spiritual warrior sees each test as a blessing, because it is a chance to mature spiritually and move closer to God. When we recognize each test or challenge as a positive event, we approach it with zeal and enthusiasm, knowing we are engaged in consciousness-raising. Each test is a chance to prove that we are focused and sincere about becoming spiritual beings.

Even Great Teachers Were Tested

Many temptations appeared before Jesus while He was praying and fasting in the desert. Satan taunted him, saying, "If you're the Son of God, turn these stones into bread!" Then Satan challenged his faith, urging: "You have been fasting, so you must be starving. Go ahead then; pray to your God for bread." This prompted the famous reply of Jesus, "Man shall not live by bread alone, but by every word that proceedeth out of the mouth of God." Then Satan presented another temptation, offering Jesus great riches if he allied himself with the devil instead of with the Divine Father. That is the point at which Jesus shouted, "Get thee behind me, Satan!"

Satan challenged the Buddha in the same way. Before his enlightenment, the Buddha was a sheltered prince named Siddhartha who lived in the royal palace until the age of twenty-nine. Then he left to discover what was going on in the outside world. As the story goes, first he saw a diseased person, then a decrepit old man and finally a corpse.

After observing these different stages of life, Siddhartha renounced the world and went to live as a monk. But soon he realized this was dry renunciation. True renunciation must be done with knowledge and genuine detachment, rather than avoidance like an ostrich with its head in the sand. So Siddhartha decided to sit under a *bodhi* tree until he achieved liberation. Whatever it took, he would remain fixed in this position until death. It was at that stage that Satan appeared, trying to convince Siddhartha that he had no right to seek liberation.

Other great saints also faced severe difficulties in fulfilling their commissions. St. Teresa of Avila had to run away from home to practice her life of renunciation and simplicity. St. Francis of Assisi disowned his parents in public. St. Thomas Aquinas, a celibate monk, was locked in a cell with a prostitute in an attempt to get him to break his vows.

These experiences let us know what we can expect.

Without a doubt, we will be tested at our weakest points. That is why self-regulation and renunciation are so important: they help make us strong enough to resist the attacks that will surely come our way.

Working on Our Own Consciousness

Several years ago, as I spoke to a group of so-called revolutionaries and diplomats from another country, I emphasized the importance of renunciation and regulation. When leaders continue to smoke, drink and otherwise indulge themselves, they become easy prey for adversaries who seek to tempt them at their most vulnerable points. Such temptations are bound to occur. Indeed, one of the first goals of espionage is to discover the enemy's weaknesses in order to exploit them as effectively as possible. Self-indulgent persons cannot protect themselves against these attacks, so how can they possibly guide others?

I told this group of revolutionaries to first work on themselves. If they were sincere in their intentions to raise others' consciousness, they had to first get their own "acts" together and strengthen their own consciousness. If not, they were likely to endanger people and lead them to destruction.

In general, as we engage in conscious-raising activities we put pressure on those in our environment to change. However, we must embody the transformation that we are expecting in others. As we do so, we "walk our talk" and gain power that is truly honorable and enduring. All other forms of power are temporary.

Genuine power is based on integrity, principle-centeredness, inner realization, and the ability to act in alignment with higher consciousness. Those who possess such power become love and knowledge in action. In other words, healing the self also heals the community. If we wish to serve others, we must take a serious self-inventory and root out the obstacles that prevent us from advancing in our level of consciousness.

The Vedic tradition recounts the story of Lord Chaitanya, a divine incarnation who lived in Bengal about five hundred years ago. The story recounts Lord Chaitanya's cleaning of the Gundica temple. His actions in cleaning the temple represented the process of purification for human beings dedicated to spiritual life. Later, Lord Chaitanya cleaned the outside of the temple, representing the grossly materialistic aspects of consciousness, so that no dirt could be carried inside. In this way, Lord Chaitanya taught those around him about the importance of prevention.

Next, as Lord Chaitanya cleaned, he worked with his own hands and used his own clothing to wipe the dirt away. By these actions, he was demonstrating that we must search within ourselves and do our own inner work of purification. He was reminding us that, as spiritual scientists, we are microcosms of the outer world and that we have to look inward.

When Lord Chaitanya cleaned the Gundica temple, He worked hard to wash away the subtle impurities that might not be immediately visible. This type of almost-undetectable contamination can destroy the "devotional creeper," which is the immature, vulnerable sprouting of love and dedication that occurs in the early stages of spiritual life. Even a small amount of impurity can cause trouble in this beginning phase; if it is not rooted out, such impurity can grow like a weed and choke the young creeper. Lord Chaitanya was demonstrating that it is not enough to cleanse ourselves of obvious external forms of pollution. We must examine ourselves more deeply for the subtle, hidden kinds of dirt that can cause serious difficulties later on.

Weeding Out Saboteurs of Devotion

An impartial, investigative attitude is a vital tool for all spiritual warriors, because subtle interferences can arise at any moment to pull us away from the path of right action. Such an investigative attitude enables us to see the patterns of the mind clearly and weed out our destructive thoughts, feelings and behaviors in order to serve those around us better. This is not a task that is accomplished once and then forgotten. We must exercise constant vigilance to keep our mind free from self-centered preoccupations and available for service.

One of the most venomous weeds to take root in the heart of a spiritual warrior is the attachment to name and fame. If we have a strong desire to distinguish ourselves from the crowd, to be better than others, or to be noticed and appreciated, we are not acting in a selfless way, and our so-called "service" is actually self-aggrandizement and a means for feeling important. Another dangerous saboteur is envy, which is the total opposite of love and selflessness. Envy interferes with our ability to see and hear truthfully, and distorts our perceptions to such an extent that our behavior can become extremely damaging to others—and to ourselves.

We cannot understand spiritual realities by scholarship alone. Although study is important, the path to spiritual realization is through dedicated, selfless service. As we offer service to others with no expectation of reward, the Lord in the heart becomes more available to us and provides for our needs—because we have removed the veils that hide the truth.

Self-Protection

As we purify our own consciousness and become more effective spiritual warriors, we must keep in mind that we are in a wartime situation. To fight effectively, soldiers must know how to protect themselves. The art of self-protection is an essential component of our inner work and our endeavor to serve others. Instead of being naive, we must see circumstances as they are in order to improve our resistance to negative influences, obvious or subtle.

On commercial airlines, at takeoff the flight attendants instruct passengers in the use of oxygen masks, reminding them to secure their own masks before assisting others. In the same way, to be effective spiritual warriors we must protect ourselves first. Otherwise we are of no use to anyone. The greatest protection of all comes from our unconditional, unmotivated, uninterrupted devotional service. Such service opens us up to a flow of divine love and protection in all circumstances.

Our minds are extremely vulnerable to influence from the media and the electronic devices that surround us. Self-protection for spiritual warriors involves being vigilant about the mind at all times, minimizing television viewing, excess computer work and any other habits that lead to passivity, inertia and mental "absenteeism." We must also immunize ourselves against a mob mentality and degraded mass consciousness by including processes of purification as a regular part of our lives.

As spiritual warriors, we must not forget the help we are constantly receiving from higher beings in this universe. At the same time, we must be aware of the tremendous influx of lower beings who are attempting to neutralize us by polluting our minds and hearts. These harmful entities are always on the prowl for new victims and are continually seeking out ways to direct us toward darkness.

The Value of Discernment

To avoid a "herd mentality," spiritual warriors must learn to be discriminating. They must understand that the root causes of destructive behavior can generally be traced back to a common origin—lust or the desire for sense gratification. Even those who start out with the best of intentions can turn into abusers if they are attached to sense pleasures, because eventually they reach a point where they will stop at nothing to fulfill their insatiable desires.

As spiritual warriors, we must not allow this "herd mentality" to capture us. Instead, we must keep ourselves apart, ready to lead the herd as a result of our purity and commitment. For this, we must be able to resist our lower urges and guide others to genuine spiritual shelter—a difficult task in a society that bombards us with temptations at every turn. Although these principles of discernment are simple to understand, they are important because they have a deep impact on our ability to maintain our strength.

"Normal" is Not Natural

We must resist the temptation to be "normal," because those who are now considered normal accept the values and practices of an insane world. In modern society, for example, normal people strive to accumulate as many commodities as possible, because they believe that their success and personal worth are linked to the number of possessions they have acquired. As the joke goes, "The one who dies with the most toys, wins." If we espouse this viewpoint, the toys we have to play with form the measure of our personal worth. Unfortunately, this notion confuses acquired material worth with our inherent worth as spiritual beings.

As spiritual warriors, we must go beyond this narrow conception of human life. This means that in every situation we must ask "Why?" and "How?" and "What will that lead to?" We should constantly examine the ramifications of our thoughts and actions—and seek to discover the laws behind them. Ultimately, we will learn who the Lawmaker is and how to be in harmony with His laws. We will discover that we do not want to be lawbreakers, because we do not want to experience the painful consequences of our actions—especially when we violate spiritual principles. If we disobey *material* laws, we may "get away with it" for a time. But we are always caught when we break *spiritual* laws, because the Lord resides in the heart of each of us and is eternally aware of what we are doing.

Despite the materialistic focus of our modern society, growing numbers of people are becoming spiritually aware, seeking to understand the nature of reality and the purpose of human life. Many have developed an awareness of spiritual principles and have had experiences that transcend the "normal" material consciousness. Such experiences can serve as catalysts for them to access a deeper level of spirituality—in which they can experience a dynamic, personal relationship with God and discover the joys of the higher, nonmaterial realms of existence.

The Impact of Subtle Phenomena

For the most part, our problems are far deeper than the obvious social evils of oppression, imperialism, nationalism and even poverty. Many of our greatest complications exist on the subtle level. Spiritual warriors, in addition to being materially competent, should learn to master these subtle aspects of existence. We are not interested in skating over the surface of issues, as the average materialist does.

Spiritual warriors must be sensitive, alert and meticulous in all their dealings if we are to make a positive contribution to the level of collective awareness. We must be especially discerning in the area of our inner experiences. Many people engage in meditative practices that cause them to enter altered states of consciousness. Without proper guidance, however, the deeper levels of consciousness we reach through meditation can sometimes cause a lack of integration with our surroundings. Some of those who once practiced intensely in such areas as *Kundalini* yoga, complicated breathing exercises or other mystic disciplines without proper instruction and guidance are now in mental institutions because they became seriously unbalanced. Others who divulged their visions to people who could not understand what was happening also became labeled as mentally ill. Their mental state was considered negative and dangerous.

We must not forget the perspective of history here. Not long ago many intuitive, spiritual women and men in Europe and America were convicted of witchcraft, deprived of all their property and tortured, hanged or burned. The Middle Ages produced inquisitors who, acting as authorized church judges, brutally killed many so-called "heretics"—essentially people with a different vision of God than the one authorized by the church. Remember that Joan of Arc only became a canonized saint several centuries after her burning at the stake, and that this style of punishment was not unusual for the times. On the other side of the Atlantic, America experienced the Salem witch trials and executions. Today, keeping these historical precedents in mind, we should always be truthful, but remain cautious about baring our souls indiscriminately.

Sound Vibration

Another aspect of our environment that requires careful discernment is sound—who we talk with, what we talk about and what we hear. Even if we are not aware of it, sound vibrations have a powerful effect on us. For example, if we engage in frivolous, speculative or gossipy conversation, we weaken our vital energy and interfere with our spiritual development. Such behavior causes us to become off balance and consequently makes us more open to attack.

Remember, in one sense the body is just a collection of vibrations, and it stands to reason that sound has an effect on matter. Instead of using drugs to numb their patients against pain, certain dentists use specific sound vibrations that alter consciousness to such an extent that medication is not necessary. As another example, researchers have discovered that different kinds of music either enhance plant growth or retard it. Plants thrive with classical music, but they can barely survive, and even die, when rock music is played around them regularly.

Rock music also has a tremendous effect on the human *chakras,* or energy centers—it can intensify lust and incite us to act in degrading ways. Generally, when we listen to this heavy music we feel aggressive, lusty, egocentric and animalistic, because the music is intensifying these energies. That is why we must be so attentive to the quality of sound that we allow in our environment—sound can determine our level of consciousness even when we are unaware of its influence.

Dark Night of the Soul

Above all, in our growth process, we must be prepared for what is called the "dark night of the soul." This can be a very challenging period. This is a time of danger and opportunity: The danger is that we may succumb to defeat and despair, and the opportunity is that we are receiving an unprecedented chance to put many old, destructive patterns behind us. The "dark night of the soul" offers us the possibility of attaining genuine self-realization—liberation from the painful cycle of birth and death. Yet, with all that it offers, it is truly a "dark night," often accompanied by a devastating feeling of loss or an acute sense of loneliness. We are likely to feel totally misunderstood, unappreciated and unloved, and we may experience profound separation from everyone and everything we have held dear. Quite simply, this is because to fully gain ourselves, we must first lose ourselves.

In the Christian tradition, Saint John explains that as the light dawns and the higher law begins to act, it stirs up our fears and throws us off balance—even to the point of sinking into a profound depression. We may question whether God Himself has completely forgotten us. During this period, all of our secret, long-held desires and fears must appear before us so that we can transcend them.

Seasoned spiritual warriors meet this challenge with a smile and remain happy. First of all, we are secure in the knowledge that the Supreme will not give us more than we can handle, and second, if the situation is becoming truly unbearable, we can persevere in the certainty that a positive change is just around the corner.

The beautiful aspect of the dark night of the soul is that, as we penetrate all the layers of selfishness and suffering and begin to release our old negative patterns, we finally become the vibrant person that we really are. What follows the dark night of the soul is a high level of attainment accompanied by an abiding experience of profound joy. To reach that level, though, we must remove the countless layers of dirt encasing our hearts and consciously choose to ally ourselves with the forces of goodness and transcendence.

Choosing Our Path with Care

As spiritual warriors, we must be especially vigilant about choosing our spiritual path. We should accept things favorable to devotional service and reject things that are unfavorable. Many of us have a problem deciding what is favorable or unfavorable; we have so many choices. In our local holistic newspaper, for example, there are pages and pages advertising astrologers, massage therapists, acupuncturists, and so on. We can find almost anything we want. It is wonderful to see so many people going beyond orthodox, traditional methods and frames of reference, but it can be dangerous, too, because wherever there is spiritual potency, there is also the opportunity to fall prey to negative energies.

We should recognize that the guidance received from channeling and similar activities is not necessarily wise or spiritual. We must look at the life of the channeler and remember that God is not so weak or desperate that He will transmit His message through someone who lives an impure life. We must always evaluate the message carrier and the quality of the message.

We must be at least as careful as we are when we go shopping. When we shop, we usually know what we are looking for and evaluate our purchases carefully. The same is true in the "spiritual marketplace." If the situation can genuinely help us in developing love of God, then it is appropriate. But we must first be sure, through vigilant observation, that the person or group actually has what we are looking for and is not just giving lip service to attractive ideas or slogans.

We all have free will, and because we are in a world at war, we must make our choices with care. Negative forces will tempt us at every turn and use a variety of subtle approaches to neutralize our potency. That is why self-observation, vigilance and purification are so important.

We should choose a bona fide tradition and go deeply into it. If it is properly bona fide, it will naturally help us appreciate other genuine traditions. But if it is not deep, it will make us more self-righteous and sectarian, because we will feel that we have the only answer. However, even worse than sectarianism is the refusal to accept any rules, regulations or authority about what is proper. If absolute truth does exist, then a bona fide tradition will transmit it directly, without watering it down to make it acceptable to those who are not serious.

When we start relying on our own ideas, we get into trouble. Then *Maya* laughs at us, saying, "Oh, you are going to try to defeat me on your own? Who do you think you are? We'll see about this." But when we are backed up by the Lord—*Maya*'s boss—then we have a chance. Then we are humble enough to receive the grace of love and protection that the Lord provides.

The Importance of Commitment

We must draw a line between eclecticism and a lack of commitment. Sometimes, people do not want to commit to anything and have no interest in working on themselves. To avoid facing this unpleasant truth, they call themselves "eclectic." On weekends they may go to the mosque and on Mondays to yoga. Tuesdays are dedicated to Tai Chi, Wednesdays to Bible study and Thursdays to color therapy. Every day finds them in a different place, and each week brings new interests and explorations.

At the end of the month, when they are exhausted from going from one place to another, their next item of business is to learn stress management. At some point, after running from one religion or spiritual path to another, they may even start believing that this "God stuff" just doesn't work. After all, they have not discovered any benefits! Then they decide to dedicate themselves solely to making money—at least that is tangible and immediately gratifying.

This is an unfortunate state of affairs. It is up to each individual to seek the appropriate teachings and go forward, but everything that we want to purchase has a price. Materially, we pay money or offer something in exchange. If we want to learn a trade or profession, we must spend time and effort to achieve the goal. Spiritually, the price for advancement is our dedication and commitment. We need to keep our focus. We should not be unchaste or disloyal to our own tradition, and we should be eager to have a sense of identity—but a profound one that transcends superficialities and connects to the universality of all teachings. Otherwise, we just dabble here and there, practicing mental gymnastics that do not lead to any substantive change. We must be honest with ourselves and discover just how serious we are about spiritual life.

We should ask three basic questions of any system we encounter. The first question is, "If I am perfect at this practice, what can I expect to achieve?" Once you have heard the answer to this question, you may decide that you do not care to proceed any further, or you may find that the goal is exactly what you have always wanted. The second question is, "What are the means for attaining the goal?" The answer to this question enables you to decide whether you are willing to pay the price to get there. The third question to ask is, "Who has already reached the goal and how do they live their lives?" We should carefully scrutinize those who have supposedly reached the goal to discover their true situation in life. If we feel aligned with the answers to all three questions, then we can "go for it." If we do not, then we should look somewhere else.

There is a widespread tendency in today's society to avoid commitment. This is an enormous problem. People are afraid to "miss out" on anything; therefore, they prefer to remain theoretical, open to all the choices that might be available. This translates into a tendency to observe spiritual paths, evaluate them, speculate on them, experiment with them and do everything except explore them deeply enough to gain any genuine benefit. People need to become more serious and realistic in order to gain the necessary stability in these turbulent times. Theories, speculation or endless internal debates eventually produce only frustration. We need a practical approach to living, one that offers specific ways to make our lives better and also help those around us.

We cannot afford to squander our precious energy by saying, "Yes, I'd like to hear him when he comes back again to speak," and then carrying on our business as usual. Instead, if we are serious, we will go home and say, "This speaker said something important. I want to see how it can work." Then we apply it in daily life and evaluate the results. Is there now more desire to serve God, help others and experience the wonderful love that the Lord has in store for everyone? Or have we become lazy and slipped back to our old habits?

Purity is the Force

Purity offers a general solution to the problems facing society, and provides an ideal focus for our personal spiritual practices. We must remember that constant vigilance is necessary in this polluted world, where nothing remains pure on its own. As the Bible and other scriptures teach us, Satan cannot harm us unless we weaken our resolve and yield to temptations. Just as the potential for disease is all around us, so are opportunities for self-degradation and hurtfulness. In either situation, it is only when our resistance is low that harm can overtake us and wreak havoc.

Calling on the Names of the Lord

At this period in history, we are heavily under siege. What can we do in our times of desperation, when we have exhausted all our material resources? We can call on the names of the Lord. Reciting or chanting the holy names is a beneficial practice at all times and in all circumstances.

The Quar'an (17.110) tells us, "Call upon Allah or call upon the Beneficent God; whichever you call upon, He has the best names" The Quar'an also declares that since the most beautiful of all names belong to the Lord, we should call upon Him by using them. The teachings of Zoroaster remind us to repeat the holy names, as do the scriptures of the Baha'i faith, which claim that the names of God carry the most powerful vibrations of any sound and have the greatest effect. In addition, in the *Bhagavad-gita* (10.26) Krishna says to Arjuna, "Of sacrifices, I am the chanting of the holy names."

This emphasis upon the names of God is not just an Eastern tradition. The Book of Mormon admonishes us to cry unto the Lord for mercy in the morning, in the afternoon and in the evening. The Christian Bible tells us in Romans 10:13 that whoever calls on the name of the Lord shall be saved.

Psalms 113:3 says that from the rising of the sun to its setting we must praise the names of the Lord—not just when we need food in our refrigerator or want a higher salary and a new car. We should be turning to God for everything at all times.

Even in daily life, we catch someone's attention by calling out to them. For example, perhaps an acquaintance is trying to sneak away and avoid notice. "Brother Jones, wait a minute!" we shout. We have caught his attention. Or maybe a lazy employee is trying to go to sleep before finishing his work for the day. If we are weary enough of this behavior, we may call him by name and say something like, "Wake up! You've been sleeping all week long! You've been sleeping lifetime after lifetime. Wake up *now!*"

Although chanting the holy names is powerful for us as individuals, it is even more potent when done in groups. When we join in unison with others to invoke the Lord, our personal call is amplified. This demonstrates once again the great importance of community and the necessity for congregational activities to deepen our spiritual life and our connection with higher realms.

Devotion

Devotion is necessary in developing and maintaining purity. Through devotion, we learn to transcend the ego, relinquish our selfish desires and be of service in the world. When we are devoted to something greater or higher than ourselves, our motivations are not based on self-interest, competition or greed. That is why, as spiritual warriors, we must constantly monitor our level of devotion. As we dedicate ourselves to serving the Lord with all our hearts, the Lord will reciprocate by giving us increasing abilities to serve even more. If we are genuinely devoted to the Lord, and if we radiate that devotion to others, we can create a powerful spiritual environment that will help countless people discover true meaning in their lives.

Health and Healing

Spiritual warriors must be attentive to the issues of health and healing. Without giving undue emphasis to the importance of the body, we must still love and care for this instrument of service so that it can be of use to others. Before we choose a health-care modality, we must choose health itself, and resolve in our minds that we will not settle for less than vibrant well-being. This is an age in which borderline health is dangerous, because there are innumerable threats to our wellness. As we enter this new century, there is a strong possibility that unknown diseases will begin to engulf the planet.

Disease is often a matter of consciousness, as modern research in psychoneuroimmunology demonstrates. Yet in this society, countless people succumb easily to the pervading climate of lower consciousness, reinforced by such phenomena as television, music and the movies. Because of this, many of us may not be able to resist these diseases, and only those who have prepared themselves through a combination of love and self-discipline will have a reasonable chance of survival.

At the same time, the expanded consciousness of twenty-first century humankind has given us a chance to explore additional aspects of a holistic worldview and its expression throughout the world community. In considering all these, we should always remember the importance of being practical. In other words, whatever works, "go for it"—once we are certain that it works not only for the short term, but also for the long term.

Modern society offers a variety of ways to deal with sickness—homeopathy, Reiki, acupressure, acupuncture, reflexology, color therapy and many more. When we speak of a holistic approach, we are talking about physical, emotional, mental and spiritual aspects. New modalities are constantly being developed, and old ones are being rediscovered. It is important to realize, however, that no single approach will work for everyone. Some diets and remedies will work in one culture but not in another, or for one type of body or personality but not another.

The ultimate essence of these systems is to stimulate the body to heal itself, doing whatever is necessary to free the organism's natural healing forces. As we seek healing for ourselves, it is also extremely important to consider the global impact on the environment and other life forms. Actually, as in all our actions, we must take into account everyone and everything—past, present and future. If a remedy does not include all of these aspects, it is relative and transitory, and its effects are temporary. We must always evaluate the implications of our choices.

When we consider a healing process that addresses past, present and future, we are talking about karma. In an analysis of karma, the principle of holism is particularly significant. However we look at the body and try to heal it, we are inviting complications if the method does not address the karmic component. If this aspect is ignored, no matter how accurate the physical diagnosis or how skillful the physician, our remedies will fail to save us.

Karma and Healing

Disease is actually extremely personal and specific. A disease is the culmination of an individual's personal karma from this and previous lives. The end result of any remedy is intimately related to the state of mind of the diseased individual and of the practitioner. This is why the same treatment can be given to two people with different results. One person may heal quickly while another heals slowly, or one will die while the other recovers fully. This is the karmic factor, which is not just theoretical or ethereal. Universal law works like civil law: in alignment with the law, we thrive; in opposition to the law, we suffer.

Illness and constant turmoil are unnatural. Armed with this

understanding, we realize that to heal and lead a balanced life, we must first eliminate everything that diminishes our ability to be the powerful, dynamic and loving beings that we are.

Let us take some examples. A person experiencing a severe legal problem is perhaps dealing with a carryover of karma from a previous life. An individual with a chronic disease may also be reaping results from destructive activities in a previous life. How does this occur? The process is not hard to understand. Each time we die, we give up the physical body and the subtle, or astral, body takes the soul to its next existence, carrying with it the imprints of our experiences and the traits from our previous lives. These traits will eventually manifest in various ways throughout our lifetime.

If we develop our inner vision, we can confirm these truths for ourselves. In some, this ability is a natural gift. Certain people can look at a face and discern that person's earlier lives. Just as some individuals can read auras and see signs of a disease before it physically manifests, others are aware of their own previous existences.

Keep the Goal in Mind

As spiritual warriors, we should explore alternative healing methods—but always with the true goal in mind. The main reason we want to have strong, healthy bodies is to equip ourselves for service. When we are healthy, we can resist negative influences, wage war against corruption and help others attain higher consciousness through our own example. If we are merely keeping our bodies fit, we have not accomplished much. Even animals are capable of eating, sleeping, mating and defending—this is not very impressive. As *Homo sapiens*, we are supposed to pursue higher values and self-realization above everything else. The opportunity of this human life is a special gift that God gives His courageous and obedient sons and daughters. We must not waste it.

We must remember that the all-time greatest healer is love. Love invigorates; it revitalizes; it inspires; and it attunes us to the rhythm of life. Our beliefs about love and our life experiences of intimacy or alienation greatly affect our physical health. The power of love is so great that all of us, consciously or unconsciously, seek love and joy in everything we do. Unfortunately, though, many people have a distorted understanding of love and so produce conflict and unhappiness in their lives.

As spiritual warriors, we have a responsibility to recognize genuine love and to act accordingly, sharing it with others. And what is genuine love? Essentially, love is a deep understanding of ourselves and others. Real love means connecting with the essence rather than with superficialities. When we love, we can appreciate a person's true nature beyond the outer shell, and we can see the reality of the individual regardless of behavior, appearances or value systems.

Questions & Answers

Question: I recently talked with a dear friend who told me that I am too motherly, overprotective and controlling, and that I preach too much. Another friend has told me that I am not forgiving enough for hurts that have happened to me. This same friend has also said that she holds on to things herself and does not forgive others, and that this is an obstacle to her spiritual development. What advice do you have about this?

Answer: There is a difference between trying to serve and trying to fix. If we try to fix someone, we assume that the other person is incomplete while we are complete and know how to set the other person straight. This is arrogance, is it not? When we are so sanctimonious, we are invalidating the other person and reinforcing the very helplessness that we are supposedly trying to remedy. But if we are genuinely interested in serving others more fully, we can approach the situation in a less self-righteous and overbearing way.

We can express our love, ask how we can help and demonstrate that the situation is hurting us because it is hurting the other person. Then we can join with the person to brainstorm for viable alternatives and offer support for taking positive action. In this way, the resolution of the problem becomes a collaborative venture, instead of an adversarial "win-lose" relationship.

It is helpful to receive feedback from others. This feedback points us to aspects of ourselves that need improvement, and often we are either completely unaware of our character defects or have deliberately pushed them out of our awareness. Others are doing us a service to point them out. Even if we eventually find that we have no problem in that particular area, the fact that another person raised the issue means that we have a difficulty to address in the relationship. If we care about that individual, we will want to stop provoking the reaction. Either way, we have something to work on in ourselves.

As to your other friend, you have noticed that in the process of giving you feedback she is reflecting upon her own behavior. It can be very interesting to see how such an exchange takes place. Those who genuinely try to help us will automatically help themselves. It takes courage and humility to speak in this open, self-revealing way. It is also a sign of genuine caring to tell someone an unwelcome truth, because the consequences may be uncomfortable. We have the tendency, even when someone asks us directly for feedback, to say to ourselves, "I don't want to answer this truthfully. I'm going to have to deal with her for the rest of the year. If I tell her what I really think about her, things are going to get really tense. Why doesn't she just go ask someone else!" It is a sign of great love and selflessness to speak truthfully in a clear yet compassionate way that the other person can accept and act upon.

Question: You are urging us to become more holistic, and you also say that some of our health issues and illnesses are psychosomatic. But when I go to allopathic health practitioners, they discourage alternative methods of healing. What should I do?

Answer: This holds true for both mental and physical health practitioners. All it means is that, at a certain point in our spiritual careers, we have to decide where we will place our faith: In God's medicine, or in man-made substances and practices that can prove detrimental. Also, we must remember that traditional Western medicine—the allopathic approach—is extremely addictive. It almost seems designed to make you dependent. When you take these allopathic "shortcuts," you damage your body's recuperative capacities and set yourself up for ongoing medical care, because, for example, the medicines may kill "good" bacteria along with the "bad" and cause imbalance in the metabolism.

It can be even worse at times to consult traditional professionals in the area of mental health. We have to be extremely careful. If we have deep meditative experiences as a result of our metaphysical practices, and if we speak about them, orthodox professionals may not always understand what is happening to us. As a result, some spiritualists and transcendentalists will wind up in mental institutions because they have divulged metaphysical visions to some "textbook" therapist. There is a dire need for therapists with a connection to higher consciousness.

With longer and more intense practice, we will experience deeper levels of consciousness. We may get flashbacks from previous lives, but this should not frighten us. On the contrary, those who consider themselves sane in this insane world have a real problem. Anyone who tries to be "normal" in this madhouse is in a real difficulty, because to be "normal" means to be crazy from a spiritual viewpoint.

As your longing grows to experience spiritual reality,

your cries will be heard. If you persevere, the universe will definitely respond to your spiritual yearning—but you have to persist in faith.

Question: We have been talking about how difficult it is to be anti-material in a material society, while at the same time maintaining ourselves by working at jobs, paying bills and fulfilling our daily responsibilities. How should we behave in the workplace—particularly how we can remain humble? Often in the workplace, that quality is misunderstood.

Answer: The question implies that being humble means being foolish, inactive or naive. Yet Jesus was being extremely humble when He went into the synagogue and overturned the tables of the moneychangers. He was humble in the sense that He was totally surrendered to divine will, doing what needed to be done in the moment without any concern for Himself. Being humble does not necessarily mean keeping quiet. It means being truthful and unafraid to represent that truth, refusing to be distracted by any desire for distinction, adoration or profit.

Humility may mean inactivity in some cases, but in other cases it means being even more active than usual. Humility is not just a matter of tolerating situations. It means being true. For example, we would not tolerate our child taking harmful drugs. We would not say to ourselves, "Well, I'm just going to be humble and put up with this because I'm a wonderful parent and I want my child to be creative and self-expressive." Of course not. You would be extremely foolish, cowardly and irresponsible. Humility not just a matter of being tolerant.

In order to act humbly, the question to ask ourselves is, "In this situation, what will produce the higher good—action or inaction?" If addressing the issue head-on will result in a greater good, then that is what we must do. Humility means evaluating situations in terms of the well-being of everyone involved, not in terms of our own comfort and security. It also means being willing to take action upon our conclusions after the evaluation has been made.

Spiritual life is always about selflessness. But selflessness is active, not a state of inactivity. We must always keep in mind that being humble means being honest, truthful, straightforward and ready to deal with the consequences, whatever they may be. The world's greatest spiritual teachers were humble in this sense, even if it meant that the whole world turned against them.

Chapter 9

Guidelines for responsible action

We Are Always Acting

As we have understood from our discussions of karma, every action produces a corresponding reaction in the universe, one that will eventually find its way back to us. Another important aspect of this understanding is that, by our very nature, we are always active. Even if we decide to remove ourselves from society and live on a mountaintop, we will still be active to some degree. When we sleep, our consciousness remains active. In the *Bhagavad-gita*, Arjuna inquires about this point, and the Lord instructs him, explaining that we should devote all our activities to the development of our spiritual life instead of trying to avoid activities (and their corresponding karmic reactions). As we do this, even our ordinary actions of eating, working and caring for our families begin to transcend the material platform.

Today, people have a mistaken idea about spirituality, considering it to be impractical and abstract. Naturally, many of us are intrigued by abstraction because it holds a certain mystique, but the end result of this false notion is that we have divorced spirituality from our daily lives. We have "faked ourselves out" and performed a kind of misguided surgery, cutting out our spiritual essence and leaving a shell that gives the illusion of being the only reality. Consequently, we do not realize that we were intended by our Maker to be guided by spirituality in all of our interactions.

We do not realize that the true measure of our spirituality is how we interact with our environment and the living beings around us. We think that love and spirituality are sentimental feelings in the heart that make us "feel good" and require no commitment or action on our part. But love is a verb, and ultimately, so is spirituality.

Because spirituality is not separate from everyday life, it is not what we do in a church, temple, mosque or synagogue that makes us spiritual; it is what we do everywhere. Cooking a meal and offering it with love to others can be a spiritual act. Tending a garden, nursing a baby, massaging an elder, carrying packages for a neighbor, even greeting someone with a genuine smile or praying for someone other than ourselves—all these are acts of spirituality if they are done as service in remembrance of God. The opposites of these actions are behaviors based on total self-absorption and an undue obsession with our own importance, perspective and materialistic agenda.

If we approach all our activities from a spiritual warrior's perspective, then we will be doing our part to raise consciousness, even when confusion and negativity surround us. Despite our idiosyncratic tendencies, propensities and capabilities, we all share a common responsibility to do what we can, wherever we are, to make a difference in the collective consciousness of the planet.

Helping and Serving

Serving is different from helping. All souls are equal creations of God, even though there may be some differences between material bodies and consciousness. Our common perception of "helping," however, does not reflect a relationship between equals. When we "help" someone, we are using our own power to rescue those who are apparently of lesser strength, all the while accepting their frailties from our supposedly superior vantage point. Sometimes in relationships we magnanimously tolerate others, meaning, "I recognize your existence. I accept that you are flawed, and I tolerate your flaws because I am so wonderful." Although we may not say it, or even think it consciously, we are placing ourselves in a higher position. People feel this sense of inequality and resist it to the point that it will interfere with our ability to communicate.

When we "fix" a person, we perceive that individual as broken and believe that their broken state requires us to act. We do not see the wholeness in the other person or trust the integrity of life within them. When we "fix" or "help," we may inadvertently take away from people more than we give them. Our behavior implies that they do not have the resources to deal with the situation on their own. If we do things in such a dehumanizing or demeaning way, we diminish the self-esteem of others and cause damage, even with the best of intentions. In order to be of real service, we must be attentive not only to doing the right thing, but also to doing the right thing in the right way. Otherwise, despite our efforts to improve the situation, we may unintentionally cause greater conflict and unhappiness for ourselves and others. The spiritual warrior's commitment does not stop at helping others. We must be truly selfless servants.

Serving is different from "helping" or "fixing." Service rests on the basic principle that life is a sacred, holy mystery. When we "serve," we do so in the consciousness that we belong to life. In contrast, when we "help," we see life as weak, and when we "fix," we see life as broken. In either case, we see ourselves as above or separate from the wholeness of life. When we really "serve," we empathize and make a sincere effort to understand what is required. Once we realize what is needed, we bring all our resources to the forefront to assist. The gesture of serving occurs between equals and originates in humility, selflessness and love.

When we serve, we do not impose our power or seek anything for the separated self. We draw from all of our experiences, and the wholeness in us serves the wholeness in others and the wholeness in life. We serve with gratitude for the opportunity, and not with a grudging attitude that can affect the atmosphere at least as much as our good deeds, canceling out their benefits. Service is an ongoing, reciprocal relationship between people, whereas "helping" incurs debt, as in: "I've helped you and now you owe me." When we "help" someone, they owe us one. On the other hand, serving brings healing because it is mutual and there is no debt to repay.

The Humility of Service

There is a natural humility that comes from the recognition that we are not above the problems that others are experiencing. In fact, we can see problems in others primarily because those same problems exist within us. This understanding forces us to come to terms with the fact that we are not strong enough to "fix" anybody. Our well-intentioned egocentric efforts repeatedly fail to have the desired effect until we recognize that forces far greater than us are at work, and that our job is simply to be conduits and facilitators for the help that is being made available by God and His agents.

Still, as we grow spiritually and learn to let this divine empowerment flow through us, we may find ourselves wanting to share these blessings and realizations with others. Most of the time, our actions and our state of consciousness will have a beneficial effect on others with no deliberate effort on our part. On other occasions, though, we may need to speak out. Although people may not accept what we have to say or may not be interested, it is our duty to offer the best we have.

We must have the courage to act upon what we know and the compassion to use all that we are, to find a way to get the message across effectively. To know that we have something to offer and to not try to share it is selfish and cowardly.

You do not help me by reinforcing my nonsense or by speaking or acting in a way that reinforces the absurdity of my behavior. You serve me by your understanding and your willingness to remove my complacency about my current situation. You may grab my hand or you may come behind and push me. It is good to understand me, but if you do not lovingly give me a shove and pull, then you are not my true well-wisher. On the other hand, if you try to force me to live according to your own desires and make no attempt to understand me, you are not my well-wisher either.

Better still, you can lead me by showing me the successes and lessons of your own example. I can have more faith in what your are doing and saying because I can see the effects for myself. I am not interested in hearing theories. I want to see the solutions in practice so that I know I can trust the help you are offering.

We want to feel sincerely that "your problem is my problem," which is in fact the case, because the people around us are part of the environment that we experience. Everything is interrelated and we are never isolated. It is not enough for us to simply go about our own individual projects effectively, pushing others out of the way so that we may do some "good work." We should always explore what we can do to inspire and assist others to perform their own service as well.

We are all eternal servants—of God and of each other. As we recognize this truth, we open ourselves up to strong internal connections, great blessings and even divine intervention. Events that result solely from our material, intellectual expertise do not reflect spirituality. It is when circumstances in life unfold beyond our normal understanding and capacities that we recognize the presence of God personally coming through us to do His will. As we allow the Divine to act through us, we will witness amazing developments, far beyond our wildest dreams. If, on the other hand, we function based only on our own abilities, the results will be mediocre at best.

Seeking Divine Empowerment

Consider the example of a martial arts *dojo.* Within these confines, the best students always display great prayerfulness, concentration and reverence toward teachers and carriers of the tradition. These students understand that their teachers' knowledge has not come cheaply, and, because theirs is a rather mystical art, they realize that obedience to their teachers' commands summons great mercy to them while fighting.

Similarly, spiritual warriors always summon permission, assistance, guidance and love from senior authorities. Wherever we may be incompetent to accomplish a goal, our predecessors' aid is indispensable. The ultimate victor is always that group or individual most closely aligned with God's will. Receiving the blessings and endorsement of predecessors is a large part of the potency contained in almost all spiritual activities.

In the *Bhagavad-gita,* Arjuna's victory over an army far superior and better equipped than his own is a clear example of divine empowerment. The Bible tells us that when Joshua fought the battle of Jericho, the walls came tumbling down. But what happened? How did he do that? After Moses passed on, Joshua took over as general and told the children of Israel that he had to continue the mission despite all odds. When the army reached Jericho and saw their mighty adversaries and those powerful walls, many became frightened and confused. They believed the obstacles before them to be insurmountable.

Yet, like all true spiritual warriors, Joshua was not deterred. He told his army not to worry and to remember God, who had already shown Himself many times. "Why are you going to forget about Him at this point?" he asked them. God had instructed him: "Let the trumpet blow, reserve your energy, focus on the target, and be calm about what is to be done and why. It must be done. Circle around for six days and on that seventh day when the trumpet blows, all of you together shout."

For genuine spiritual warriors, an apparently insurmountable obstacle is cause for excitement, because we wonder what our wonderful Lord will do. The journey becomes an adventure with an unknown outcome. Perhaps He will bring order to chaos, clean up the nonsense and perform some kind of miracle—making the impossible a reality. Everything is based on our level of devotion and commitment. The real workers for God are almost gleeful when there is a problem that requires the Lord's intervention because they know that the Lord will never let them down.

Understanding Power

Different types of power influence individuals, communities, nations and the planet. Ultimately, the degree of love expressed determines the nature of the power and its effect on the environment. On the other hand, the extent of our envy and lust determines how far away from the Source of love we have strayed in our spiritual evolution. The Vedic tradition teaches that the inhabitants of this earth planet have come here because they are trying to usurp the power of God and seek to align themselves with another kind of power that can help them to achieve their goal. In other words, human beings want to play God. Our entire world history is dominated by the struggles of individuals, institutions, races and political parties grabbing for power while trying to minimize God as the ultimate source of all power.

As members of a materialistic civilization, many Westerners believe that power means the ability to manipulate people and resources, largely because these are the examples that are available. However, this is not genuine power. True power, which is internally based, is the ability to manifest whatever is needed without taxing the surrounding environment. As we develop a greater emphasis on love and devotion in our communities, we will develop tremendous power to make positive changes happen. This is because we will be aligned with divine power—not our own limited capabilities. Otherwise, we may encounter constant frustration and struggle as we rely on external resources to shape our world, because all material things are temporary and will eventually disappoint us—especially when we need them the most.

Identifying Types of Power

In fact, various types of powers are available to us all to a greater or lesser degree, according to the intensity of our desire and efforts to acquire them. Part of our duty as spiritual warriors is to recapture these various powers and use them to benefit others. When we have power, we have ammunition to make things happen; otherwise we are no more than sentimental philosophers.

The question then becomes whether our power is aligned with God and His agents or not. A true spiritual warrior is wary of misusing power, realizing that ultimately all power belongs to God. We should never forget that the dark forces are also extremely powerful, and they can cause great damage. It is our responsibility to have the discernment to recognize the difference and to align our power only with the highest.

Physical Power

The first and most obvious type of power is physical power. When physical strength is the law by which an individual or group functions, we tend to see a great deal of struggle and abuse such as corruption, war, genocide and ecocide. Although this behavior is extremely animalistic, many societies still function on this level.

Institutional Power

The second kind is institutional power, found in governments, churches, political parties and other organizations. In this type of power, the structure, rules and survival of the organization tend to become ends in themselves while the essence—the original purpose—is forgotten. Institutional power often becomes a matter of leaders occupying figurehead positions and acting in an extremely superficial way, minimizing the genuine care and growth of the people they are supposed to be serving. Most of the available energy is directed toward maintaining the strength and coherence of the organization and the privileges of the leaders.

Viewed in this way, institutional power is not far removed from physical power and violence. In another sense, though, it is worse, because it causes psychological suffering. People who are mistreated by institutions can feel an even greater sense of betrayal, frustration and apathy than victims of physical violence, and many of them can become anarchists. Any situation in which the institution becomes an entity unto itself—as if it were in fact the essence—has the potential to be extremely dangerous because myopic power can hurt, abuse, and exploit people.

Despite the risk of disappointment and corruption, institutions can also serve to bring individuals together to develop their consciousness. Such institutions require leaders who are attuned, powerful, loving, compassionate and focused on truly serving their constituents. In other words, they require spiritual warriors.

Emotional Power

The third category of power is emotional power. Emotional power affects our passions and emotions. It is the power that makes us worship entertainers and athletes as if they were God Himself, to such an extent that we may fall into a trance-like ecstasy or faint in their presence. We all know people who have pictures of movie stars, sports heroes or famous singers on their walls. These "star-struck" individuals dress like them, talk like them, walk like them, and—if we mention some tidbit about them—drop what they are doing and want to hear every last detail. They may stand in line for hours to buy a concert ticket, or wait outside a building ten stories below, not even sure that the object of their affections is at home in the apartment above. This phenomenon unleashes a tremendous amount of power, and that is why certain destructive, scheming individuals with a variety of agendas have infiltrated the entertainment field in order to affect the minds of millions of people.

Academic Power

Next is academic power. Academia has enormous influence in Western civilization. Anyone who has associated with "academic types" knows that our society attributes a tremendous amount of power to these individuals and their mental gymnastics. Although the academic world has a culture of its own, it has a huge impact on the larger society. What these so-called teachers promote actually becomes accepted as the standard of truth and knowledge just because of the powerful mystique they possess in this culture.

The types of power listed so far are essentially material and/or psychological. They are developed by our material efforts and can be used for the upliftment or degradation of society depending on our motivations. They are also temporary: Physical strength can wane, political power and fame can be great one day and gone the next. Even our academic notoriety can vanish overnight when our theories are replaced with new ideas.

Intuitive Power

God and our own spiritual essence guide us from within at all times, however it is up to us how much we listen and pay attention to this guidance. We must also discern what is guidance and what is the influence of our senses and environment. As we develop the ability and trust to hear and let ourselves be guided by this divine inspiration, we develop amazing insight and the capacity to inspire others.

Sacred Power

Sacred power results from following standardized formulas and bona fide systems, teachers and prophets. As people engage in austerities and selfless service, they naturally develop empowerment in harmony with the laws of the universe; they open themselves up to inspiration from higher realms. When directed properly, sacred power can propel them toward transcendence and divine power.

Divine Power

Divine power is the greatest of all, because it contains the highest adoration and appreciation for the Source of all power. Divine power comes to those who realize that they must emulate the lives of the most advanced saints—showing mercy, tolerance, full surrender and love for all of God's creation.

Divine power manifests when we become humble enough to fully offer ourselves to God to be used like puppets. We have reached the highest level of spiritual attainment at this point, when we totally surrender all personal agendas and desires. Then the direct energy of the Lord can enter so that we begin to act in accordance with what He wants to accomplish. Our work is then done as if God is doing it Himself. In Vedic terminology, such empowered individuals are called *avesa avataras,* and this divine power, known as *daiva,* is considered infinitely superior to *purusakara,* which is strength generated by one's own intelligence and abilities. It is this divine empowerment that every spiritual warrior lives for.

Keeping Spiritually Attuned

Moses was one of the most spiritually attuned people of his time, and as a result, God gave him a special task in a period of great calamity. The Lord provided Moses with special sight and direction to help him carry out his assignment. We, too, must be tuned-in to the Lord's mission, not only for our own personal survival, but also for the sake of all the innocent people being victimized by the destructive mindsets of the modern world. We must keep alert to the issues plaguing us because every resident of this planet in some way shares a destiny. If we prepare properly, we may circumvent crises that would otherwise be inevitable.

When we dedicate ourselves to serving the divine will, our capacities may expand in incredible ways. For example, as a youngster, I had an extremely bad stutter that required years of speech therapy. And yet, whenever I discussed holy topics and spirituality, I was fluid and coherent. By the Lord's grace, around that time I became a child evangelist on radio and television. It was as if the Supreme Lord was directly reminding me that He was the one doing the talking.

When presidents, kings or other leaders speak, the idea is not for them to communicate on their own account, but rather to serve as mouthpieces for the Lord. Originally, leaders were meant to act as mediums or as connections to the higher kingdoms. The role of a spiritual teacher or guru emphasizes this connection even more. That person's duty is to act as a "spiritual postman" who delivers transcendental messages to the right addresses.

As for how spiritual warriors should live, Jesus Christ gave us many perfect examples. So did the Buddha and prophet Muhammad, as well as many other great teachers. Once again, we must ask ourselves, why are we not following these examples? We may call ourselves Christians, but are we really Christ-like? If we are Buddhists, are we truly Buddha-like? If we are Muslim, do we behave as Muhammad did? We should be looking at the behavior of Jesus Christ, the Buddha, prophet Muhammad and other great spiritual emissaries for examples of how to conduct ourselves.

When we live for ourselves, we do not care so much about how we affect others. But as we become more spiritually oriented, we specifically concern ourselves with what we say, what we do, why we do it and how we do it, based on how our actions affect the community. This is not overkill, obsession or paranoia. It is perfectly appropriate, because spiritual life is about eternal community and dynamic relationships with God as the nucleus.

As spiritual warriors, our duty is to replicate the original atmosphere of the spiritual kingdom wherever we go. We are not just waiting for a "pie in the sky" outcome or biding our time on earth until we ourselves go to the spiritual kingdom, oblivious to all the pain surrounding us in the meantime. We have an important mission to uplift others and support their spiritual evolution.

Being Responsible Leaders

Although leaders can help others enormously, they can also hurt them more profoundly than anyone else. People give their leaders attention, love and surrender. Successful, God-centered leaders can provide their constituents with more care and guidance than almost anyone can. But when leaders—particularly those who claim to be dedicated to God—fail to put the Lord at the center of their activities, then not only do others experience pain, but they also lose faith in God. As spiritual warriors, we should internalize this truth and constantly remember the importance of integrity as we fulfill our responsibilities.

This is especially true of the spiritual relationship between priest and congregation or guru and disciple. Such a connection is extremely powerful, invigorating and supportive if it occurs according to the proper system. However, when it is misused it can become tyranny and the worst kind of abuse, because it can affect every aspect of existence.

Many people are atheistic these days because of the extreme hypocrisy they have witnessed in so-called spiritual communities. They have lost interest in God and religion because many supposedly "God-centered" people are not genuine. These atheists may not have been strong enough to separate the corruption of the institution from the purity of the actual source.

At the same time, in terms of our own evolution, we must always remember that no religious or spiritual institution in the world can fully save anybody. Sometimes people hide behind institutions, avoiding self-purification. Spiritual institutions are designed for creating a certain atmosphere that allows people to interact, grow and develop their personal relationships with God. Sometimes people confuse the institution with the teachings themselves, to such an extent that they become "burnt out" and forget that these institutions are training grounds—imperfect by nature. We are all ultimately responsible for our own commitments. What happens to us at the time of death is based on the mercy of our mentors and our individual attainments and consciousness, not necessarily upon the institutions with which we were affiliated.

True spiritual warriors are not armchair philosophers. Let us follow their example. As we enter the twenty-first century, we can no longer afford to come together to just "talk about things." As spiritual warriors, we must stop procrastinating and immediately put issues on the table for quick evaluation and implementation.

Unfortunately, the modern paradigm has created the "no-show" leader who sits isolated in an ivory tower pushing buttons and commanding armies. We need to restore the courageous, theocratic leadership of bygone eras when generals gladly accompanied their troops into combat and fought with them in the trenches as qualified and enthusiastic warriors. People would therefore respect them and follow their command. Today's world desperately needs leaders willing to "put their lives on the line" for the collective welfare.

When we select leaders, the rule of thumb should be that we never allow people to represent us who are not ready to roll up their sleeves and make genuine sacrifices on our behalf. Leadership is necessary and welcome, but true leadership means attuning to higher blessings and then sharing these with others by all means available. Such a leader is a true servant-leader, connected with divine power.

Being Alert and Strategic

The situation is relatively simple when we encounter an enemy who is visible and tangible, wearing a particular uniform. It is far more difficult to fight an enemy such as degradation, which is of a more subtle and pervasive nature. We cannot easily fight confusion, lust, and greed if we do not know how to recognize them and root them out.

Those who study the martial arts understand the science of converting energy and using it against an opponent who is projecting energy. Practitioners learn how to channel and sidestep. Like the story of David and Goliath in the Old Testament, sometimes our oppressor wants us to lose faith, because then we lose our greatest weapon. But even when we are armed with faith, we cannot fight oppressors on their own terms. We would be foolish to fight our enemies using the weapons they are most expert with. We have to learn how to get around the opposition's strengths while making the most of our own.

A true spiritual warrior will say: "Whatever it takes, I'm going to be someone who makes a difference in the collective consciousness, starting with how I lead my own life. I'm going to be concerned about others, but I'm not going to try to fit in and appease those who are already caught up in materialistic patterns." Consider firefighters who must risk their lives to save others. While this is part of their job, if they become careless and sacrifice themselves trying to save one child, then they will not be available to save countless others in the future. In a similar way, as spiritual warriors we must always be ready to extend ourselves to help others, but not to the point that we become lost in the process.

We cannot have the upper hand in combat if the enemy has powerful weapons and we show up on the battlefield with a little stick, thinking, "Oh, we are really going to do some great fighting today." We must assess our weapons, and be able to match or do better than our opponent. Remember, in the spiritual arena, these weapons are not material, but spiritual: Love, humility, faith, compassion and the examples we show by our own behavior. If we fight like Arjuna in the *Bhagavad-gita*, totally surrendered to the Lord's will, we can overcome even the most overwhelming odds.

Acting as Revolutionaries

Every bona fide prophet who has brought about important changes in mainstream society has been a revolutionary spiritual warrior. Their very existence was dedicated to annihilating oppression and injustice and bringing out higher truths.

To do this, they had to enter hostile environments and survive long enough to accomplish their aims.

Since being revolutionary means going against the grain, and being spiritual also means standing out and thinking independently, it stands to reason that if we are spiritual, we are naturally revolutionary. It also follows that as spiritual warriors, we must be revolutionaries. To be effective as revolutionaries, we must draw upon powers much higher than ourselves. Those who attempt to be either spiritual or revolutionary, but not both, are simply dabbling reformists who can have no major impact.

As we examine history, we discover a great number of spiritual revolutionaries who paid a high price for their truthfulness. One example is Zoroaster, a Persian mystic, who was stabbed to death because he tried to engage in consciousness-raising. Another example is Socrates, who was put to death because he supposedly poisoned the minds of the youths with anti-material notions. Buddha was stoned and harassed by orthodox Hindus. The Prophet Muhammad's life was threatened by assassination attempts. Jesus was crucified. Saint Teresa of Avila, a nun, had to sneak out and run away from home to practice her life of holy simplicity and renunciation. The founder and leaders of the Ba'Hai faith were often threatened. The parents of St. Thomas Aquinas, a celibate monk, locked him up with a prostitute, hoping that he would break his vows. Saint Francis of Assisi gave away all his possessions and rejected his parents in public to pursue his vocation. In India, there were assassination attempts on Ramanujacarya, Bhaktivinode Thakur and Bhaktisiddhanta Swami.

The list goes on and on. These saintly individuals, and many others, sacrificed everything to remain true to their vision. In many such cases, although it appears that these people suffered needlessly, they actually made a conscious choice to achieve a purpose. From another, higher perspective, since they were totally surrendered to divine will, how could they have done otherwise? After all, how can someone afraid of death teach us that we are not our bodies? How can teachers urge us to know we are eternal if they fear death themselves? How can teachers exhort us to give up all attachments if they cling to anything? Paradoxically, through their renunciation and martyrdom they have attained immortality.

Being Revolutionary in Today's World

One sure sign of our potency as spiritual warriors is the strength of the reaction we provoke from the negative forces. If, as agents of light surrounded by negative influences, we do not "stir things up," then our light is not very bright. When we shine a torch into the darkness, it should devour the darkness and cut a path for others. Then we are fulfilling our roles as spiritual revolutionaries.

Right now, all around the world, our religious and educational institutions are under siege, and we must take notice. For example, certain evangelists are among the most powerful mind programmers in existence. We have to start taking control back by kicking out corrupt leaders, just as Jesus acted against the moneychangers in the temple.

Jesus went directly to places of worship because the corruption of these spiritual places was causing great degradation in society at large. Relatively speaking, it is not so bad when complications are of a political, social or economic nature, because these difficulties are to be expected; they arise out of materialism. However, when the spiritual foundations of a society begin to decay, peoples' hearts become devastated because spirituality is supposed to be the most uplifting and unifying experience that gives meaning to existence.

So what did Jesus do? He started knocking heads and turning over tables. The truth is revolutionary! His actions made an impact at that particular time. Of course, we are not asking you to start turning over church pews and breaking temple windows—you could spend your whole life doing that and still not make a dent. There are too many iniquitous situations to deal with. We do not always need physical or material force to make a difference. What we are requesting from you is something far more effective: Use the sacred and divine powers of righteousness, love, piety and chastity to affect the collective consciousness. These natural qualities are disarming and heart-melting. They penetrate to the core of people's hearts and can bring about genuine healing.

A word of caution is in order here: As we use these powers in the service of healing, we must not be naïve. A useful reminder of this point is the biblical account of Jesus riding into Jerusalem on a donkey. The people of the city gave him the "red carpet" treatment, putting their coats down, placing palm fronds at his feet and calling out joyfully to him with great intensity—the same ones who would later take his life or at least acquiesce to his crucifixion. Let this serve as a warning. Whenever people give us the red carpet treatment, we would be wise to take a careful look at their ulterior motives.

Today our situation is similar to that of Jesus' time. Some of the world's greatest contemporary conflicts are the result of spiritual confusion and insincerity. One religion is fighting another; one ethnic group is cursing another and nations are falling apart. It has gotten so extreme that many people are even cursing God. Naturally, the forces of oppression become exhilarated when this type of outcome occurs.

When we commit to a strong spiritual life and discipline, we are taking a most revolutionary stance. We are saying that we refuse to be blind fools. We will not be docile and passive, nor will we anesthetize ourselves to avoid noticing that the house is on fire. We are denying the selfishness that turns a blind eye to the misery of others as long as we have some degree of temporary comfort.

Standing Firm

Some of us have already experienced harassment because of our genuine desire to combat ignorance. It is widely known that prophets are little respected in their own homes. Therefore, we must be prepared to face intense challenges as we work on our own "turf." The Supreme Lord often arranges for those who are the closest to us to be our biggest tests, allowing us to clearly see the choices before us. What do we really want—the spiritual or the material? Constant challenges will confront us, whether in the form of those most dear to us or other external forces.

Hopefully, none of us will have to undergo tests as severe as those experienced by many of the world's greatest teachers. But if we are serious about becoming anti-material and understanding the nature of the soul, we will not escape challenges completely. Not only will the average people of today consider our behavior quite radical, but also we will be serving the Supreme Personality of Godhead, the most envied Person in the world, while living in the abode of His enemies and offenders. For the most part, we will find ourselves surrounded by people totally dedicated to corrupt business as usual. Those of us who are seeking an easy ride will soon discover that spiritual environments and spiritual commitments are not for the faint-hearted.

If we know ahead of time that we will have tests, when they come we can undergo them with a certain measure of zeal and enthusiasm. Instead of trying to avoid them, we can understand that they are part of the experience that will eventually qualify us to go back home to the kingdom of God. These tests allow us to demonstrate our loving commitment to the Lord, even to the point of engaging in warfare for His glorification. Knowing and remembering this should constantly bring solace to our hearts, even in the most difficult times.

Evaluating Our Actions

Above all, spiritual warriors are servants of the Lord engaged in action for the benefit of others. In the midst of the fray, how do we identify right action? Several methods are available to weigh and measure the morality and feasibility of an action.

One alternative is to imagine what the results would be if a majority of the people performed a similar action. It is said, "We judge a tree by the fruit it bears." Something that is properly aligned will produce beneficial results if the majority of people carry it out. However, when many people indulge in something that is wicked, the resulting misery and contamination leave many victims.

Therefore, as we evaluate a potential action, we can ask ourselves if the action would add to or detract from the progress of human civilization if masses of people performed it. If everybody engaged in abortion, what would be the state of society? Would we have a future? If everyone espoused some kind of sectarian religion, would there be any sense of unity with diversity? If everyone thought that they had the one and only answer to the world's problems, would there be any means of communication? If everyone took to chauvinism, racism, nationalism or tribalism, would we have a viable planet? Clearly, we would not. Most importantly, we should ask ourselves: "Are my thoughts and actions pleasing to God?" Who, by the way, is always watching.

To summarize, we must evaluate every potential action on this basis: If masses of people did it, would it create a higher good? Would God be pleased? This is how ancient culture functioned. Members of a village would feel too embarrassed to do anything hurtful, and could not bear the feeling of letting their community down. Nowadays, because of everyone's laxness, the most successful people are those who can get away with being the most dishonest. For example, drug dealers frequently have the best houses and nicest cars. Very often, the most ingenious minds are used to either invent or defend the most deviant and debilitating behaviors. We must do everything we can to transform this state of consciousness.

Questions & Answers

Question: I read somewhere that if you want to be great, you must shun people of a lower mentality and with less ambition. One author says it is critical to avoid people who do not think at a high level and who are despondent and pathetic. Is this a practical approach to life?

Answer: That is not only totally impractical, but it reflects the kind of arrogance that has caused the inhuman world order we now have. Where do you stop? First you avoid these people. Then you consider them unworthy, so you ostracize them or banish them to another region, or you even try to eradicate them from the face of the earth. So this idea has the germ of genocide in it. In persons of evil intent, it can be an excuse for great suffering and destruction. Today, for example, genetic engineering has the potential to rid the planet of "undesirables." Yet who would decide what is undesirable, and would the result really enhance the general welfare?

We have to be very careful of these ideas, and of our own ambitions that may lead to this kind of thinking. Years ago, some people thought that rainforests were extraneous and that the land could be put to better use. They had no idea what havoc they were inviting. Everything in creation has its use and purpose, even if we cannot see its value. In our ignorance, we tamper with the natural order at our peril.

I cannot overemphasize the danger of this kind of thinking. It is at the origin of much juvenile delinquency, because parents treat their children in a similar manner. In their search for intellectual stimulation, career advancement or social acceptability, parents have abandoned their children for "higher" company, leaving them in the care of others. The children, who sense this neglect, are hurt and angered by it to such an extent that they try to inflict pain on themselves and others.

For the world to survive, great numbers of people must

become God-conscious. They must do their best to think in the way that God thinks. As spiritual warriors, we must take the responsibility of leading and guiding others, making every effort to educate them and elevate them. We should not complain about the burden. Just imagine the uselessness of a teacher without students or a parent without children. Students serve their teachers with their ignorance. Children serve their parents with their innocence. Without these, the cycle of giving and receiving—the very process that gives life meaning—breaks down.

We all have to live together. At the same time, if people around us are constantly draining us in different ways, the quality of our service will decline. That is why we must learn to protect ourselves by radiating love so that others are uplifted by our presence and we do not become depleted by theirs. This involves making our resistance stronger through prayer, meditation and spiritual company, so that we can serve as a nucleus of inspiration for others.

We must become our brothers' and sisters' keepers. We should not shun someone in a difficult situation. We should extend a helping hand. When we do that sincerely, we will find ourselves helped in turn by higher forces. "Modern" people do not seem to realize that the more we help others, the more our own supply of energy and blessings will increase.

The spiritual warrior should be hungry for truth, knowledge and good association—wherever it can be found. My spiritual mentor once said that it is the qualification of great thinkers to pick up the best from the worst. The intelligent should find nectar in a stock of poison, should accept gold even from a filthy place, should accept a good qualified spouse even from an obscure family, and should accept a good lesson even from a street beggar. We can take knowledge from anywhere. There should be no sectarianism. Wherever true knowledge is available, we should accept it. That is the real position of knowledge seekers.

Question: What is the role of knowledge in connection with service? Is it more important to be knowledgeable about scriptures, or to engage in some type of service?

Answer: Both are significant. The more we understand why and how to do the proper thing, the more we will benefit. However, when something is potent and positive, even if we do not fully understand it, there will be some benefit in being a part of it. The highest spiritual connections cannot be made with intellect only. We must each connect with our entire being. This can happen through knowledge connected with compassionate, selfless service.

Once the vice-chancellor of Benares University came to visit the great spiritual master Bhaktisiddhanta Saraswati Swami, who was known throughout much of India as being a very learned scholar. The vice-chancellor explained that he needed answers to some very difficult scriptural questions. Bhaktisiddhanta in turn requested him to go next door to the temple and assist the priests in washing the worship paraphernalia. The vice-chancellor replied, "No, I am asking a very difficult question that they will not be able to answer." However, Bhaktisiddhanta insisted that he ask the priests. When he approached them with his questions, they replied, "Well, we're busy now washing these articles, but when we finish we can try to answer your questions." Even though he was a famous, prestigious scholar, he removed his suit jacket, rolled up his sleeves and humbly began to assist. After the brass was cleaned, he returned to Bhaktisiddhanta who asked him if he had received the answers to his questions. The scholar replied, "Yes. While I was helping to clean the paraphernalia, the answer automatically came to me." Bhaktisiddhanta then explained that spiritual life cannot be fully understood through intellectual ability, but that a proper service attitude brings the necessary insight and understanding. This is an example of the potency of service performed with humility.

Question: With the world heading toward a potential crisis at some point, what should we do? Are we supposed to withdraw from society or should we spend our time preaching and getting the message out?

Answer: The servants of God are always full of compassion—they are not "salvationists." "Salvationism" means that, above all, I am concerned with attaining my own liberation regardless of others. It is a materialistic, egotistical attitude and gradually escalates into different levels of selfish behavior. We must always be willing and available to serve others to the utmost of our abilities. However, just as a doctor must be careful to keep healthy when dealing with sick patients, spiritual warriors must be careful not to get drawn into the materialistic mindset while interacting with materialists.

As mentioned earlier, our duty as spiritual warriors is to create the original environment of the spiritual kingdom wherever we go. We do not want to go to heaven or the spiritual kingdom alone. We do not isolate ourselves and become oblivious to all the suffering around us. Naturally, we will not want to associate ourselves with certain activities because they are not in harmony with who we are. This is not running away or avoiding a situation; it is simply a matter of being selective. When we are selective in a mature way, our experiences are of a higher quality and we get less distracted from our goals.

Spiritual warriors should be focused, always recognizing and appreciating the unusual blessings we have somehow had the good fortune to receive. We should feel great compassion for the materialists who are captured by gross sense gratification and also for those who have acquired a little knowledge and then refused to go further. It is our responsibility to help wherever we can.

Question: How do we find our path, our purpose, our mission or what we need to accomplish? How do we find out what that is if we really do not know?

Answer: You can offer a simple prayer. "Dear Lord, please put me in whatever situation is best to help me to love you unconditionally." But we must be careful in interpreting the response. In general we do not know what we have experienced in previous lives and what kind of karma is following us. Consequently, we are often unaware of the games the mind and intelligence will play with the signals and messages we may receive. We have many ways to rationalize anything. We should be particularly suspicious if the "answer" reinforces our ego and makes us feel important.

The more serious we are spiritually, the more willing we will be to pray like this: "Dear Lord, I am yours. Use me as necessary. I understand that you have in mind the best thing for me. I know that you are the best friend, the best lover, the best caretaker, and the best provider, and that all of my difficulties are because I am interfering with Your plan for me. Therefore I am now making a tremendous leap of faith and asking you to take away my interference. Just make me do the things that are best." Pray like that and you will see things happen in your life. Of course, then you may have to pray another prayer: "Dear Lord, help me deal with it!"

Chapter **10**

Serving the world community

Creating a Viable Future

An African proverb says: "We have borrowed the future from our children, rather than inheriting it from our ancestors." Indeed, the future belongs to our children—it is theirs, not ours. It is our duty, our obligation and even our joy to protect that future for them at all costs.

As spiritual warriors, we have a significant role to play in safeguarding this future. To preserve a viable planet for the next generation, we must balance and integrate the spiritual, metaphysical and material aspects of our present reality. Recognizing the need for a more natural way of life, we can strive to live in harmony with nature and in full awareness of our environment, understanding the ebb and flow of nature's various cycles. We can also appreciate the importance of finding our true independence by depending on God in all circumstances while at the same time applying techniques of spiritual awakening in our daily lives.

We are in the midst of a serious shift in global consciousness, and many spiritual warriors will be significant players in this transition. We are moving away from a culture of taking toward a culture of giving. We should revel in the fact that this is a time of spiritual harvest and that many of us are gardeners who will help in this harvest period. As each of us releases our own negative patterns, we advance spiritually and enable our role in this harvesting to expand. On the other hand, if we fail to work out these patterns and remain subject to our lower impulses, we do a great disservice to ourselves and also to the world. We must fulfill our responsibility as spiritual warriors to model new thought patterns and behaviors so that we can help create new communities based on wholesome, natural interactions.

True Culture

God has given human beings a framework for wholesome living in the form of true culture. True culture exists when a society recognizes and supports spiritual principles as the legitimate foundation of human life, and organizes all its structures and activities to enable people to progress toward the goal of spiritual liberation.

One of the universal elements of true culture is dance. Like music, expression through dance is found in all ancient cultures. For instance, while Lord Chaitanya was traveling through India, there were constant gatherings where intense dancing and chanting the names of God would go on such that the chanters were bound together in states of ecstasy and love.

What is the role of culture? Culture provides an environment that encourages certain kinds of growth. In laboratories, for example, scientists use certain chemical solutions to create cultures; without these environments, the growth of particular cells would not be possible. A woman's womb is also like a culture, made up of the elements that foster her embryo's development. When the woman's internal environment is altered by foreign and unwanted elements such as tobacco or intoxicants, the growth of that embryo can be stunted or deformed. In addition, proper food digestion requires a particular bacterial culture. In general, the Almighty Creator has designed natural habitats and environmental cultures in which all living beings can thrive.

The Supreme Creator and His agents always equip their creations with precisely what they need to fulfill their purpose. For example, bees are perfectly equipped to draw honey and kangaroos have the ideal pouch to hold their offspring. As human beings, we are provided with a mind and intelligence that precisely suit our intended purpose of elevating our consciousness.

Human life is meant to be more than just eating, sleeping, mating and defending. Indeed, the animals are far more expert in eating, sleeping, mating and defending than we are. If the human form were meant only for these activities, then God somehow got it wrong and gave us the improper equipment to fulfill our purpose. But we can be sure that God, nature and biology never get it wrong. We are meant to use our equipment to claim our full spiritual heritage.

We must notice what has real, lasting value and treasure what is truly sacred. In today's world, this means that we must revitalize the human spirit. Rather than continuing on our bad-bargain shopping spree, sacrificing tradition for fads, wisdom for information, loyalty for popularity and lust for love, we must learn to be more discerning, integrated, interdisciplinary and philosophical. Instead of running after short-term pleasures that eventually disappoint us and provide no lasting happiness, we must learn to seek the pleasures that take time to accumulate yet later provide joy and exhilaration. Everything has a price. If we are willing to pay the price of perseverance and commitment, then we will be qualified to receive our rewards accordingly. This is the approach of true culture.

The same can be true of our daily work. We all work in order to provide for ourselves in a world that seems hostile to our basic existence. Yet there are ways to bring about higher states of being that move beyond simply existing. For example, we can each dedicate our work to the benefit of the whole and offer each action as a service to something greater than ourselves. Real, ancient culture was designed to do just that. As spiritual warriors, we can be attentive to techniques for developing this higher state of consciousness wherever possible in modern society.

A Spiritual Nucleus

We should appreciate both the purpose and process of culture. In ancient cultures around the world, a spiritual nucleus held each society together. There was an understanding of extended family, of motherhood and fatherhood as a service and responsibility that extended the longevity and quality of the community. In almost all these cultures, God played a central role and the people understood the higher purpose of human life. Indeed, although our spiritual essence is encased in a material body, we are always metaphysically endowed and spiritually competent. We simply need an environment that encourages us to invest time and energy in bringing that spiritual competence to the surface.

True culture is based upon four principles: austerity, cleanliness, mercy and truthfulness. These principles are fundamental to our purification and surrender to God's will. As we look back over millennia of human history, these four principles were the prominent features of the first age, the Age of Truth. In that age, almost every human being was a qualified priest or yogi of the highest order. Beings of such strong character were not at all seduced by the deluding energies of Maya.

In modern times, we must make a determined effort to reinstate these principles as the foundation of our civilization.

As spiritual warriors, we must live by eternal spiritual principles and measure what is wrong and what is right by a spiritual yardstick—and encourage others to do so. As we find spiritual solutions to material problems and fulfill our role as representatives of spiritual culture here on the material platform, we will experience the dynamics of spiritual life more fully and help build true culture wherever we go. Although many challenges and difficulties may confront us, our relationship with God and our awareness of who we truly are will give us great strength.

Combining the Best from East and West

The ancient Eastern model of culture considers people to belong to the whole—as parts of the universe, parts of nature, parts of their communities and parts of their family units. It assumes that people are intrinsically responsible and will therefore commit themselves to the well-being of future generations. Members of African culture live by the mindset "I am because we are." They recognize how much they have received from their ancestors and the extent to which their tribal community and extended family nourish them. Because they do not feel separate, they accept responsibility for preserving the gifts they have received for those who will come after them.

The modern world has an unprecedented opportunity to combine Eastern and Western traditions into a harmonious synthesis. Aware of this, Srila Prabhupada, the founder of the International Society for Krishna Consciousness, made a significant contribution when he brought the best from the East and connected it with the best from the West. Srila Prabhupada explained that, materially, India is like a lame man and spiritually, the West is like a blind man. Separately, East and West have serious difficulties. Despite its clear vision, the East is materially challenged by resources and expertise, and struggles for advancement. At the same time, the West lacks spiritual vision despite its numerous material accomplishments. Srila Prabhupada chose to combine the vitality of the West with the wisdom of the East to create a worldwide movement that could help usher in a new era for humankind.

The marriage of East and West need not be an idealistic attempt to create a utopian society. Instead, it can provide practical knowledge that helps us create an environment based on eternal spiritual principles rather than external superficialities. When practiced at its highest level, this combination of Eastern and Western thought can be a powerful vehicle for disseminating the Supreme Lord's message—it is not demigod worship or impersonalism, but selfless service to humanity and to God.

The Sacred Art of Dying

Many ancient cultures had profound teachings about death and dying. We can study these teachings in such writings as the Egyptian and Tibetan *Books of the Dead* and India's *Bhagavad-gita* and *Bhagavata Purana*. These cultures were not morbidly focused on death, but rather understood that death is a natural part of the cycle of life. Such texts prepared people for the hereafter and made their transition easier.

Since many of these cultures engaged in astrology, palmistry and other intuitive practices, many people could estimate in advance the time of their death. Consequently, they would prepare by praying or by visiting sacred shrines and temples. When they fell ill, they would often go to a sacred pilgrimage place to sleep in a shrine or temple because they knew that while the physical body was at rest their subtle body could connect with other dimensions and be rejuvenated.

Spiritual warriors must acquaint themselves with some of these practices in order to understand first-hand that concrete information is available about death, the hereafter and the

Reestablishing True Culture

To a large extent, our present environment is unnatural, and this unnatural condition is a consequence of a serious imbalance in our approach to life. We must regain control of our lives and habitats. We must restore our school systems back to a state that does not require metal detectors as we usher in the students; where we do not have to experience chaos and carnage as our children terrorize their classmates and teachers. We must regain our very sanity. To reestablish a healthy, natural environment, we must rediscover the divine harmony and order inherent within ourselves and express it in the world. That is why, as spiritual warriors, it is so important to do our inner work of self-observation and self-purification. Only then do we become prepared to play our role in establishing a true culture based on tolerance, respect for nature, simplicity, self-sufficiency, and loving community. Once established, such a culture will perpetuate a positive cycle, fostering in turn the development of whole, healthy, joyful human beings and provide promise for the future of the world.

Tolerance and Interfaith

True culture is based on inclusiveness, tolerance and acceptance. Now more than ever, spiritual warriors must use good judgment, because there are forces on the planet actively trying to fragment society and create anarchy. Unfortunately, the world's religions are particularly susceptible to divisive tactics. As spiritual warriors, we cannot allow ourselves to fall into such a trap, fighting others over such details as the "correct" name of God. Let us examine this particular example a little further. Most people have more than one name. With the wide variety of languages on the face of the earth, how could the Supreme Source of all things have only one name? There is at least one name of God in every language, and many traditions have multiple names for various circumstances. Yet some elitists have created the false, absurd notion that they have gained the special favor of the Lord and that no one else knows God's name.

Despite the fact that all of God's spiritual emissaries have given us a similar message, today their followers are killing, maiming and sabotaging each other. The fundamentalists of the world, regardless of their sect, say that everyone else is going to the devil. Sometimes intense conflict even occurs within the same religion. Many Muslim, Buddhist, Hindu and Christian groups cannot even be on the same podium with members of another group within their own tradition. In the Bible, John 1:12 states, "As many as received Him, to them He gave the power to be sons of God." The Bhagavad-gita tells us that we are all parts of the same God and that we are suffering particularly due to improper use of the senses and the mind. Also in the Bhagavad-gita (4.11), the Lord states: "As all surrender unto me, I reward them accordingly. Everyone follows my path in all respects." The most significant concern is the quality of our surrender to the Godhead.

Connection with Nature

Genuinely spiritual culture is in harmony with the cosmos, with nature and with natural laws. In modern society, surrounded as we are by artificial environments, we will all benefit from a closer relationship with the natural world. We inherently understand that a natural environment is important for our rejuvenation. People spend money to rent or buy property with a scenic view, and fix their homes or apartments to look natural. They install fountains and use plants, mirrors and natural backgrounds to give a sense of connection to nature.

It is important to spend more time in nature, going to parks, to the forest and the country. We can take time to commune with the elements and talk with the plants and the insects. This is not merely trivial sentiment. When we are near streams, rivers or water or walking in the park, we feel a sense of rejuvenation because we are imbibing some of the natural energy that has been taken from us by artificial surroundings.

Doing things more naturally is also more in alignment with the divine order, which allows us to be more transcendental. This is because a natural lifestyle sensitizes us and enables us to commune with the essence within and around us. It is extremely difficult to be spiritual when our materialistic desires and habits entrap us, and we are acting wrong, eating wrong, thinking wrong—deluded and distracted by many of the artificial concoctions of this society. How, then, can we aspire to transcendence?

Simplicity and Self-Sufficiency

Spiritual culture is focused upon the kingdom of God and serves as an arena in which human beings can learn to love God more. A spiritual warrior's eyes are always open. Knowing the dangers of selfishness and greed, we embrace practices that help us break the bonds of this material realm. This is the real meaning of simplicity and self-sufficiency.

The natural order is very simple. Much of what society has given us is artificial, encouraging us to lust after commodities. The more commodities we possess or the more toys we acquire, the greater is our supposed "success." We have developed a consciousness based on quantity, but not quality. Yet everything that humankind needs for growth, progress, and proper communal, social and familial interaction is readily available. The quality of our lives simply depends on how we use, misuse or abuse what we have received. When there is too much abuse—whether in this life or a previous one—then higher forces will impose deprivation. This is why we often see many people, even "innocent" children, born into and remaining in abject poverty.

A life of simplicity and self-sufficiency creates a potent antidote for almost all material ills because it does not feed the flames of materialism and brings about a harmonious attitude toward Mother Nature. Simplicity helps us recognize the essence of life and, because it provides few external factors to distract us, makes us less vulnerable to temptation. We gain more control of our environment and experience less stress.

We must also be careful not to over-collect possessions. Those who place a high value on property often have trouble in interpersonal relationships. They frequently carry a burden of guilt for their greed, pride and selfishness and are concerned about losing what they own. Over-collecting has deprived them of the necessary time to get personally acquainted with people, and so they try to fill the void with more possessions to cover up their loneliness. We should always remember that hoarding violates the natural order and can create many problems. Rupa Goswami, the great renunciate of Vrndavan, India mentions that over-collecting and over-endeavoring for mundane things will cause stagnation and destruction in spiritual life. As an exemplary representative of spiritual community, he is endowed with great authority to advise others on what to implement and what to avoid.

His famous book, *The Nectar of Instruction* offers clear guidance on what activities are beneficial for the success of the individual and society at large.

We can learn to live more simply by using natural resources in a proper, balanced way rather than abusing and exploiting them. When we recognize and connect with the earth as a living organism we naturally feel more whole and secure knowing that we are in harmony with our surroundings, resting on our mother's bosom. When we develop a genuinely respectful attitude toward our environment—not just in words, but in actions—we receive more assistance and protection from all the wonderful guardians provided by our Mother-Father God.

We must move toward self-sufficiency and live in accordance with divine law. Self-sufficiency allows us to be independent, and it is natural to have control over the variables in our lives. We must remove ourselves from the "opulence" that technology has convinced us is a necessity. When we depend on these technologies excessively, we live an unnatural life, experience mental and physical stress, and have few inner resources to fall back on when difficulties arise. When we are slaves to luxury, we are vulnerable and we miss out on the real joys of life.

Today many people are taking courses in sociology and psychology, yet they cannot begin to fathom how much their own minds will be devastated during trying situations. There is nothing wrong with studying abstractions like psychology and sociology, but we must go beyond them for a real understanding of our nature. Many people cannot even function for a few days unless a television set or some other source of non-stop noise is available; silence makes them crazy! That is how unnatural they have become.

One of the principles related to personal self-sufficiency is the importance of good nutrition. As spiritual warriors, we must always remember that our body is our armor. We should follow a highly nutritious, natural and vegetarian diet. We should be careful not to be "fast-food" vegetarians, trying to subsist on fried, canned and frozen foods, because this will eventually backfire. Instead, we can grow our food on the land, and then prepare and eat it. We should eat as much natural, raw and living food as possible—fruit and vegetable juices, roughage, sprouts and green leafy vegetables.

The culture of devotion is a more subtle aspect of self-sufficiency. If we are strong, self-reliant spiritual warriors, we will not allow our minds be captured by any system whose inherent nature is degrading to the soul. This is why self-sufficient rural living can actually be quite revolutionary. A life dedicated to simple living and high thinking, beyond the allure and imprisonment of modern culture, gives us the higher consciousness to resist material enticements and become strong spiritual warriors. Those who have made a commitment to offset negativity and ignorance in the world must simplify and streamline their lives in order to create room for what is more valuable.

Strength in Community

Around the world, spiritual culture is intimately related to a strong sense of community. One great ploy of the negative forces in this age is to divide everyone by means of personal ambition and the desire to distinguish oneself from others. Yet throughout history, the most God-conscious people have often been extremely modest and have belonged to an organized group or order.

Many indigenous peoples in Africa, India, Tibet and South America lived (and still do) in closely-knit communities, where their strong affiliation can be seen in their manner of speech, dress, work and worship. They have received sufficient strength to withstand cultural and spiritual erosion through this unity of will and action. Together, they have been able to penetrate many artificial and flamboyant expressions of individuality and reach more profound levels of intimacy and understand more subtle aspects of existence.

Community is the law of "safety in numbers" in action. We can unite in large groups to chant and pray together, protecting ourselves from harm and evoking tremendous power that creates a protective bubble. A strong community can give us wonderful guidance and security to help us cope with our daily challenges. That is why we should continually refresh ourselves in the company of other spiritual warriors.

Members of a tightly knit community have the interests

of the whole at heart and become their brothers' and sisters' keepers. Being our brothers' and sisters' keepers means loving one another as we love ourselves. We cannot muster the faith to care for anyone but ourselves if we fear resource shortage or do not truly understand who supplies these resources. Nothing material lasts forever, but the love we give to another and the sacrifices we make for something greater than ourselves do endure because they come from a higher source.

The natural and innocent love that we imbibe in a close community burns away behaviors that are unnatural and unhealthy. Thus, we grow spiritually in such an environment. In addition, our ancestors appreciated that love and fear affect a person's immune system. At one time, it was openly acknowledged that some persons died from heartbreak, and even today, medical science understands that people who receive fewer hugs and less affection are more prone to degenerative diseases. Community life can be good for our health.

Creating Community

Community is not simply a system or a set of concepts and ideas; it is a living organism whose personality is the aggregate of each individualized consciousness. Like any living being, community has unlimited potential, yet must be protected and nourished in order to develop fully. Community is like our own physical bodies, which support many living organisms. When all the parts are functioning together harmoniously, then the body is healthy and its experiences are dynamic, auspicious and directed to the well-being of all.

We can create community by several methods—by crisis, by accident, or by design. When people come together in crisis, their relationships may not be lasting, because the situation is temporary and based on external conditions that are affecting people at a particular moment. Community can be formed accidentally as well, but there will be no glue, or purpose, to seal the relationships.

In contrast, community by design has a purpose and plan for coming together. At the root of the word "community" is the idea of communion—meaning wholeness, communication, cooperation and commonality. Without these elements, there is only pseudo-community, where people come together to discover what they can take or use rather than what they can become, what they can share and how they can serve. Often we hide behind institutions and situations and become impersonal.

Yet a sense of community only emerges as a result of honest communication, cooperation and fellowship. Community with nothing to communicate is simply an artificial grouping without life. When a community has genuine vitality, the members have something to communicate and share with each other. Each member is straightforward while at the same time being sensitive to the feelings of others. Real community is never exclusive. When the nucleus of a community is strong, it becomes flexible enough to balance, adjust, expand and include the new. Real community is never exclusive or ambiguous. A community truly based in spirituality is always ready to inspire everyone to realize that God is there for them.

Four Principles of Community Building

In most ordinary communities, people mechanically go about their business, tolerating the trials of daily life while suffering underlying feelings of anxiety. Yet, as spiritual warriors, we do not want ordinary communities; we want vital, living environments in which people can thrive. As we have seen, this can occur when we elevate our individual consciousness, which in turn boosts the community atmosphere and uplifts the environment. The success of a community is based on what the individuals bring into the environment.

Remember the spiritual warrior's checklist from chapter 7:
1. Sense control and mastery of the mind
2. Humility
3. Fearlessness
4. Truthfulness
5. Compassion and pridelessness
6. Material exhaustion and disinterest in material rewards
7. No idle time
8. Patience and selflessness
9. Firm faith
10. Perseverance
11. Curiosity and enthusiasm to learn and grow
12. Surrender to divine will

We are going to give you another set of four important tools which, in combination with the spiritual warrior's checklist, are sufficient to raise individual and collective consciousness, connect community members with divine power and provide solace as we face the challenges of becoming transcendental. Reflect on these tools as a daily meditation, and make the choice to shift your consciousness:

1. Treat everyone you encounter as if the success of your spiritual life depends upon the quality of your interactions with them.

2. Reflect upon the person you love the most, and aspire to treat everyone with that same quality of love.

3. View all conflicts as your own fault first.

4. Realize that the people in your present environment might very well be the people with whom you will live out your life, and who will be with you at the time of death.

The first two technologies are closely related. If we recognize the spiritual significance of each encounter and offer every person the same quality of love that we direct toward our most beloved, our interactions are bound to be positive and uplifting. We will immediately experience an elevation of consciousness, because others will feel—consciously or unconsciously—that we truly care for them. We are not simply tolerating them or having a business exchange with them. This positive energy will rebound and return to us.

These first two technologies are not always easy; indeed, they are often extremely difficult. Other people sometimes treat us unkindly or abusively. Yet we should persist in treating them as if our spiritual life, or even our physical life, were hanging in the balance and depended upon our behavior. God has arranged for the associations that we have—people are in our lives and pass through our lives for a reason. Spiritual warriors look for the lessons to be learned and take advantage of the associations whether the other person does or not. When we treat each person wholeheartedly in this way, we will quickly recognize that God is everywhere and in every person.

Most parents are patient and forgiving toward their children. Imagine how powerful that type of loving care could be when directed toward a co-worker, a next-door neighbor or a stranger on the highway. We have all noticed the deterioration in people's behavior these days. On the roadways, we have probably witnessed drivers blaring their horns at cars that inadvertently "cut them off," and then accelerating in order to "get even" with the offenders. The people around them become understandably fearful and try to avoid getting caught in this mini-drama. The atmosphere becomes highly charged with negative energy.

Yet if these angry people had viewed the offending drivers as their most beloved, their responses would have been more forgiving and patient. While they may scold their most beloved, they do so based on concern for the beloved's well-being, not based on rage, which can quickly spread throughout the surrounding environment. We should not condone reckless behavior, but we certainly do not need to contaminate the atmosphere with poisonous feelings, which are often far more harmful than the original transgression. When we truly have people's best interests at heart, then even if they make a mistake, they will feel our goodwill, and the interactions between us will be more pure and true. Such an attitude will affect both parties in a positive way, just as "road rage" can negatively afflict so many people. Such positive behavior creates powerful, cohesive communities.

The third technology is to view any problem in a relationship as our own fault first—whatever the issue may be. As long as we consider the difficulty to be caused by another person's wrongdoing, we are closed to our own contribution to change and healing. All we do by engaging in blame is to intensify the conflict—we help neither the other person nor ourselves. But if we see the problem as our fault—the consequence of our saying something that was misunderstood, or of not offering proper assistance, or of failing in some way we are not even aware of—then we can move beyond material consciousness to a higher level. It is at this higher level that conflicts get resolved, and, at the very least, we have established a good starting point for trying to reach a harmonious outcome.

We are in a wartime situation and do not have time for personality problems! Personality is simply something we picked up this lifetime based on some acculturation, and it is something that we will change in this lifetime or lose in another. Personality is simply some "stuff" you have picked up, so drop it if it is unhealthy! We do not have the time to be stagnated or slowed down because someone looked at us a certain way, said something rude, ignored us or did not understand us sufficiently.

Remember to not see conflict as something negative, but as an outgrowth of the diversity that characterizes our thoughts, attitudes, beliefs, social systems and structures. Most importantly, we should see it as a time to grow and learn how to serve each other better. Conflict requires at least two people to have life, and therefore it only takes one individual to be strong enough to create healing instead of conflict. If we have enough concern for others, we can find the strength to help and to look beyond our own ego. We must realize that the quality of our life is dependent on how we serve others—this is the position of very advanced souls. Even if someone offends an advanced soul, the more advanced soul takes the humble position in always accessing God consciousness, humility, and devotion. They have loving feelings even toward their greatest enemies—this is transcendental consciousness; not material consciousness or mixed devotional consciousness. They relate to the God presence in each person, and in this way they experience God consciousness everywhere and in everyone.

The fourth spiritual technology is to associate with the people in our environments in the mood that we are sharing our lives with them, and they may be the people who are there for us when we die. We must truly attempt to understand this idea, which is not just a theoretical proposition. God has arranged all our relationships, and it is up to us to use them for our greater spiritual good. Our consciousness is deeply affected by the company we keep and the environments in which we immerse ourselves. If we live with others, we must make every effort to enhance our associations with them to create an uplifting atmosphere.

The nature of our consciousness at the time of death determines our next existence. If our consciousness is proper, we will enter directly into the spiritual kingdom. If not, we may become distraught as we recognize the missed opportunities caused by our lack of commitment. That is why the quality of our association with others is so important. Those with whom we spend our lives can help us use this precious human form wisely—and we can do the same for them—so that at death we will be spiritually prepared.

Building Strong Families

A tribe exists in East Africa that understands and utilizes the power of community, the power of rites of passage and the power of mantra—the use of sound to affect our circumstances. In this particular tribe, birth is not viewed merely in physical terms, but also as the arrival of the soul in a new environment.

When a couple is ready to procreate, the woman first goes out into nature to contact—through deep, contemplative meditation—the soul that will come into her womb. In her meditation she tries to hear the song or mantra associated with that soul. Once she hears that song, she shares it with her husband. Together they sing the song as they unite to conceive a child.

The consciousness of the man and woman during sexual relations determines the quality of the soul that they will bring into the community. The men and women of this African tribe understand the importance of consciousness, and they act in a deliberate manner to invite a highly evolved soul into their family.

In the modern world, far too many souls are conceived in an environment of lust and violence rather than love. No wonder so many children are violent! When the consciousness at conception is based on greed, manipulation and self-centeredness, the children born of that union are quite naturally oriented toward selfish individualism. Such egocentricity leads to many problems and, for some children, becomes the start of a violent, frustrating, empty life.

In this same African community, once conception has occurred, the mother and father sing the mantra to the growing child in the womb. The child's consciousness is already being influenced in a positive manner by external sound vibrations, even while the fetus is in the mother's body. Before the birth, the mother and father share the song with the midwives and the community elders so that they can join together to invite the child into the world during the birthing process.

In a true community, midwives and elders should participate in the births of all children. Important events in our lives should not be undertaken alone. As the child in this African tribe grows and passes through the different stages of life, the same mantra is sung. For every celebration, every achievement, and even every major difficulty, the community sings the same mantra to create intimacy and provide support.

Yet in Western culture, people struggle to survive because they do not receive the cultural support to help them move through issues and adjust to different stages of life. Rites of passage are important to reinforce our sense of belonging and to help us clearly understand our responsibilities within the community. Rites of passage also give community members an opportunity to honor our life transitions and to indicate what is now expected from us. Most of all, rites of passage remind us of our place in the whole and of the connection of our individual lives to a higher, spiritual purpose. Because modern society does not have true rites of passage, we often make choices based on relative, transitory values without an understanding of ancient wisdom and without blessings from higher realms.

In this tribe, the use of the person's mantra continues into old age and even after physical death. Just as community members once invoked the birth of that soul by means of a particular sound vibration, they now sing the mantra after death to ensure a safe journey and glorify the soul's relationship with God. They acknowledge that the soul is passing on to its next existence and hoping that the soul will return directly to its home in the kingdom of God.

These rituals form a stark contrast to a lifestyle based on technology and gross materialism. Modern society engages in behavior that does not develop our inner faculties, fails to reinforce our experience of the divine and cannot move beyond what we see, hear, feel, touch and taste. Such a lifestyle is extremely limited, and many of today's problems stem from this restricted view.

We must be more family oriented if we want to be successful at nation-building and improving the environment we live in because the family is the microcosm of the planet. When family units begin breaking apart, we should understand that society is on a rapid path downward. Civilization and higher consciousness decline rapidly when the family unit means less and less.

Cooperation and Community

Cooperation can occur in communities in different ways and in different forms. For example, cooperation can be vertical or horizontal. The idea of simply serving—a superior, the boss, the manager, the elder, the mentor, or the guru—is vertical. All too often, when community members have reverence for the people in authority they have little time for anyone else. Real cooperation must go beyond the vertical level to include the horizontal level as well.

Horizontal cooperation is even more important than vertical, because the way we relate to our peers demonstrates our true level of evolution. Our pattern of dealing vertically with authority represents only one aspect of ourselves—one that is often a facade anyway. Our true selves show in the horizontal direction because we have to make genuine connections with people. This is not always easy. Actually, the more we succeed in relating closely to our peers, the more powerful our vertical connection becomes, because we purify ourselves in the process.

A community gains its strength from the quality of its relationships. Indeed, every aspect of creation is involved in relationship, and, as spiritual warriors, we should view all interactions in terms of the kinds of relationships we want to achieve. Relationships within communities must be strong, or anything the community builds will be temporary and cosmetic.

If we think that individualism is more important than community consciousness, we are inviting endless rounds of problems and divisions. We must understand that everything is connected and that everything affects everything else. We must treat whatever God has given us with reverence and learn how to use it properly rather than abusing it.

Addressing Conflicts in Community

Whenever people come together, differences are inevitable. Yet differences need not be divisive. Actually, when a community has a strong nucleus, such difficulties will not cause lasting problems. As spiritual warriors, we must learn to value differences and understand how they can be assets rather than threats. A strong community will appreciate the diversity among its members, understanding how it can enrich and strengthen the group.

In a community, we are constantly affecting the consciousness of others and, in turn, others are producing an effect upon us. The Lord arranges for community members to help one another grow. For example, at times we may find ourselves obligated to work with someone whose personality we dislike—yet by associating with that person we may discover an opportunity to learn, or teach, some lesson. That is why, if we choose to, we can view conflict as an exciting adventure in self-discovery. This attitude will make the resolution of conflicts go much more smoothly and we will begin to see conflict as simply a natural outgrowth of the diversity that characterizes our thoughts, attitudes and beliefs. The constructive use of conflict can bring out alternatives in thinking and behavior for the benefit of all parties, providing creative solutions to the challenges of community living. Most importantly, we can consider conflict as a process that helps us discover ways of serving the needs of others better.

The success of a community is directly related to its ability to resolve conflicts. We should expect problems, but success depends upon how we deal with those problems. A community that cannot master the resolution of conflicts in a healthy way can gradually deteriorate and ultimately self-destruct.

Maintaining a Positive Community Environment

When people meet, their conversations often focus on personal difficulties: "Let me tell you how bad things are. I've got so many problems—I mean it's really bad. You don't know how bad it is. My health is so bad. I've got so many creditors; my lights were turned off yesterday; my water is going to be turned off; my car is going to be repossessed; my bicycle has a flat tire. I don't know what to do." The litany goes on, reporting one problem after another.

Although it makes sense to share our problems with each other, what happens when every single encounter with a particular person requires us to listen repeatedly to a laundry list of suffering? After a while, we try to avoid such people, because we hear nothing positive and are tired of such a resolutely negative perspective on life. Without being artificially optimistic, we can always find something good in our experiences, even the most painful ones. Difficult people offer us a challenge to see their good qualities, which do exist beneath the surface if we are willing to look for them. When we consciously decide to see the good in others, we are better equipped to discover the meaning behind all our encounters. The person who drives us crazy is in our life for a reason. Unless we look deeply at the situation we cannot discover the lesson and we will find no solace.

Just as we should always seek the good in people and situations, we should also maintain a positive environment in our communities. This means not letting nonsense run rampant, because it will only drag down the rest of the community. If people under your leadership are acting badly, you must put an end to such behavior. By allowing negativity to flourish, you are perpetuating disorder and therefore not serving the community properly.

Although we cannot make a person or a group behave in a certain way, we can certainly reinforce behavior—both positive and negative. This is a power that we should always keep in mind. If we do not succeed in changing negative patterns for the better, we may have to refuse further contact. For example, a doctor's role is to diagnose and treat disease. If a patient refuses to comply with the doctor's orders, then the doctor may say, "I cannot accept you as a patient." Otherwise, the doctor would be a cheater because the patient would be paying money and not receiving proper care.

This is like a parent whose child has begun to run wild. A loving parent who cannot change a constantly intoxicated child, for example, may have to say at some point, "You are not going to do this in my house! I love you too much and I'm not going to see you coming home drunk like this. If you are not going to change, then you have to move out. I'm not going to support your behavior or accommodate your lifestyle." This is not to say that we should immediately reject people if something negative happens. We have already discussed the importance of being able to resolve conflicts, but in some cases we run head-on into the same wall over and over and must take more effective action.

A few resolutely negative members of a community can gradually destroy the community bond. People inherently know this; that is why parents are so particular about their children's friends. When we are around negativity it will begin to affect us; it is contagious.

The same is true about positive people. Our emotional and mental states create an energy field that affects others. Everything is alive, including the unseen atmosphere that surrounds us. When we uplift other people, we enable them to extend that same positive energy to others in their own environment. The positive energy ultimately returns to us in countless ways. As we create a positive, uplifting environment, we help our communities at the same time that we are helping ourselves. Maintaining a positive environment will minimize problems and help those around us to flourish.

Make the Commitment

This period in history is an extremely important time for making serious commitments. As spiritual warriors, our basic commitment should be to develop greater God-consciousness. There is no time to waste. Around the planet, the communities in which spiritual warriors live must become so powerful that everyone becomes surcharged with spiritual energy. People should feel that they have entered another dimension when they visit these communities. They will see the love and respect that spiritual warriors have among themselves and be inspired to join our powerful community, or create their own. That is how the positive energy can spread.

We must have so much love for each other that we constantly encourage each other to be loyal to their vows, to be loyal to their process and to be loyal to their natural position as eternal spirit souls. Please hear this call to arms for strong spiritual warriors—join our spiritual battle and take your natural position as servants to your beloved Lord. If we do this, we will feel solace in our hearts even in the most difficult times.

Questions & Answers

Question: You stressed the importance of health, nutrition and communing with nature... do you include the importance of exercise in that category? I am wondering because I have noticed in my life that any time I feel overwhelmed or overworked, if I can go outside and walk for even 15 minutes, my head feels much clearer. I don't know if it's the actual exercise or maybe the smiles and pleasantries I exchange with people I encounter, but I do know that I feel energized and more focused. Could you address that?

Answer: Yes, exercise is very important for your consciousness to maintain a high level of resistance against the negative energies—too often people discount the benefit exercise has upon their mind and consciousness. It is easy to see the benefits to your body. When we are in anxiety our body will tense up; that stress does not simply remain in our mind. Exercise such as walking relieves some of that tension and elevates the consciousness, especially if we are able to walk in pleasant places like parks, woods or near the water. But when we walk we should remember to be "mindfully walking" and we should try to share some love and compassion with the people we come in contact with. This sharing will come back to us in so many positive uplifting ways. If you are so upset that you don't even want to see people then just go to the park and show a little love toward the birds and the crickets or the dogs and cats, and that will come back to you also. It is very dangerous to not be mindful of our health.

We must develop mindfulness in all of our activities. Everything has an essential nature and ultimately the essence of everything is the Supreme Personality of Godhead. Mindfulness means being able to perceive and bring out the essence—how to constantly see God in everything and everywhere at all times. Our breathing, our walking, our hearing, our speaking, our eating, all of these things can take on such deep potency and can enhance our spiritual life or they can cause us to become distracted, causing our life to be mundane, and we will feel empty. We want to feel nourished inwardly and we want to be radiant externally—we want to be love in action. People should feel uplifted and inspired by our association. They should want to associate with us more and feel good about themselves and about life. When someone is carrying a lot of compassion and devotion they automatically make others feel good. They make us want to rise to higher levels of achievements. They cause us to want to be more loving because love, compassion and devotion are contagious. We have our choice—whether we are going to be sufficiently mindful and connect with the auspicious and beneficial, or allow ourselves to be disturbed and drained.

We are compressing a lot of information to make it easily accessible for you. We do not speak simply for the sake of your entertainment or our own distinction. We want you to apply these things to your life, see how they work and share them with others. The time for just talking about things has passed. The time to merely conceptualize and reflect has passed. We can no longer come together just to talk about things.

We want to create the kingdom of God even here, and we can begin by hearing and trying to share. We encourage you to run, run in these days as fast as you can, trying to absorb yourself deeper in spirituality. If you do not run fast enough you will remain stagnated and intoxicated by the nonsense that is going on, and you will not reach the treasures you are entitled to. Go for your treasure, beloved!

Question: What is our responsibility as a group to the collective karma of the planet and our society?

Answer: We have a very great responsibility. The Vedas describe karma in very intricate detail. There is what is known as *prarabdha* karma, karma that has already matured and for which we have already received the reactions, *aprarabdha* karma, which has not yet matured. There is the karma *bijam*, which is still in the seed stage, and the karma *kuta*, which is an even earlier stage. Not only is there individual karma, gender karma, race karma, tribal karma, national karma, and universal karma, but there is also the karma of specific groups.

As one of these groups, spiritual warriors must develop teamwork, strong families, powerful commitment and a willingness to guide, help and complement one another. Not a day should go by where we do not recognize the importance of selflessness and caring for one another. As our actions become increasingly positive, then our collective karma becomes more beneficial and affects other aspects of the community. We can see this phenomenon acting very powerfully in people who have strong faith and devotion. Their faith and devotion are infectious.

One of the reasons for the degradation of today's world is the negative karmic energy accumulated in our environments. As spiritual warriors, it is our task to transform this energy through our own examples. We should live in such a way that we become karma-free, without creating new problems to entrap us. Then the people we meet will not drag us down with their negativity, but instead will be uplifted by our naturally radiating positive energy.

The greatest service we can do for others is to live an exemplary life as carriers of devotion and as models of love in action. We can help others realize that God is available to everyone, has no favorites and offers them a love that knows no bounds.

Question: I've attended your lectures and have read most of your books. You are very eclectic and you have the ability to present difficult subject matter in a simple format and make complex issues seem easy to resolve. I have two basic concerns: First, the acceleration of sectarianism over the last decade, and second, so many spiritualists who began very focused in their missions are becoming discouraged, depressed and are moving to the sidelines. What can you offer that can give us more faith and determination in our missions as spiritual warriors?

Answer: *The Mahabharata*, a classical Indian epic, is a story of two families in conflict. King Duryodhana, the head of Kuru dynasty, is determined to destroy the sons of the Pandu dynasty. One way he tries to do this is by directing a great mystic yogi named Durvasa Muni, with his several thousand disciples, to visit the Pandavas at an inauspicious time. Durvasa Muni was known to invoke curses upon those who disappointed or offended him. Duryodhana's idea was to send Durvasa Muni to dine with the Pandavas after they had already completed their meal, in hopes they would have nothing to offer and that he would curse them in anger.

Yudhisthira, the head of the Pandavas welcomed them, but asked that they first go bathe in the river and make prayers before coming to eat, in accordance with the traditions of the time. Draupadi, the devotional wife, was asked to prepare the meal. In complete desperation, she prayed to Krishna that she had nothing in the house with which to prepare a meal, and could not receive her important guests properly.

As she prayed, Krishna appeared Himself and demanded to be fed as well. Draupadi, now fully broken-hearted, wept that there was nothing to offer her Lord either, except a grain of rice that was stuck at the bottom of her unwashed dish. Krishna, however, happily accepted this, and was fully satisfied by the love and devotion behind the offering. As Krishna was satisfied, Durvasa Muni and his disciples at the river also felt fully satisfied, as their hunger had mystically disappeared. Having no appetites, they became embarrassed that they would not be able to eat if they returned to the house. So they left the river and went home.

The important purport of this story is that if we have the right consciousness to serve others, and if God is satisfied, many miracles will take place in spite of whatever challenges or difficulties we are confronted with.

Another story, also from the Vedic tradition emphasizes the same theme. Once there was a little sparrow that laid her eggs on the shore of the ocean, but the waves carried the eggs away. She asked the ocean to return her eggs. The ocean, of course, did not respond. She then threatened that she would use her beak to scoop up the ocean. As she began to pick up water in her small beak and carry it away, everyone laughed at this impossible task. However, as she continued to toil, one beakfull at a time, the news spread at last to Garuda, the supernatural bird, about her problem. He was pleased by her determination, and came to the earth planet, offering to join in the sparrow's efforts if the ocean did not return her eggs. The ocean, realizing that Garuda was fully capable of the task, was horribly frightened and returned the eggs.

This is the position of the focused spiritual warrior in these difficult times. Yes, the problems we are confronted with are awesome and seem insurmountable, but we should never forget that if we can just play our role with sufficient perseverance, the Supreme Lord will send us helpers. This is the nature of spiritual warfare.

Let me leave you with a few thoughts to keep in mind as you embark upon the path of the spiritual warrior.

Always remember:

There is only one Supreme God. And as we all surrender to the Godhead, we are rewarded accordingly.

There is only one nation: The nation of humanity. Although there are many different races, genders and tribes, we all share similar human desires, and the soul is the same in everyone.

There is only one religion: The religion of love. One great spiritualist once said, "It's good to be born in a religion, but not to die in one." There are many religious philosophies, and many institutions, but ultimately the science of religion is based on becoming a deep lover of the divine couple, Mother-Father God, and of all life.

There is only one language: The language of the heart. We communicate in so many ways, but our most profound and universal communication is through the heart. We are all seeking the ultimate solace for the heart—the highest knowledge, the greatest love and eternal existence. My dear beloved spiritual warriors, we have a lot of work to do on ourselves and our world to attain this pure solace.

Index

abortion 83, 86, 249
academic power 238
advertisements 128, 129, 131, 132
African philosophy 27
agriculturally based societies 28
AIDS 17, 58, 83, 84, 199
alcoholics 31
alien abductions 53
Allah 166, 218
alpha state 130
alternative healing 222
American Dream 26, 27
angels 18, 50, 100, 116
Applewhite, Marshall 136
archangels 116
architecture 101
Arjuna 88, 177, 218, 229, 244
Aryan 96, 97

Ascended Masters 45
asuras 12
atheists 40, 125, 137, 242
attachment 94, 107, 151, 153, 208
attunement 124
austerities 18, 190, 194, 239
austerity 68, 258
avesa avataras 240
Ba'hai 175, 218, 245
barter 26, 29
battle of Jericho 234
Bhagavad-Gita 57, 146, 164-166, 172, 218, 229, 234, 244, 260, 262
Bhagavata Purana 260
bhakti yoga 172
Bhaktisiddhanta 245, 252
Bhaktivenode Thakur 245

Bhavisya Purana 46
Bible 9, 50, 58, 73, 116, 158, 162, 175, 185, 216, 218, 234, 262
bodily comfort 133
Book of Mormon 218
Bowan, Carol 59
Brahama-Vaivarta Purana 57
Buddhism 27, 33, 44, 165, 174
calamities 10, 17, 35, 37, 38, 41-44, 57, 168
Caldwell, Janet Taylor 42
Camus, Albert 134
Carroll, Lewis 39
cataclysmic events 39
Cayce, Edgar 41, 42
Celts 51
chakras 213
chanting 125, 173, 218, 219, 256
chastisements from God 17, 58
chemical and biological warfare 49
child abuse 16, 83, 85, 94
children 12, 28, 32, 55, 58, 59, 75-77, 80, 81, 85, 86, 90, 91, 129, 132, 139-141, 152, 186, 204, 234, 250, 251, 255, 261, 264, 270, 273, 274
Christ 87, 241
cleanliness 258
cloning 54, 55
collective welfare 138, 243
collective consciousness 25, 52, 80, 93, 116, 149, 156, 230, 244, 247, 269
collective awareness 211
collective dreams 21
Collins, Jack 34

combat 4, 100, 180, 188, 196, 243, 244, 247
comets 49, 50, 55
commercials 107, 130-132
commitment 5, 15, 86, 123, 143, 154, 196, 203, 210, 215-217, 230, 231, 235, 248, 257, 266, 272, 279, 282
communalism 20, 90
communication 22, 139-141, 249, 268, 285
community 3, 4, 20, 29, 30, 33, 35, 61, 75, 80, 117-119, 140, 141, 144, 146, 161, 169, 184, 188, 192, 206, 219, 220, 241, 249, 255, 258, 259, 261, 264, 266-269, 273-279, 282
community consciousness 276
compassion 10, 13, 32, 73, 170, 181, 187-190, 233, 244, 253, 269, 280, 281
computers 22, 26
conception 140, 210, 273
conditioned mind 39, 182, 184
conflict 4, 24, 94-96, 98, 185, 223, 231, 262, 271, 272, 276, 283
consciousness 4, 5, 10-12, 16, 19, 21, 24, 25, 31-33, 38, 39, 49, 50, 52, 54, 65, 66, 73, 76, 80, 82, 83, 88, 90, 93, 95-100, 103, 104, 112, 116, 119, 130-133, 140, 142, 149, 150, 153-156, 161, 165, 170, 171, 173, 175, 176, 182-184, 189-191, 195, 196, 198, 201, 204, 206-209, 211-213, 220, 222, 225, 229-232, 237, 242, 244,

245, 247, 249, 256-259, 261, 263, 266-273, 275, 276, 279, 280, 283
Constantine, Emperor 33
corruption 25, 67, 74, 222, 237, 242, 246
cosmic arrangement 37
Council on Foreign Relations 115
courage 31, 32, 52, 224, 233
crime 10, 21, 37, 74, 81, 83, 86, 97, 143
culture 16-18, 20, 23, 26, 28, 32, 33, 42, 53, 56, 61, 64, 65, 67, 68, 72-75, 79, 80, 83, 89, 90, 93, 94, 96, 98, 102, 116, 118, 119, 121, 128, 144, 147, 149, 156, 165, 166, 169, 172, 178, 191, 220, 238, 249, 256-259, 261-263, 265, 266, 274
curiosity and enthusiasm to learn and grow 181, 196, 269
daiva 240
Dalai Lama 44
dark night of the soul 213, 214
data processing 22
death 20, 34, 42, 47, 50, 56, 94, 97, 102, 119, 136, 166, 199, 205, 213, 242, 245, 246, 260, 269, 272, 274
demigods 99, 100
democracy 91
demonic energy 90, 100
demonic energies 82
demonic agenda 101, 104, 113, 123
demonic forces 15, 98, 120
demons 12, 88, 96, 99-105, 107-110, 114, 116, 120
depression 13, 104, 115, 134, 138, 213
detachment 37, 67, 187, 205
determination 153, 283, 284
devil 96, 127, 205, 262
devotees 38, 100, 169
devotion 72, 156, 207, 219, 235, 236, 265, 272, 281-283
devotional creeper 207
Dickens, Charles 39
dinosaurs 43
disasters 13, 17, 36, 41, 42, 46, 49, 50, 56, 71, 137
discernment 209, 210, 212, 236
disease 10, 21, 30, 34, 36, 50, 145, 149, 166, 199, 218, 220-222, 278
disinterest in material rewards 181, 190, 269
divine power 13, 239, 240, 243, 269
divine intervention 18, 175, 233
Dogon 51
domestic violence 98
Draupadi 283
dreams 21, 41, 42, 173, 234
Dronacarya 177
drug addicts 31, 149
drug abuse 17, 82, 144
drugs 13, 65, 77-79, 82, 96, 104, 107, 108, 111, 112, 145, 149, 160, 212, 226
Druids 51
dull mind 151, 152
dullness 151-153

Durvasa Muni 283
Duryodhana 283
dwelling 151-153, 173
earth changes 38, 41, 46, 57, 199
ecocide 30, 161, 237
economic exploitation 70, 89, 104
ecstasy 139, 159, 160, 182, 238, 256
egocentricity 75, 273
Egyptians 51
elder abuse 16
Elizabeth Clare Prophet 45
emotional power 238
empowerment 17, 34, 79, 176, 178, 190, 232, 234, 239, 240
entertainers 64, 238
enthusiasm 24, 153, 181, 196, 204, 248, 269
envy 170, 208, 235
Europeans 25, 94, 97
evil 25, 72, 94, 95, 99, 115, 116, 118, 124, 129, 133, 162, 163, 250
extraterrestrials 44, 50, 51, 53, 55
faith 10, 26, 67, 72, 74, 120, 150, 178, 181, 194, 195, 199, 205, 218, 225, 233, 242, 244, 245, 254, 267, 269, 282, 283
families 28, 31, 34, 107, 118, 140, 172, 229, 273, 282, 283
fanaticism 4, 22, 48
fantasizing 130, 151
fear 18, 32, 48, 49, 52, 88, 95, 98, 104, 132, 138, 155, 167, 182, 187, 246, 267
fearlessness 181, 186, 269
firm faith 181, 194, 269

four principles of community building 268
Franklin, Benjamin 160
free will 105, 108, 142, 215
freedom 86, 105, 106, 125, 134, 135, 161, 191
gambling 66, 67, 101, 108
Ganga-devi 57
Garuda 284
gender problems 22
genetic engineering 54, 250
genocide 30, 97, 109, 137, 237, 250
global consciousness 256
global suffering 38
global warming 46, 47
God 10, 11, 17, 18, 26, 29, 31, 32, 38, 45, 50, 51, 56, 58, 64, 67, 72, 73, 78, 83, 89-91, 94, 97, 99-101, 115, 118, 120, 122-125, 137, 150, 160-163, 167, 169, 170, 172, 174-176, 178, 182, 183, 185, 186, 189, 190, 192-194, 196-201, 203-205, 211-218, 222, 230, 232-236, 238-242, 247-249, 251, 253, 255-263, 265, 266, 268, 270, 272, 274, 276, 279-284
God-consciousness 32, 90, 279
government 48, 52, 69, 70, 81, 82, 113-115
grace 199-201, 215, 240
Greek philosophy 27
greenhouse effect 46
guilt 172, 173, 264
guns 80

healing 29, 30, 33, 144, 145, 161, 206, 219, 221, 222, 225, 232, 247, 271, 272
health 29, 31, 34, 67, 131, 141, 142, 144-146, 168, 199, 219, 220, 223-225, 267, 277, 279, 280
Heaven's Gate 136
herd 129, 209, 210
Hickey, Marilyn 152
higher consciousness 4, 16, 19, 31, 38, 52, 95, 98, 142, 183, 184, 198, 206, 222, 225, 266, 275
Hinduism 27, 165, 174
Hippocrates 144
Hitler 94
holistic 17, 30, 99, 142, 146, 214, 220, 224
homicide 13, 30, 142, 161
horizontal cooperation 275
humility 10, 153, 181, 184-186, 188, 201, 224, 226, 232, 244, 252, 269, 272
Huxley, Aldous 39, 40
hypnotic regression 42, 166
illicit sex 58, 83
impersonalism 171, 260
impious 11, 32, 100, 116
impious influences 32
impotent spiritual leaders 13
incarnation 42, 207
incest 16, 83, 85
Indians 44, 51
Industrial Revolution 26, 90
Information Revolution 26
institutional power 237

interfaith 4, 261
International Monetary Fund 115
intoxication 77, 137, 164
intuitive power 239
invisible government 114, 115
Isaac Asimov 39
Islam 27, 45, 117, 174
Joan of Arc 212
Jonathan Swift 39
Judeo-Christian 45
Justin Martyr 167
Justinian, Emperor 27, 167
Kali-yuga 57
karma 40, 89, 167, 168, 175, 190, 221, 222, 229, 254, 281, 282
Kaunda 19
King, Dr. Martin Luther 87
kingdom of God 97, 170, 172, 186, 248, 263, 274, 281
Krishna 57, 88, 218, 259, 283
Kuti, Fela Anikulapo 97
Larry Dossey 145
leadership 4, 32, 33, 66, 91, 243, 278
liberation 3, 68, 125, 161, 189, 190, 205, 253, 256
Chaitanya 207, 256
love 8, 10, 12, 13, 23, 32, 38, 39, 56, 58, 63, 72, 73, 76, 84, 85, 96, 97, 119, 122, 125, 136, 137, 139, 140, 142, 159, 163, 176, 178, 187, 189, 190, 192, 193, 196, 202, 206-209, 215, 217, 220, 222-224, 230, 232, 234-236, 239, 242, 244, 247, 251, 254, 256, 257, 263, 267,

269, 270, 273, 278-285
love in action 39, 280, 282
lust 8, 10, 63, 64, 68, 76, 82, 84, 85, 130, 149, 190, 213, 235, 243, 257, 263, 273
Mack, Dr. John 53
Mahabharata 46, 283
Mahatma Gandhi 87
mantra 189, 273, 274
manvantaras 46
martial arts 234, 243
Marxism 19
Mason, Glen 94
Masons 89
mass production 22
mastery of the mind 181, 269
material exhaustion 181, 190, 269
materialism 16, 18-20, 26, 30, 31, 40, 51, 56, 91, 94, 102, 107, 118, 119, 121, 149, 163, 171, 179, 207, 211, 230, 235, 244, 246, 253, 263, 264, 274
matricide 30
Maurya, King Ashoka 33
Maya 162, 163, 203, 215, 258
Mayadanava 88
Mayan 44
media 51, 66, 67, 85, 86, 104, 107, 111, 113, 117, 129, 140-142, 209
medical care 29, 225
meditating 125
mental illness 13, 29, 90, 138, 141, 142
mental health 67, 141, 142, 225
mental discipline 153
mercy 38, 56, 74, 141, 176, 189, 200, 201, 218, 234, 239, 242, 258
metaphysical 31, 40, 54, 88, 114, 134, 145, 225, 255
midwifery 29
millennium 4, 28, 35
mind control 45, 110, 128, 129
mode of goodness 164, 165, 168
mode of passion 164, 165
mode of ignorance 137, 152, 164, 165
modern civilization 116, 140, 149
modes of material nature 142, 164
money 18, 29, 64, 69-71, 77, 80, 83, 103, 106, 107, 110, 113, 120, 131, 132, 143, 199, 216, 262, 278
Moody, Dr. Raymond 43
Moses 234, 240
Mother Earth 36, 69
Mother Nature 37, 91, 161, 264
Mother-Father God 161, 169, 172, 182, 200, 265, 284
munis 147
Mussolini 94
Mystical Christianity 27, 174
Mystical Islam 27
Mystical Judaism 27
mystics 50
mythology 51, 110
Narottama Das 33
Native Americans 27, 44, 97
natural disasters 13, 17, 49, 71, 137
nature 11, 16, 17, 21, 26, 28, 32, 37-39, 44, 49, 65, 67, 70, 84, 85, 87, 91, 93, 100, 102, 103,

105, 109, 125, 134, 137, 138, 142, 148, 155, 161, 162, 164, 169, 186, 211, 223, 229, 235, 242, 243, 246, 248, 255, 257, 259, 261-265, 272, 273, 280, 284
negative thoughts 133
negative influences 17, 93, 180, 208, 222, 246
Mandela, Nelson 87
Nigeria 72, 98
no idle time 181, 192, 269
Nostradamus 41
nutrition 265, 279
Obasanjo, General Olusegun 20
Winfrey, Oprah 53
Origen 27, 167
ozone depletion 47
Parliament of World Religions 3-5
patience 181, 193, 194, 201, 269
perseverance 1, 181, 195, 257, 269, 284
personalism 171
pharmaceutical drugs 78, 79
pharmaceutical 77-79
physical bodies 84, 130, 158, 267
physical power 236, 237
physicians 29, 33, 144-146
pious 32, 39, 82, 100, 116
politicians 31, 69, 78, 139
pollution 21, 36, 47, 69, 70, 167, 207
pornography 16, 83, 85
power 5, 9, 12, 13, 16, 18, 25, 30, 32, 38, 48, 66, 67, 69, 70, 73, 80, 82, 86, 88-90, 99, 101-103, 105, 106, 108-110, 112-116, 124, 130, 132, 146, 155, 163, 167, 170, 185, 186, 189, 199, 206, 223, 231, 232, 235-240, 243, 262, 266, 269, 273, 278
Prabhupada 259, 260
pralaya 46-48
praying 125, 173, 176, 205, 230, 260
prediction 41
pridelessness 181, 188, 269
propaganda 63, 110, 121, 156
Prophet Muhammad 122, 174, 241
Protestant Reformation 24
psychiatrists 90, 131, 143, 144
psychic 8, 40-42, 54, 56, 89, 109, 110, 129
psychic manipulation 109
psychic phenomena 8, 41, 56, 110, 129
psychological warfare 129
psycomantium 43
purification 58, 91, 133, 161, 168, 196, 207, 209, 215, 242, 258, 261
purity 12, 16, 41, 64, 95, 99, 117, 154, 210, 217, 219, 242
purusakara 240
pyramids 43
qualities of a spiritual warrior 179
Quar'an 10, 50, 73, 116, 166, 218
racism 4, 10, 16, 19, 22, 37, 96-98, 249
rajas 137, 164
Ramanujacharya 189
rape 67, 72, 83, 85
rationalization 151-153

regulation 82, 181, 184, 206
reincarnation 27, 28, 42, 59, 165-167
relationships 11, 12, 23, 29, 30, 51, 55, 61, 83, 84, 118, 127, 139-141, 160, 161, 169, 183, 231, 241, 242, 264, 267, 272, 275
religion 9, 33, 55, 63, 72, 73, 98, 120, 123, 157, 158, 174, 175, 178, 181, 216, 242, 247, 249, 262, 284
religious sectarianism 22, 123, 174
religious intolerance 16
Renaissance 23, 24, 26
revolutionaries 206, 244-246
righteousness 95, 115, 116, 180, 247
role models 64-66, 80, 135, 140, 145, 146, 148, 190
Rupa Goswami 264
Ruth Montgomery 42
sacred power 239
salvationism 253
samadhi 171
sanskrit 8, 46, 122
Sartre, Jean Paul 134
Satan 94, 162, 205, 218
Satanism 104
sattva 137, 164
schools 53, 62, 73, 76, 80, 81
science 24, 26, 39, 88, 119, 131, 161, 172, 178, 243, 267, 284
scriptures 8, 25, 27, 35, 36, 44, 50, 51, 55, 73, 95, 100, 102, 103, 114, 116, 137, 147, 152, 162, 163, 168, 175, 178, 186, 189, 193, 194, 218, 252
secret societies 89, 113-115
self-gratification 23, 117
self-knowledge 10
self-protection 98, 208, 209
self-restraint 201
self-sufficiency 112, 261, 263, 265
self-sufficient 5, 21
selflessness 84, 181, 193, 194, 208, 224, 226, 232, 269, 282
sense control 169, 181, 269
sense gratification 31, 62, 65, 66, 82, 86, 98, 108, 142, 156, 165, 169, 209, 253
service 4, 5, 19, 26, 29, 32, 67, 97, 118, 119, 161-165, 169, 172, 173, 176, 182, 190, 191, 196, 197, 208, 209, 214, 215, 219, 220, 222, 224, 230-233, 239, 247, 251, 252, 258, 260, 282
sex 58, 64, 83, 85-87, 96, 107, 160
sexism 16, 96
sexuality 83, 87
Shaw, George Bernard 39
simplicity 28, 62, 205, 245, 261, 263, 264
sin 67, 95, 148, 196
sincerity 153
slavery 89, 90, 101, 105, 113
slaves 55, 90, 101, 105-107, 156, 191, 265
social reform 161
solace 4, 7, 13, 93, 118, 248, 269, 277, 279, 285
souls 66, 73, 76, 87, 102, 110, 125,

133, 138, 146, 162, 170, 179, 182, 188, 190, 200, 212, 230, 272, 273, 279
sound vibration 189, 212, 274
spiritual rejuvenation 133
spiritual warrior checklist 180
spiritual warriors 1, 9, 11, 13, 17, 32, 36, 56, 74, 93, 100, 101, 120, 124, 129, 137, 146, 148, 153, 154, 157, 159, 163, 167, 172, 177, 181-183, 192, 197, 198, 202, 203, 207-211, 214, 219, 222, 223, 234-237, 241-246, 248, 251, 253, 255, 256, 258-261, 265, 266, 268, 270, 275, 276, 279, 282, 283, 285
spiritual technology 178, 272
spiritual bankruptcy 52, 144
spiritual nucleus 258
spiritual warfare 12, 156, 179, 180, 195, 284
spirituality 4, 9, 62, 73, 93, 111, 120, 123, 137, 149, 154, 157, 173, 174, 178, 186, 187, 201, 229, 230, 233, 240, 246, 268, 281
Srinivasa 33
St. Jerome 27
St. Francis of Assisi 205
St. Thomas Aquinas 205, 245
St. Teresa of Avila 205
St. Clement of Alexandria 167
Stalin 94
Stern, Dr. Jess 42
Stevenson, Dr. Ian 59
Sufism 174

suicide 13, 30, 55, 90, 134-139, 142, 144, 161
Supreme Godhead 26, 172
surrender to divine will 72, 181, 197, 269
Plath, Sylvia 135
tamas 137, 164
Taoism 27, 165
teachers 10, 11, 62, 117, 122, 124, 175, 186, 190, 203, 205, 227, 234, 238, 239, 241, 246, 248, 251, 261
technology 26, 28, 30, 39, 42, 44, 61, 62, 87-89, 129, 150, 178, 265, 271, 272, 274
television 7, 26, 27, 45, 52, 53, 56, 64, 72, 76, 77, 85, 105, 107, 108, 130-133, 150, 151, 209, 220, 240, 265
terrorists 48
tests 38, 162, 164, 194, 196, 198, 203, 204, 248
The West 17, 28, 79, 166, 259, 260
The Divine 26, 56, 66, 115, 117, 158, 175, 200, 205, 233, 240, 261, 263, 274, 284
tolerance 73, 149, 201, 239, 261
Torah 9, 50, 73, 116
transcendental consciousness 272
tribalism 4, 16, 22, 37, 98, 249
Trilateral Commission 115
truthfulness 181, 187, 188, 245, 258, 269
Tubman, Harriet 87
Twain, Mark 39
UFOs 51, 53, 56
Vaisnavism 33

Vedas 8, 10, 12, 46, 50, 88, 116, 281
Vedic predictions 46
Vedic scriptures 51, 55, 100, 103, 137, 147, 162, 189
vegetarian 168, 265
violence 55, 64, 73, 76, 77, 80-82, 85, 89, 98, 112, 133, 142, 168, 179, 182, 202, 237, 273
Virgin Mary 45
Woolf, Virginia 135
voidism 171
war 10, 15-17, 32, 46-48, 59, 73, 80, 82, 99, 111, 116, 193, 195, 215, 222, 237
weapons 9, 10, 33, 48, 49, 68, 80, 128, 132, 141, 196, 197, 244
Western society 17, 23
Western medicine 30
witchcraft 212
women 54, 55, 73, 83-86, 96, 135, 212, 273
World Health Organization 29, 141
World Parliament of Religions 3
worry 10, 31, 234
worship 25, 64, 71, 72, 101, 143, 174, 238, 246, 252, 260, 266
yogis 27, 40, 50, 109
Yudhisthira 283
Zecharia Stitchin 54
Zohar 45
Zoroaster 218, 245
Zulu 51